ENCYCLOPAEDIA OF INDIAN GOVERNMENT: PROGRAMMES AND POLICIES

ENCYCLOPAEDIA
OF
INDIAN GOVERNMENT:
PROGRAMMES AND POLICIES

Vol. 12

Agricultural Development

Edited by

Satish Tiwari

ANMOL PUBLICATIONS PVT. LTD.

NEW DELHI - 110 002 (INDIA)

ANMOL PUBLICATIONS PVT. LTD.
4374/4B, Ansari Road, Daryaganj
New Delhi - 110 002

Encyclopaedia of Indian Government: Programmes and Policies

First Edition, 2000

ISBN 81-261-0515-1 (Set)

PRINTED IN INDIA

Published by J.L. Kumar for Anmol Publications Pvt. Ltd., New Delhi - 110 002 and Printed at Mehra Offset Press, Delhi.

Contents

Preface

Encyclopaedia of Indian Government: Programmes and Policies contains authoritative information on about fifty departmental policies and their future developmental programmes.

Organised to be completed in 40 volumes, this gigantic work covers Agriculture; Atomic Energy; Chemicals and Fertilizers; Coal; Commerce; Communication; Culture; Defence; Education; Environment and Forests; External Affairs; Finance; Food & Consumer Affairs; Food Processing Industries; Health and Family Welfare; Home Affairs and Internal Security; Human Resources; Industry; Information and Broadcasting; Labour; Law, Justice and Company Affairs; Non-conventional Energy Sources; Ocean Development; Parliamentary Affairs; Personnel, Public Grievances and Pensions; Petroleum and Natural Gas; Planning and Programme Implementation; Planning and Statistics; Posts and Telegraphs; Power; Rural Development; Science and Technology; Social Justice and Empowerment; Space; States Affairs; Steel; Steel and Mines; Sugar and Edible Oils; Surface Transport; Textiles; Tourism; Urban Development; Water Resources; Women and Child development etc.

Based on the information derived from authoritative sources, this work contains authentic facts and figures. I am deeply beholden to all the scholars whose writings are cited or substantially made use of in the present work. I am also thankful to Anmol Publications Pvt. Ltd. for undertaking publication of this encyclopaedia. I am solely responsible for shortcomings in presentation of matter.

Encyclopaedic in nature, this will prove a dependable reference work for scholars and academics besides those appearing for different competitive examinations.

—**Satish Tiwari**

1
Introduction

The National Agenda for Governance, inter alia, has given a call for creating a hunger-free India. Department of Agriculture and Cooperation committed itself to this avowed objective by setting out on the task of doubling food production in the next 10 years besides generating additional employment and incomes in rural areas. In order to achieve these tasks, a separate provision of Rs. 1400 crore has been earmarked for Special Agriculture Programmes in the Ninth Five Year Plan period.

The South-West monsoon in 1998 was the Ninth successive normal monsoon in terms of quantum and distribution of rainfall for the country as a whole. Notwithstanding the two major weather related setbacks that occurred in May-June 1998 creating unprecedented heat wave conditions in the Eastern India and again in October, 98 resulting in rain/flood damage to standing agricultural and horticultural crops, the country has achieved a remarkable acceleration in overall growth in agricultural production in the year 1998-99. The expected growth rate in foodgrains production this year is likely to be around 3.9 per cent.

Crossing 200 million tonnes mark in foodgrain production

During the year 1998-99, the country is likely to cross the landmark figure of 200 million tonnes in foodgrains production, an all time record. The expected rice production is 84.48 million tonnes and that of wheat 70.63 million tonnes, a much higher production level than that of the earlier best of 1996-97 i.e. 81.3 million tonnes and 69.3 million tonnes of rice and wheat respectively. The year is also likely to witness a record pulse production of 15.19 million tonnes against the earlier best of 14.5 million tonnes in 1996-97. The sugarcane production is likely to touch a new high of 282.68 million tonnes against 281 million tonnes of 1995.

On farm water management

A Centrally Sponsored Scheme for increasing agricultural production in Eastern Region (Assam, Bihar, Eastern Uttar Pradesh, Eastern Madhya Pradesh and some districts of West Bengal) with a thrust on utilisation of ground water potential with an outlay of Rs. 500 crore during the Ninth Five Year Plan is under consideration of Government. An estimated area of 2.5 lakh hectare is expected to be brought under Arrigation, yielding an additional production of 10 lakh tonnes of foodgrains every year.

Achievements in horticulture

Some of the notable achievements in the horticulture sector during the year are:

— Record plan allocation of Rs. 222 crore

— Additional area of 1.5 lakh hectares under horticulture crops

— Additional area of 35,000 ha. brought under micro irrigation

— Record harvest of Onion (47.2 lakh tonnes) and Potato (23.5 million tonnes);

— All time high production of pepper (1 lakh tonnes)

Technology mission for north east

Technology Mission for Integrated Development of Horticulture in North Eastern Region including the state of Sikkim has been proposed with a tentative outlay of Rs. 500 crore to utilise the horticulture potential of the region scientifically, consolidate the gains made so far, remove constraints and give an impetus to horticulture growth, by coordinating the efforts of various agencies committed to the cause of area horticulture development. The impact of the mission will be as detailed below:

— area expansion;

— improved production and productivity of horticulture crops;

— creation of post harvest management and marketing infrastructure;

— revitalise processing industries;

— export enhancement;

— promotion of overall development of the region by creating sustainable employment opportunities in the region.

Technology mission for integrated development of vegetables

In recent years, vegetable production has come under increasing demand and supplies crisis, resulting either in periodical glut or scarcity causing distress to both the farmers and the consumers. Integrated development of vegetables involving production, handling, post harvest management, transport and marketing is vital to ensure remunerative prices to farmers and competitive prices to consumers, by promoting effective linkages between research, development, marketing and processing in mission mode.

The focus of Technology Mission with an outlay of Rs. 50 crore for Integrated Development of Vegetables will be on/off season production of vegetables, productivity increase, reduced post harvest losses and processing. The impact of Technology Mission, when launched, will be to increase the production of vegetables and bridge the gap between the demand and supply for quality vegetables, all through the year, in all regions of the country' avoiding the potential of periodical glut and scarcity resulting in distress to farmers and consumers.

Technology mission on cotton

To be implemented in major Cotton growing States, the mission envisages setting up of 4 mini-missions with an estimated investment of Rs. 698 crore over the next five years. Productivity of Cotton Lint is estimated to increase from 256 Kg/ha to over 415 Kg/ha.

Thrust on rainfed farming through watershed development approach

During Ninth Plan, the National Watershed Development Project for Rainfed Areas (NWDPRA) has been significantly restructured. Paradigm shifts in the implementation strategy for allowing greater flexibility, decentralisation, higher involvement of watershed communities, linkages with credit institutions to mobilise resources and ensuring long-term sustainability have been achieved. It is expected that as a result of the restructured programme of NWDPRA, agricultural production and productivity in these areas will considerably improve in the coming years.

In view of expansion in the programme, a considerably higher resource allocation to the tune of Rs. 225 crore has been made during 1998-99, as opposed to Rs. 155 crore during last year.

In the revised guidelines of NWDPRA, greater attention will be paid for treatment of Special Problem Areas affected by salinity, alkalinity, aridity, waterlogging and ravines encroachments etc. within micro watersheds.

A special programme-Watershed Development Project for Shifting Cultivation Areas (WDPSCA) being implemented in the North Eastern States, has been thoroughly redesigned for implementation during Ninth Five Year Plan. Watershed Development through Externally Aided Projects The various on-going Externally Aided Projects founded by World Bank, EEC/ EU, KFW/ GTZ, DANIDA, SDC, FAO/UNDP, etc. are continuing during Ninth Plan. These projects continue to play a complementary role in the national project in helping evolve and replicate sustainable watershed models based on innovative approaches and technologies to serve as testing laboratories in diverse agro-ecological conditions.

The Integrated Watershed Development Project for Hills (5 States) sponsored by the World Bank and currently under preparation will become effective in Mid-1999. In the second phase, the State of Uttar Pradesh, in addition to Punjab, Haryana, Himachal Pradesh and Jammu & Kashmir, has been included. Three other projects in Orissa, Andhra Pradesh and Haryana are under various stages of preparation. The formal negotiations with the World bank assisted U.P. Diversified Agricultural Support Project has taken place and the Project finalised for its implementation with effect from October, 1998.

Additional financial support expected to be received from various externally aided projects during 1998 has been estimated at Rs. 205 crore, which will enable to take up 0.30 million ha. additional area for treatment.

Soil and water conservation

The on-going Centrally Sponsored Schemes of Soil Conservation in the Catchments of River Valley Projects and Flood Prone Rivers have been thoroughly restructured on a project approach. The programmes have been redesigned for:

— Greater location specificity measures

— Community participation

— Sustainability

— Scientific monitoring

— Evaluation and impact assessment

The implementation of the project would result in:

Increase in crop yield on an average by 2 quintal per ha. Reduction of sedimentation rate from 16 tons per ha. per year to 5 tons per ha. per year.

Of the total geographical area of the country nearly 174 million hectares suffer from degradation in one form or the other. The following efforts have been made for reclamation of problem soils in the country:

The on-going Centrally Sponsored Scheme for Reclamation of Alkali Soils has been thoroughly restructured on the lines of the successful World Bank sponsored U.P. Sodic Land Reclamation Project.

Externally Aided Projects under implementation for reclamation of problem soils are:

(i) U.P. Sodic Land Reclamation Project Phase 11 (Rs. 1200 crore)

(ii) EEC Supported Ravine Rehabilitation Project EEC Assisted Project for Reclamation and Development of Alkali Lands in U.P. and Bihar

Three new Centrally Sponsored Schemes are being launched for:

(i) Reclamation of Shallow and Medium Ravines in six States

(i) Reclamation of Acid Soils in the North Eastern States and

(i) Reclamation of Coastal Saline and Sandy Lands

A Project Concept Document is under preparation to address the second generation effects of the Green Revolution in the country.

National Agricultural Technology Project (NATP)

National Agricultural Technology Project (NATP) sponsored by the World Bank was launched in November 1998 to address specific system constraints, weaknesses and gaps in research and extension. The "Innovations in Technology Dissemination" component of NATP is to be pilot tested over a five year period in 24 districts of six states, namely; Andhra Pradesh, Bihar, Himachal Pradesh, Maharashtra, Orissa and Punjab.

During the year under report, şeries of Workshops were held involving participating States to concretise various aspects of the project Agricultural Technology Management Agencies (ATMAS) have been established in first phase project districts and draft strategic research and extension plans formulated. Investment proposals for the selected districts to augment infrastructure support were considered and approved by the National level Technology Dissemination Management Committee in its meeting held on 30th November, 1998.

Women in agriculture

Central Sector Scheme, "Women in Agriculture" is in operation since 1993-94 in seven States, namely; Maharashtra, Kerala, U.P., Punjab, Haryana, Rajasthan and Himachal Pradesh. Village based training programmes of farmwomen, skill upgradation programmes for link workers, result demonstrations, study tours and Mahila Goshtis are organised for transfer of Technologies. The scheme is proposed to be expanded to 28 districts of 19 States/UTs during Ninth Plan with an estimated outlay of Rs. 17 crore. About Rs. 100 crores have been mobilised through Externally Aided Projects (Bi-lateral) to cater to skill upgradation and capacity building of farmwomen in 80 districts of 6 States, namely; Andhra Pradesh, Karnataka, Tamil Nadu, Gujarat, Madhya Pradesh and Orissa.

Rational use of fertilisers

The prices of Phosphatic and Potassic fertilisers were maintained at the 1997-98 levels by giving higher subsidy to encourage increased consumption. This also helps in more balanced fertilisation since fertiliser application had shifted unduly in favour of nitrogen through urea after decontrol of Phosphatic and Potassic fertilisers. The price of urea was increased from Rs. 3660 per MT to Rs. 4000 per MT in the interest of fiscal sustainability and balanced nutrient application. While the modest price increase would not have serious adverse impact on the farmers, it would help in containing fiscal deficit. The change in relative prices of the fertilisers would also encourage more balanced fertiliser application.

Seed production and distribution

Various Seed Development Schemes being implemented by the Department will ensure increased availability of quality and certified seeds to farmers from the level of 73.27 lakh tonnes of certified/quality seed for the year 1998-99. A Scheme on Seed Bank is proposed to be launched during Ninth Plan with an outlay of Rs. 50 crore approximately, which will provide for storing of seeds of important crops in various agro-climatic regions depending upon the requirement.

A pilot scheme on Seed Insurance is proposed to be launched which will cover the risk factor involved in production of seeds in the event of any unforeseen situation, thereby promoting quality seed production.

To ensure availability of good quality seeds to farmers, a system of release and notification of varieties evolved as a result of research has been instituted.

Alongwith augmented production, Seed Certification Programme has been strengthened to ensure that certified seeds are available to farmers easily. With increase in seed production, simultaneous thrust has been on increasing export of seeds, which presently constitutes about 1% of the total world trade in seed sector.

Plant varieties protection bill

A legislation for Protection of Plant Varieties & Farmers' Rights is proposed to be enacted with the objective of protecting intellectual property rights of the plant breeder thereby making the fruits of research in India and abroad available to Indian farmers. The breeder or owner of a variety will get protection legally to control its production and marketing.

It will stimulate investment for research and development and ensure availability of high quality seeds to the farmers. It will protect farmers' rights, which include their traditional rights to sell, use, exchange, share or sell their farm produce of the protected varieties.

The varieties preserved or developed by farmers will be registered under the proposed legislation as farmers' varieties. The farmers/farming community will be rewarded for conservation/development of their varieties by getting suitable compensation, if the new varieties are developed from their variety.

De-reservation of farm implements

Availability of quality farm machines/equipments to have farmers at competitive prices has been the prime concern of the Department of Agriculture and Cooperation. In this direction, the Department has been pursuing with the Ministry of Industry for the dereservation of the manufacture of the agricultural implements and machines from the purview of the Small Scale Sector. At the request of the Department, Hon'ble Finance Minister in his Budget Speech, 1998-99, announcing that the farm implements and tools would be excluded from the list of items reserved for manufacture by the Small Scale Sector. The Department of Industrial Policy and Promotion, Ministry of Industry, have, issued a notification on 23.2.1999 dereserving six items of agricultural equipment, out of 41 items under the reserved list.

Plant quarantine

A UNDP Project on Plant Quarantine is going on to upgrade and modernise the facilities available at the 5 major plant quarantine stations, namely; New Delhi, Mumbai, Chennai, Calcutta and Amritsar. Building construction is going on at Chennai and Calcutta. The new plant quarantine station near the international airport at New Delhi has been inaugurated in December, 1998 with latest equipment of international standards like electron microscope etc. Skills of PQ functionaries by way of fellowships and study tours and other training progr mmes in India and abroad are being upgraded.

Integrated pest management

Integrated Pest Management (IPM) is an environment friendly ecological approach for managing pest problems with minimum dependence on chemical pesticides. IPM approach is the best mix of the pest control techniques and agronomic practices for total crop management on a sound ecological footing. During 1998-99 (till January 1999), about 505 farmers field schools have been organised wherein 1662 Extension Officers and 14,764 farmers have been trained in IPM practices. 1823 million laboratory reared bio-control agents have been released in the field which covered an area of 5.30 lakh ha.

Banning of hazardous pesticides

Two hazardous pesticides-methomyl 24% formulation and phenyl mercury acetate are being banned and another two hazardous pesticides—methomyl 12.5% and phosphamidon 85% SL—are being phased out. The final notification is to be issued shortly after vetting from the Law Ministry.

Amendment to insecticides act and rules

To make the law more stringent in order to ensure quality control and proper check on spurious pesticides, amendment to Insecticides Act, 1968 and Rules thereunder are being carried out.

Agricultural credit

The emphasis on Agricultural Credit has continued to be progressive institutionalisation for providing timely and adequate credit to farmers for increasing agricultural production and productivity. Providing better access to institutional credit for small and marginal farmers and other weaker sections to enable them to adopt modern technology and improved agricultural practices, has been one of the major objectives of the country's agricultural policy.

The flow of institutional ground level credit for agriculture and allied activities has increased from Rs. 15169 crore in the year 1992-93 to Rs. 30976 crore in the 1996-97. The total credit flow from all agencies is expected to go up to Rs. 38054 crore in 1998-99.

Kisan credit card scheme

To provide instant credit facility to farmers for their agricultural operations, a model Kisan Credit Card

Scheme has been launched in 1998. Until now the scheme has been introduced by the State Bank of India and also its 5 associate banks as also by:

Category of Banks	No.
Commercial Banks	29
Cooperative Banks	52
Regional Rural Banks	39

RBI/SLBC are monitoring the scheme at the National/ State levels.

Rehabilitation package for revamping of the Cooperative Credit Structure (CSS)

Requirement of Agricultural Credit, a critical, input for increasing production and enhancing productivity is increasing and likely to touch Rs. 60,842 crore by 2002. The revamping efforts covers the following:

— The package includes legal, financial, operational and administrative measures.

— It comprises cleansing of balance sheets, Voluntary Retirement Scheme and Computerisation.

— Requirement of funds has been estimated at Rs. 6687.40 crore.

— Amendment to the National Cooperative Development Corporation Act, 1962

The National Cooperative Development Corporation (NCDQ was established in 1963 to undertake planning and promotion of programmes for production, processing, marketing, storage, export and import of agricultural produce, foodstuffs and other notified commodities on cooperative principles. With the passage of time, it has been felt that the NCDC's mandate needs to be broad-based, and amendments to the NCDC Act have been necessitated in the light of experience. The NCDC (Amendment) Bill is in the final stages of drafting and is expected to be introduced in Parliament shortly. The main features of the amendments are:

— Expansion of NCDC's scope to include Animal Husbandry, Forestry, Horticulture, Pisciculture etc.

— Extension of NCDC's coverage to livestock, industrial goods, handicrafts and the service sector.

— Provision of loans directly to cooperative societies on appropriate security to be furnished by the borrower.

Amendments to multi-state cooperative societies act, 1984

To set the pace for cooperative reforms and to strengthen the democratic management of cooperatives, it is proposed to effect wide-ranging amendments to the Multi-State Cooperative Societies Act, 1984. The changes are based on the report of the Committee on Model Cooperative Law, set up by the Planning Commission in 1991. The amendments to the MSCS Act are expected to be introduced in Parliament shortly. Broadly, the following issues have been addressed in the proposed legislation:

— Greater degree of autonomy for Multi-State Cooperative Societies

— Reduction in the control and level of intervention of the Government

— Establishment of Quasi-judicial Dispute Settlement Authority

— Provisions for safeguarding the interest of members

— Removal of some restrictive provisions on the functioning of societies

— Freedom of societies to determine their own priorities.

Agricultural marketing

On transfer of the subject of Agricultural Marketing from the Department of Rural Development, Ministry of Rural Areas & Employment to the Department of Agriculture & Cooperation, Ministry of Agriculture in December, 1998, new initiatives have been undertaken to formulate and finalise plan schemes for development of a well knit comprehensive nationwide efficient and responsive marketing system at different levels right from rural markets, wholesale markets and terminal markets of national importance. Where as resources for development of rural periodic markets and improvement of services in the wholesale markets will be placed at the disposal of State Governments within the ambit of State Work Plans, the Central Government would like to embark upon scheme for development of markets of national importance, and preparedness and capacity development of agricultural production and marketing system to meet the challenges posed by the WTO Agreement.

Cold storage

A comprehensive programme for enhancement of existing cold storage capacity in the country from the present 11 million tonnes, to 12.3 million tonnes; in the next three years has been prepared with the objective to stabilise the marketing of perishable vegetables and fruits in particular and to enable the farmers to get remunerative prices for their produce, by utilising storage facilities. The sick cold storages having a capacity of 8 million tonnes will also be revived. 4.5 lakh tonnes of onion storage will be created in the next three years. The entrepreneurs will be encouraged to set up new cold storage by providing commercial loans at subsidized interest rates and capital investment subsidy of' 25%. Besides, adoption of latest technologies in cold storage techniques, pilot projects on onion storage, low energy consuming ccol stores and treatment of CIPC/irradiation on potatoes are proposed to be, undertaken to make preservation efficient, and cost effective and to minimise post harvest losses for the farmers.

Price support intervention by NAFED

The National Agricultural Cooperative Marketing Federation of India Limited (NAFED) is the Central nodal agency for undertaking price support operations for non-perishable commodities as also under the framework of the Market 0 Intervention Scheme (MIS) for perishable horticultural items.

During the year, market intervention operations were carried out for six products in various parts of the country. A record quantity of 78,495 M.T. of culled apples were procured under the MIS in Himachal Pradesh during July -November 1998 to protect apple growers of the State from the ill effects of the glut situation caused by record production of apples in the State.

With a view to alleviating the hardship caused by unprecedented rise in price of onions during July -October 1998 in Delhi, NAFED procured a total quantity 12,297 MT tonnes from markets in Maharashtra and supplied them to the Department of Consumer Affairs, Government of India and to the State Government of Delhi for retailing through their outlets. For augmenting availability of onions for sale in Delhi NAFED also imported 687 MT tonnes; of onions during the crisis. NAFED brought in onions for distribution in Delhi initially at the rate of 30 MT tonnes per day which finally went up, to around 150 MT tonnes; a day in October 1998 for sale at a concessional price through designated State agencies.

Modified Comprehensive Crop Insurance Scheme (MCCIS)

The scheme will be introduced from Kharif, 1999 season, the salient features of the scheme are:

— To cover all farmers (both loanee and nonloanee).

— Voluntary for the States/UTs; compulsory for the loanee and optional for non-loanee farmers.

— Coverage of additional commercial/ horticultural crops subject to availability of yield data.

— Actuarial premia rates (with caps). Subsidisation of insurance charges payable by small and marginal farmers.

— Sum insured unlimited and equal to the scale of finance.

— Simultaneous introduction of a Pilot Crop Insurance Scheme based on individual -farmer as a unit for disbursement of insurance compensation.

National Crop Forecasting Centre (NCFC)

The Prime Minister in the meeting of the Chief Ministers held on 27th November 1998 announced setting up of the National Crop Forecasting Centre (NCFC) for periodical crop forecasting for major crops as also for coordination and assimilation of various methodologies and technical advancements relating to crop forecasting. The Centre became operational with effect from 3rd December 1998 with a small professional team carved out of the existing resources of the Department of Agriculture & Cooperation. The State linkages on computer network for rapid data flow is envisaged in the mechanism of crop prospects tracking. Initially, the focus of tracking crop prospects will be on 13 major crops that is rice, wheat, maize, bajra, tur, gram, groundnut, rapeseed and mustard, soybean, sugarcane, cotton, potato and onions.

Remote sensing application and FASAL

The "FASAL" (Forecasting Agriculture output using Space and Land Based Observation) project has been conceived jointly by the Department of Space DOS), Ministry of Science and Technology (MOST) and Department of Agriculture & Cooperation (DAC), Ministry of Agriculture, after detailed experimentations and development of Remote Sensing applications in real time assessment of crop acreage and production assessment in the past decade. The project aims at establishing a comprehensive system for crop production forecasting in the country. Such a system is envisaged to make the forecasts on the basis of objective assessments of the parameters affecting the crop. It will require integrated use of number of technologies such as Econometry, Agrometeorology, Remote Sensing, Field Surveys etc.

The Department of Agriculture & Cooperation have accepted recommendations of the Task Force on implementation of FASAL Project. The modalities for implementation of FASAL are being worked out in the light of current initiative to set up National Crop Forecasting Centre (NCFC) and the emphasis on using modern tools of remote sensing for strengthening the system of crop forecasting and promoting crop prospects.

Macro management

In the Macro Management approach the present pattern of uniformly structured Centrally Sponsored Schemes permitting little or no location specific flexibility will be dispensed with and the Central assistance to States will be funnelled through regionally-differentiated Work Plans formulated in a multidimensional State-Crop/Intervention matrix. Central assistance to the States will thus be based -on interventions conceived by the States rather than on the basis of schemes thrust upon them by the Centre. The role of the Department of Agriculture & Cooperation will primarily be that of advocacy, articulation and facilitation to help the States in their efforts for development of agriculture. Besides, a few major programmes of national importance will also be implemented in a Mission-mode or as Central initiatives.

It is proposed to switch over from the programmatic approach to the Macro -Management mode from 1st April 1999. The formulation of Work Plans has already commenced.

Simultaneously, the Department has also taken measures to engage in a meaningful and continuous dialogue with external agencies as also to build an on-line, real-time capacity to analyse the early warning signals emerging from the farms and the markets. Action has already been initiated to evolve a fast-tract by-pass mechanism to capture data, collate it, add value and disseminate it to the appropriate destinations with a view to carve out a leadership role for the Department of Agriculture & Cooperation and to create an enabling environment at the national level for acceleration of agricultural growth.

2

Sustainable Indian Agriculture Policy

A each agro-climatic level, educational, health or connectivity stratigies will have to be integrated with agricultural and rural edvelopment strategies. Take the Eastern Plateau and Hill agro-climatic region extending from destricts like Kalahandi in Orissa to Gadchiroli and Chandrapur in Western Maharashtra and including large tribal districts in Madhya Pradesh, the growth strategy is to conserve the rainfall of around 50 cm through waershed programmes and to follow through with forest conservation and optimal cropping patterns. However, the female literacy rate in this region is less than 15 per gcent and so no techology-oriented strategy is possible without remedying this. A destinguished Vice-Chancellor from an agricultural university told me that "sowing" dates were decided by the local Bhuva (witch doctor) rather than the agricultural scientists of the region.

Community organizations are essential for both aspects as at best co-operation is an educational process and limited sharing of rights on land and water is a way out of landlessness and rack renting. It becomes difficult, if not imposible, to channel structural and limited subsidies and priority credit, to the kind of activities described above, if the land rights of the tiller of land are not clear enforceable. Collateral needed by financial institutions, for example, becomes very difficult to organize, if tenancy arrangements are not recorded. Co-operative arrangements provide a way out. Even when farming and other economic decisions are left to the initiative of the peasant, and the signals of the market,, for well-defined purpose, for example, land shaping, acquifer management, lower land water delivery systems or even specific mardeting, quality, grading or input supply requirenents, the peasant can co-operate. Self-help co-operateves with will well-defined objectives can than become the crucial interface between the country's manpower, its limited natural endowments and regional and global markets.

Focus on agriculture: While developing macro-economic parameters for the Ninth Five Year Plan, emphasis will th3e overal GDP growth rate is visualized at seven per cent per annum, then the growth in the agricultural sector wil have to be around 3.5 per cent to 4 per cent per annum in valueadded terms and the growth rate of output will be higher. The precise contours of growth in agricultural sector will be highlighted in the Agricultural Submodel of the Ninth Plan. However, as a preliminary observation, it could be stated that growth in agricultural sector would emanate from improvements in the per hectare yields of crop sector. It is also visualized that diversification and modernization of the various subsets of the agricultural sector would gain momintum in the Ninth Plan and the dynamics of agricultural growth would emanate from growth in non-food grain secters, eg cotton, oil seeds, sugar-cane, fruits and vegetables, spices, plantation crops, etc. along with the development of fesheries, animal husbandry and dairying.

Non-food grain sector: On the assumption that per capita income during the Ninth Plan period will continue to show an annual growth of around 4 per cent, greater emphasis on diversification of the non-food grain sector involving crops like sugar-cane, oil seeds, cotton, fruits and vegetables seems inescapable. Also the output levels in the non-crop based agriculture would rise faster due to (a) increasing flexibility of resource use; (b) response to changing emand conditions; and (c) the technological changes. In fact, these variables would determine the growth process in the economy during the next decade.

The assumption regarding faster growth ot non-crop based agriculture is supported by the annual growth rates of output visualized for the Eighth Plan which have been highlighted in the technical note on the eighth Plan, in which agriculture was visualized to grow at an annual rate of 3.25 per cent in value-added terms, feshing at 5.45 per cent, textiles at 5.87 per cent, wood and paper products at 7.63 per cent and leather and rubber products at 16.03 per cent. This structure of output is in tune with the structure of demand anticipated for the economy during the Eighth Plan period.

Exports: The other major development that has taken place is the fast growthof agricultural exports. It has been estimated that while a growth of 15 per cent plus annually in agricultural export may be difficult to sustain in the long run, a growth path of around 12 per cent annualy in dollar terms should be aimed at. The output implications of cven fast growth of exports are marginal in an economy of India's size, given the magnitude discussed earlier, but in selected regions, the impacts on income and imployment can be high and the technological implications anyway can be important both on agricultural production and processing and distribution.

There is much that is of concern in Indian agriculture as we enter the Ninth Plan. Agricultural fixed capital formation required to finance growth is nowhere in sight. Fixed investment which has reached a level of per cent 8.63% per cent of agricultural GDP has gone down to 8.55 percent in 1994-95. This is happening at a time when area growth has stopped and investment requirements are high so that agricultural intensification can only proceed through larger investments in land and water and yield improvements. The crisis of channelling larger loanable funds through declogging rural credit lines continues.

In the short run, wheat stocks are below requirements for the first time after more than a decade. Wheat prices rose by 10 percent in the last agricultural year and rice price by 7.2 per cent. In the first four months of this agricultural year, wheat prices rose by 18 percent over the same period last year and rice price by 904 per cent.

Per capita income in Bihar in the last fice years has fallen and that in Uttar Pradesh is constant. Apart from West Bengal, agricultural in the eastern region is not doing well. The rural male worker current daily status unemployment rate — the only major indicator of unemployment—measuring disposition of labour time has gone up from 4.85 per cent in 1987—88 to 564 percent in 1993—94, an increase of 23 per cent.

In the Ninth Plan:

(a) Land scarcity will become an acute feature of the Indian agricultural and rural economy and judicious use of land and water will be central to the growth process; India is facing for the first time population densities of the East Asian type;

(b) Community and co-operative land and water development schemes ; and self -help and other credit and marketing arrangements will be critical to the achievement of food security and agricultural output and employment requirements;

(c) Community and co-operative land and water development schemes; and self-help and other credit and marketing arrangements will be critical to the achievements of food security and agricultural output and employment requirements;

(d) The sector will have to engage in cost reduction and diversification in first—stage processing of agricultural produce like sugar refining, cotton ginning, agricultural storage and vegetable and fruit processing, if it is to maintain its momentum in the increasing access of agricultural surpluses to regional, national and global markets; and

(e) In view of all these requirements, private and public investment in agriculture will need a very substantial increase.

Delivery system

An area of priority in the Ninth Plan is to improve project implementation and delivery mechanisms and to ensure that the intended benefits actually reach the people. Further, several social sector programmes are formulated without addressing the isssue of sustainability of benefits and most programmes run with ever-increasing government budgets and thus pre—empt resources which could find better alternative uses. The Ninth Plan must introduce necessary correctives to reverse many of the unsustainable trends in the implementation of poverty alleviation programmes. Just allotting higher outlay for rural development will mean nothing unless a major streamlining takes palce in the implementation and delivery systems.

The existion schemes whose delivery costs are disproportionately high or which fail to make the desired impact should be considered for reorientation and discontinuation. It is necessary to shelve such schemes whose delivery cost exceeds, say 15 to 20 oer cent of the total cost of operating the programme. Monitoring and evaluation of programmes have to be made equally effective and purposeful. Therefore, the Centre, States and the grass roots level organizations/institutions would need to be involved to ensure the effectiveness of the system. It is encouraging that the Planning Commission would bring out compendium of evaluation studies and give wider publicity of the findings of research studies conducted and sponsored by it. This would be helpful for a meaningful public debate on issues involved.

An overall increase in the level of real wages of the unorgainzed workers will also help empowering them to be able to secure maximum advantage from the other developmental programmes of the government. The very concepts of democratic decentralozation and empowerment of the people imply a steady reducation in the paternalistic role of the State and increased emphasis on empowerment of the people themselves. It is hoped that during the Ninth Plan there will be much more attention on bringing about awareness among the unorganized workers as also on providing effective redressal mechanisms to enforce their rights. The approach document of the Plan rightly observes that one of the most important weaknesses of the Indian social sector programmes has been is inabiligy to inform the target benefiviaries about the schemes that are available and to which they have a rightful clain. The Ninth Plan will, hopefully, stress the creation and deployment of an effective information dissemination system,and the necessary redressal mechanism for making the demands effective.

Finally, of course, there is no unique way to describe an ideal gorwth process. It can be hoped that the Ninth Plan will lay down foundations for a more progressive process of planning than has been the case so far. Growth involves a dynamic interaction of linked changes. The economic endocrine gland has to be clear as to how much other matters mingt have advanced. As such, it can also be argued that little attention is required to any particular rate of economic growth so long as it is positive.

Wouldn't it then make little sense to worry whether a baby will end up five or six feet tall when the real anxiety should be whether the baby can be safely brought through the problems of infancy, childhood and adolescence? The slower rate of growth, once under way, can pick-up speed and, of course, can slow down too. But the higher gorwth rate has the prospect of slowing down only. It is desirable to have a steady growth as it has more possibility of ending up with the fastest rate of growth of the economy just as the movement on a highway gives to the motorest the highest speed. The crux of planning is to find the turnpike and reach it. Also gorwth is no longer the guarantor of trickle down effects. To what extent these plan promises are taken care of in the Ninth Plan, can be anybody's guess.

Watershed development

India is one of the countries affected by serious and vast land desertification in the world. Such areas are characterised by severe ecological degradation with denuded forests and poor protective vegetative cover causing soil erosion and decline in the productivity of the land. The water table is receding thus causing shortage of water for irrigation as well as drinking purposes. The increase in human and cattle populaltion has only added to the immense pressue on the already fragile ecosystems.

Signs of reclamation of degraded areas of late have become visible in some parts of the country such as Ralegon Sidhi and Adgaon in Maharashtra, Kabbernala and Mittemari in Karnataka, Jhansi in Uttar Pradesh and Jhabua in Madhya Pradesh. The development of these areas which until recently epitomised poverty, resourceslessness, is characterised by the adoption of watershed based development of the area and active involvement of voluntary organisations in facilitating the participation of local community.

Watershed is a geo-hydrological unit and drains at a common point. It has been accepted the world over as a scientific unit for area development. The long-term objective of watershed development is the rational utilisation of natural resources of soil, water and vegetation for increasing and stabilising the productivity of land on a sustainable basis. The benefits that would flow from the development of watersheds would include increase in sub-soil water regime, recharge of wells along the down stream of watershed and augmentation of drinking water availability. The agricultural production would be enhanced and there will be greater availability of fooder, fuelwood, small timber and raw materials for rural industries. In the process, some intangible benefits like institution building, as people get together to manage the watersheds, and increased bio-diversity of the watershed can also be expected.

Constitution of two High-Powered Committees by Government of India recently, first headed b;y Prof. C.H. Hanumantha Rao and second chaired by Shri Mohan Dharia on drought prone, desert and wastelands development can aptly be termed as turning points in the whole perception of and approach towards area development planning in the country. Both these committees have diagnosed the problem of degradation of land, water and vegetation resources and have recommended in unequivocal terms that waershed as the over—arching principle of area development will have to be adopted by all the concerned departments if 175 million hectares of drought peone, desert and wastelands are to be brought to reasonable level of productivity and ecological balance is to be restored in these areas.

It has been clearly pointed out that without taking into account the local communities' outlook and development builds upon traditional soil and water conservation measures and farming systems, any area development programme is bound to fail.

Watershed approach is currently being followed with different thrusts by different Ministries. Ministry of Agriculture through its National Watershed Development Programme for Rainfed Areas (NWDPRA) seeks to enhance agricultural production in the rainfed areas. Ministry of Environment & Forests has used it for regeneration of vast degraded forests especially in hilly and sloppy regions. Ministry of Rural Areas & Employment h;as gone further in recognising the watershed based developmental planning in its broader sense and has used it as a tool for overall economic development of rural areas by launching the Watershed Development Programme from 1st April, 1995 for implementing Drought Prone Areas Programme (DPAP). Desert Development Programme (DDP), Integrated Wastelands Development Assurance Scheme (EAS). As a result, the flow of funds for development of land, water and vegetative resources is no more a constraint. According to an estimate, approximately Rs. 5000 crore is annually available from various government sponsored development programmes for this purpose. But, co-ordinated efforts to establish longterm strategies that are coherent at all levels would need to be made to achieve the desired objectives.

A major depressant to further agricultural growth is the fact of a cut—back in public nvestment in irrigaton. The approach paper discusses this problem but, in its strategy, it does not spell out clearly how it is proposed to reverse this trend. It wuld require augmentation of resources with the State, as also reallocation of resources in favour of irrigation.

The Approach paper has mentioned cursorily the need for technological improvement and dissemination, but it has not delineated how exactly the State would go about trying to come up with new technological packages which may substantially enhance productivity. With the technological frontier having been hit, unless and until fresh impetus is received on the technological front, it would be very difficult for agriculture to grow faster.

Even though mention has been made of increasing the credit flow to agriculture, it is difficult to squqare up this recommendation with the present era of thinking about financial sector 'reforms', which envisages reduction in priority sector lending, greater emphasis on bank investments and lending going to commercially lucrative ventures, etc. If these prescriptions are put into practice, as is being done expenditously, then it is doubtful if agriculture—and without it, the subsector of poorer sections—would be able to receive higher levels of credit flows. This would act as a bottleneck in attempts to step up investment and output in this sector.

Nothing has been said in the approach paper about the need for institutional reforms, primarily in the spheres of absentee landlordism, skewed pattern of land and asset ownership, consolidation of land holdings and tenancy reforms. These factors play a significalt role in holding back growth, besides their obvious adverse repercussons on equity. These reforms have been long forgotten, but it was expected that the new government, with a left—of—centre orientation, would bring these reforms back on the national agenda. However, evidently, that has not materiallized.

Despite the abovesaid shortcomings, the approach paper needs to be commended for its emphasis on a regionally differntiated agro—strategy, accounting for factors peculiar to different regions. It has made an honest appraisal of problems confronting this sector anf it gives insight into a few solutions, although it stops short of recommending measures to resolve some basic issues.

Soil and water conservation measures are one of the essential inputs for increasing agricultural ouput in the country. These programmes were first launched during the First Plan. From the very beginning, emphasis has been on development of technology for problem identification, enactment of appropriate legislation and constitution of policy coordination bodies. While conceptual framework of soil and water conservation activities has not changed, concept of programmes has undergone considerable revision during successive Five Year Plans.

Till the end of 1993-94, an area of 2.91 million hectare out of the total treatable area of 17.59 million hectare in the catchments of River Valley Project has been treated, which comes to 16.50 per cent of the treatable area. Similarly in the case of Flood Prone River scheme till the end of the 1993-94, an area of 0.61 million hectare out of the treatable are of 4.37 million hectare has been treated, which comes to about 13.96 per cent of the treatable area.

A Centrally-sponsored scheme for reclamation of alkali (usar) soils initiated during the Seventh Five Year Plan is continuing in Haryana, Punjab and Uttar Pradesh. The major components of the scheme include assured irrigation water on farm development works like land levelling, deep ploughing, community drainage system, application of soils amendment, organic manure, etc. It is a 50:50 funding between the Centre and the concerned state on identified components. Since the inception of the scheme, an area of 3.36 lakh hectare of land has been reclaimed with Central investment of Rs. 41.78 crore upto 1993-94. During 1994-95, it is expected to reclaim 60,000 hectare of land with Central investment of Rs. 7.88 crore.

The scheme for control of shifting cultivation (CSC) was implemented with cent per cent special Central assistance in all the north-eastern states, Andhra Pradesh and Orissa till 1990-91 wherein 26,532 families were selected (out of which 18,842 families in the north-eastern states) for rehabilitation. However, in pursuance of the decision taken in the NDC meeting held in October 1990 the scheme was transferred to the state sector * ture of Rs. 61.72 crore has been reported till 1991-92 against a release of Rs. 55.67 crore.

The Planning Commission has approved for the revival of the scheme only for the north-eastern states from 1994-95. An outlay of Rs. 15 crore has been provided for this purpose. The Scheme for Watershed Development Project in Shifting Cultivation Areas (WDPSCA) of North-Eastern States is to be implemented in accordance with the guidelines of the ongoing Centrally-sponsored scheme for National Watershed Development Project in the Rainfed Areas (NWDPRA). An outlay of Rs. 16 crore has been provided for 1995-96 for this purpose.

Ground water depletion

It was with the introduction of high-yielding genotypes of wheat and rice in mid-sixties that India ushered in the era of what is commonly referred to as 'Green Revolution'. Our country has since made spectacular achievements in the field of agriculture. It is evidence by the fact that we are today not only self-sufficient in matter of food but also in a position to export food grains and other agricultural products, in addition to having comfortable food reserve to meet unforeseen exigencies. We have emerged as the largest producer of fruits and the second largest producer of vegetables in the world. But unfortunately, the efforts made during the last thirty years have not been confined to constructive measures and useful results. Frightful damage has been wrought to the basic natural assets, particularly soil, water and genetic (plant and animal) resources on which agriculture is dependent. Although some of the damage is irreparable, the wide spread growing realization of the disastrous consequences that thoughtless exploitation of nature leads to justify hope for the future. It is a happy situation that the whole world today has become very much concerned about healing the wounds inflicted by the errors committed in the wake of modernization.

Our country is today faced with serous problems of falling ground-water-table in tube-well/pump-set irrigated areas and rising water-table in canal irrigated areas. Although our policy makers, planners, administrators and agricultural scientists are very much aware of these problems, the situation is getting alarming year after year. The remedial measures taken so far do not seem to have touched even the fringe of the problems. The situation demands time-bound aggressive measures to overcome the problems which have cropped up over the years.

"The water-table in much of the country is steadily sinking. The fall in a little over a decade has been two to four metres in many states. Delhi and the surrounding states are worse, the decline being four to eight metres in the decade after 1971, with a further fall in a decade after."

The situation has become more serious in states like Haryana and Punjab. The annual ground-water depletion rate in some districts of these states is over 30 cms. As the water-table goes down, the farmers have to take their pumping sets to a higher depth for increasing the delivery of water and this involves much cost. Generally, the pumping set depth is increased once in five years.

The problem of water shortage because of sinking tube-wells has become so acute in some areas like Kurukshetra district of Haryana that the resource-rich farmers have started getting more and more submersible pumps installed which is a very costly affair. The cost involved in installation of one submersible pump is more than Rs. 1.25 lakh. These pumps fetch water from different depths. But there is limit to the depth from which even a submersible pump can tap water. If the water-table goes beyond this limit, the pump can no longer exploit ground water.

In order to make the watershed development programme effective and sustainable efficient monitoring and evaluation oare as crucial as its implementation. Monitoring provides a mechanism to supervose, direct and control the sequence of actions so that the implementation of the programme could be guided to achieve the desired objectives. An effective monitoring helps to detect the shortcomings, if any, in planning and implementation of the Programme and thus makes possible mid-course corrections simultaneously. Similarly, evaluation of the programme helps in assessing the achievements and impact and also identifying the possibilities and constraints which work as incentives or obstructions to successful and speedy implementation of the programme.

In case of watershed management with complex networking of different activities and its implementation as a people's programme, an elaborate monitoring and evaluation system will have to be evolved right through its grounding stage to the implementation phase and post-project period. Important criteria for monitoring the successful grounding of the programme could be the following:

— Institutional framework with adequate people's participation for effective delivery system.

— The existence of the legal and regulatory framework to ensure the protection of rights of different sections of society with special emphasis on the assetless and women.

— Regular and continuous technical support to the programme.

— The presence of inter-sectoral linkages kfor effective integration and dovetailing of resources.

— An efficient mechanism for release of funds to the field implementing agencies.

The tools for monitoring the implementation phase of the programme would include:

— Physical and financial achievements through periodical progress reports from the field level implementing agencies.

— Field visits to get a first hand information about the quality of the implementation through interaction with the field functoinaries and the beneficiaries.

— Seminars and workshops to get feedback on the field level difficulties and suggestions for improvement.

— Revies meeting to examine broad policy issues.

Similarly, important indicators for an objective impact evaluation of programme could be:

— Economic indicators such as income level, purchasing capacity of the inhabitants of the project area and the trend of migration.

— Changes in land use cropping pattern as a result of land development and various water conservation measures taken up in the watershed area.

— Improvement in the geohydrological regime by way of recharge of ground water and surface water bodies and enhancement of sub-soil moisture.

— Capacity building of non-governmental organisations and local community as a result of participatory working.

As the Watershed Development Programmes primarily concentrate on dry regions such as drought prone, desert, wasteland infested and sloppy areas their success would not only bring about improvement in the productivity of land and water resources and restoration of ecological balances but would also help in correcting the regional imbalances caused by the Green Revolution of 60s and 70s between the irrigated and rainfed areas. Moreover, as the Watershed Management is based on the sound principles of sustainability, the enhancement in agricultural production as a result of watershed development is not likely to be acckompanied by such harmful practices as overuse of fertilisers and pesticides, over exploitation of ground water resources and intensive farming resulting in depletion of soil nutrients. We have sufficient funds, technical expertise, instutional infrastructure and policy-framework in the form of well formulated guidelines to treat and develop our vast degraded lands. But what is required is a proper orientation of implementing agencies towards adoption of watershed based planned and integrated aproach and willingness to involve the local people in the right earnestin the whole process. This concerted endeavour by all only would help in realising the dual goals of conserving the legendry splendour and munificence of our natural resources and making of a drought free country with food for all.

The submersible pumps extract water from such high depths that they may render shallow tube-wells of other farmers around useless. "The situation is so alarming in some of surveyed villages in Kurukshetra district (Haryana) that small and marginal farmers whose shallow tubewells have dried due to ground water depletion and can not afford submersible tube-wells are getting converted as farm labour by subletting their land to those farmers who have submersible tube-wells." Even those fetching water from wells and hand pumps for drinking and other purposes fall victims to the few haves having submersible pumps around them. Thus, reckless installation of particularly submersible pumps is highly detrimental and unjustified even from the view point of equity and social justice. This is why there is so much cry about the urgency and immediacy of effective measures not only to arrest the depletion of ground water but also to replenish it. Even the Supreme Court has taken cognizance of the problem of continuously dropping water-table. "The continuous ground water exploitation led to another serious problem which is brackish/alkaline water in Haryana. The exploitation of such water spoils not only good quality of water/canal water but it also destroys the soil fertility."

Ground water must be viewed as a national, rather than regional or local, resource and an optimum-use model should be designed for irrigation, drinking and other purposes with due consideration of the interests of all the users. "Even if water is scarce in a region, through more efficient planned use, it is possible to increase the overall benefits to everyone there. To use water properly, you must look at all the trade-offs to all significant users, not must a few and not just one time."

The steady fall of ground water-table is seriously impairing the original productive power of nature. It is highly disastrous for stable and sustainable agriculture.

The results of over exploitation of ground water is hazardous to even public health. In Calcutta and the rest of the state, "the exploitation has upset the geological balance, with arsenic from the bed rock flowing into the water. In a third of West Bengal's districts, the government admitted in Parliament earlier this year (1996), drinking water has more arsenic than the maximum limit prescribed by the world Health Organisation."

"The affected area is growing by 20 per cent every year. As for the metropolis of Calcutta, heavily dependent on tube-well water, a city university study says, it is on the brink of an arsenic bomb."

The problems caused by excessive use of ground water are visible every where. "In Delhi, for instance, though most residents are blissfully unaware, the level of fluorides in the water, which can have a crippling effect over time, is well above the safe limit in a number of localities. Some places have increasing salinity problems, some have other contamination and many have a mix of all these."

The water supply department of the metropolis of Delhi pumps out 65 million gallons of ground water every day for municipal supply as a result of which water table is continuously dropping.

The pressure on ground water has tremendously increased over the last thirty years because of high-yielding varieties, intensive cultivation involving water-loving crops and dominance of such crops in the cropping patterns which require much water, on one hand and wane of traditional sources and methods of irrigation, on the other. The yield potential of high-yielding varieties in general can not be exploited without adequate and timely irrigation water obviously increases with increase in cropping intensity. Some crops require much water. Paddy is number one among such crops. It requires a very high amount of water. Dominance of crops like paddy and wheat in the cropping patterns necessitates increased use of ground water. Sustainability of agriculture underlines the need for diversion of area from the crops demanding more water, particularly paddy, to the crops requiring less water. Emphasis has to be laid on selecting such crop verities which give equivalent yields with less moisture and are of short duration. Even in respect of crop varieties, cropping patterns and cropping intensity, we must go back to the past and seek in traditional agriculture some solution to the present-day problems.

A key to successful implementation of watershed management is appropriate planning and selection of activities followed by an efficient monitoring and objective evaluation.

The efficient planning for watershed management would require efforts at both policy and implementation levels supported byan effective information analysis system.

Some requisite changes have to be brought in at the policy level so as to remove or, at least, lessen the constraints in the effective watershed management. These are as follows:

Through regularisation of genuine encroachments following a politically suitable and socially accpetable criteria so that people can undertake ecologically sound activities like agro-forestry without fear of being evicted.

Although the needs of local people as well as their management efforts is gradually being recognised as desirable and even essential, their involvement in the process of conceptualising these efforts in a cohesive manner is still only marginal. The local population's aspirations are as important—as a potential benefit or as a potential constraint—as those of the government and, therefore, should find accommodation in the development process through appropriate policy measures.

At the district level various develkopment activities are carried out by different Departments of Central and State Governments in a watershed areas with very little cohesion. Optimum benefits can be obtained by creating a Watershed Mission at the district level which would pool resources and technical expertise and take up the watershed treatment in a comprehensive manner.

It should be appropriately amended to rehabilitate oustees from illegally occupied forest uplands. They should also be given priority in employment under various employment programmes.

The development activities under watershed development being primarily land based, the area development programmes tend to benefit the land owners more than the landless. Though the landless people may benefit to a small extent in terms of wage labour and greater availaability of drinking water, fuelwood, grasses or forest based usufructs from the village common lands, the landed class would be benefitted substantially by way of greater availability of water for irrigation, development of their lands and the improved cropping patterns. This inequity is bound to cause social tensions between the already polarised rual community into the rich and the poor. Any developmental endeavour with such overtones of social inequities would be socially unacceptable and thus would not be able to sustain for long.

An apropriate mechanism with adequate legal and institutional support will have to be devised to provide adequate income generating opportunities to the landless and assetless in the watershed area. This may involve among others, allotment of land to the landless and granting of rights over trees and other usufructs.

These have to be redesigned to diversify the rural economy and provide full benefit of the value addition to the local inhabitants. For example, establishment of wool processing units, tanneries, food processing and other agro-based industries in such areas will raise employment and income for local people. This would also supplement the income generating avenues for the landless.

Following measures may be taken at the implementation level:

It should get greater attention as the degradation of uplands has far reaching ecological consequences especially for low land people. People inhabitating uplands should be given some incentive for not taking up intensive agriculture.

Under the Integrated watershed management, close cooperation and assistance form various government agencies is reqauired, like the Ministries of Rural Areas & Employment, Agriculture and Cooperation, FOrests and Environment, Education and Commerce (for export of agricultural and forest priduce).

Greater productivity from developed watersheds would demand a better and extended marketing facility for the forest and agriculture produce which must be created by appropriate institutional and economic measures.

Target groups for training would be policy planners, administrators, technical experts, extension agents, village leaders and workers. Sufficient books and extension materials should be printed in the local language and made available for trainees.

Awareness raising including dissemination of relevant information to the field functionaries and the community is of prime importance and should be taken up on a regular and continuous basis by a district level task Force drawing persons from amongst technical experts, fold artists and social motivators.

Since watershed management planning would require the collection, storage and analysis of a wide range of physiographic as well as socio-economic data both spatially and temporally, an efficient and state-of-the-art information system is required to be incorporated in the very concept of watershed management. An essential component of planning is to make projections of future situaations under different sets of conditions. A Geographical Information System (GIS) being capable of such simulations can be a valuable tool for planning for watershed management. Recently, Integrated Mission for Sustainable Development (IMSD) launched by the National Remote Sensing Agency (NRSA) of the Department of Space, Government of India, using remote sensing and GIS techniques, has developed treatment plans for comprehensive development of watersheds in a few selected blocks of the country. The scope of the project should be widened to cover more areas so that scientific and technically sound development plans are readily available with the field level agencies. But, the scientific and technical inputs from space imageries and aerial photographs in the planning and implementation of the wateshed development programmes need to be supported by Rapid Rural Appraisal (RRA) and Participatory Rural Appraisal (PRA) involving local people for collection and appraisal of field level data.

Among the various factors responsible for steady ground water depletion is growing dependence on tube-wells/pumping sets. In fact, it is not be because of tube-wells/pumping sets as such but because of excessive exploitation of ground water through these artificial methods of irrigation that water-table is continuously dropping. There is no recharge of ground water. In order that ground water depletion is checked and effective measures taken for its replenishment, it is imperative to restrict reckless and indiscriminate installation of tube-wells/pumping sets. The number of tube-wells/pumping sets to be installed in an area should be determined considering how many of them can be sustained by ground water reservoirs. It calls for strict legislation with respect to the spacing, the depth and the quantity of the quality of pumped water to prevent its contamination. If fact, mere legislation won't do. More important is forceful implementation of the legislation. Perhaps only three states and one union territory have presently some legislation to regulate ground water exploitation.

In view of fast declining ground water resource, unavailability of adequate energy to tap it by pumping is, in a way, blessing in disguise. Had adequate energy been available, the ground water situation would have become most alarming.

While inadequacy of energy restricts the use of ground water, "the major and medium irrigation system's inefficiency is a big contributor to the ground water recharge. It would indeed be a very costly way of recharging the ground water. Further, the water recharged this way is turning a great extent of the area saline."

"The ultimate source of all water is precipitation, that is snow and rainfall. The precipitation that falls on the ground is dispersed in several ways and ultimately appears in the form of surface and ground water resources."

It is unfortunate that in our zeal and enthusiasm for modernisation, we have become oblivious of the centuries old time-tested system of irrigation where in our farmers depended mostly on surface rain water. As the situation stands today, the dependence on rainfall has drastically reduced because of increasing use of tube-wells/pumping sets and canal. In the traditional systems of irrigation, in-situ conservation of rainfall by way of such practices as bunding, terracing were very common.

The excess run-off was stored at appropriate sets in tanks, ponds and natural reservoirs for future use. We had a network of such reservoirs scattered throughout the length and breadth of the country. The impounded water was used for irrigation directly or indirectly through recharge where also used ground water for irrigation and other pursposes, digging wells without adversely affecting the ground water reserve. Numerous references to wells, tanks, ponds and natural reservoirs are found in the Vedas.

When the run-off is stored in widely scattered tanks, ponds and other reservoirs, a sizable portion of the water that infiltrates into the soil percolates deeply and adds to the ground water. So far as rain water is concerned, it has been estimated that approximately 54 per cent of the total amount infiltrates into the soil of which about 23 per cent is added to the ground water. By adopting some simple low-cost measures, it is possible to conserve upto about 65 to 70 per cent of the total rainfall.

The fast declining ground water must be recharged and the best way it can be done is In-situ conservaton of the rain water and storage of excess run-off at appropriate sites by following the age-old traditional practices which have stood the test of time. We wish and hope that decisive steps will soon be taken to revive these practices which is a must for stable and sustainable agriculture.

Farmer's education programmes

The Deptt. of Fertilizer (DOF) in the Ministry of Chemicals & Fertilizers is inter-alia entrusted with the responsibility of planning of fertilizer production, arrangements for movement and distribution of Fertilizers in terms of allocations made by the Deptt. of Agriculture & cooperation, arrangement of subsidy for indigenous and imported fertilizers including determination of rentention price and cost of imported fertilisers and administrative responsibility for public enterprises and cooperatives under the control of the Department.

The following Public Sector Undertakings (PSUs) and Cooperative under the Department of Fertilisers are carrying out agricultural extension work with emphasis on education of farmers in scientific application of fertilisers:

Besides, some of these PSUs/Cooperatives have also implemented Fertiliser Education Projects with foreign assistance.

Explaining the role of DOF as also its PSUs/ Cooperatives in regard to educating the farmers, the Department in a note stated, "It is submitted that while it will be ensured that the undertakings under the administrative control of this Department lay greater emphasis on Farmers Education Programmes, the Undertakings can at best play a supplementary role in the promotion of agricultural education and extension. Agricultural Extension and Farmers Education Programmes are the primary concern of the Department of Agriculture in the State Governments. The Ministry of Agriculture has a nodal responsibility in this domain at the level of the Central Government. This Department will endeavour to assist the State Governments. Ministry of Agriculture in the Government of India and the agricultural universities and research institutions in creating greater awareness about the balanced used of fertilisers for sustained agricultural growth and productivity amelioration".

The promotional activities undertaken by the PSUs/ Cooperatives include Farmer's Meetings, Demonstration, Crop Melas, Soil Testing etc. The following statement shows number of activities undertaken by PSUs/ Cooperatives during 1994-95:

During the course of examination of some of the PSUs on the subject *viz.* NFL, MFL, FACT, RCF, PPCL and PPL, the Committee pointed out the taking into the size and volume of business the promotional activities undertaken by their PSUs were too meagre. The Committee further pointed out that NFL which was being the largest producer of Nitrogenous Fertilisers in the country and wanted to know whether a PSU of the stature of NFL should not play a leading role in extending more and more help to farmers. NFL in a written note stated, "NFL played the role of leader, especially in the matter of providing Farm Advisory Services, facilities of farm equipments & welfare activities, in their home market comprising the State of Punjab, Haryana, Himachal Pradesh, Jammu and Kashmir and Madhya Pradesh, besides the UTs of Delhi and Chandigarh. The company has two major Urea Expansions in hand at Vijaipur in Madhya Pradesh and Nangal in Punjab. Bulk of the additional production obtained from these new expansions shall flow to the States of Andhra Pradesh, Bihar, Orissa and West Bengal from Vijaipur and Uttar Pradesh from Panipat. The Company is in the process of preparing appropriate plans to undertake Farmers Education Programmes in a befitting manner in the new territories".

In reply to another query about removing the present imbalance in use of NPK fertilizers in the country and undertaking more and more promotional activities to educate the farmers, NFL in a written note stated, "Much though per bag cost of fertilizer material plays a crucial role in the decision making process at the level of the farmers, efforts of NFL staff in the field are always oriented towards educating farmers that cheaper alternatives available to the farmers in the market are not always in the best interest of production and productivity. A pointed effort is also made to contain the growing luxury consumption of Nitrogen *vis-a-vis* Phosphates at the farmers level because of the comparative cheaper per bag price of Nitrogenous Fertiliser".

During the course of evidence of the representative of MFL, the Committee pointed out that MFL was a Urea and Complex fertilizers producing company and as such it was more important for MFL to impart education to farmers emphasising the need for using balanced use of fertilisers, CMD, MFL stated, "We recognised the importance of farmer's education had extension efforts and within our limited means we are Providing it".

When asked further whether promotional programmes undertaken by MFL should not be substantially enhanced terms, number and amount in coming years in view of the present imbalance in use of NPK fertilisers in the country, MFL in a written note informed, "Yes, but it should be done by both Industry and Central and state Govts. Further, unless efforts are taken to arrest the widening price gap between Urea and 'P' & 'K' fertilisers, any number of programmes implemented will not bear results. As long as Urea price is low on account of huge subsidy and the prices of 'P' & 'K' sources are raising every season due to factors outside the control of the industry, farmers will be tempted to use more Urea than to apply all the NPK materials, Hence, the imbalance in NPK consumption will continue to be there. However, MFL has been consistently making efforts by organising many Educational programmes to improve balance fertiliser use and also Biofertiliser use for all crops".

On the same subject CMD, FACT, also stated during evidence, "The real matter of concern is what the Chairman has pointed out, that is the imbalance. At this rate, our Mother Earth will become not good for cultivation if this imbalance continues. We have been noticing this at least for the last two years and are trying to propagate more of nitrogen in the southern States and more of phosphates in the northern States. For example, the Indo-Ganges belt has now gone in more for urea because of its cheapness but it is not good at all in the longer run.

Similarly, another problem is that at least seventy to seventy-five per cent fertiliser is phosphatic and it is getting sold in the southern States and the urea has to come in from the factories in the southern States as well as from North. So, the only way to get over this is to educate the farmer properly. We have realized this and our thrust now would be to bring down the imbalance by education the farmer more. After all, the decision is resting with the farmer, he being the land owner. They should know what would be good for the soil. This is a national question. Though we have a surplus situation on the foodgrains front, the imbalance in the fertilizer will not help in the future years. So, we understand our responsibility in this and we give more thrust to it".

Asked about the views of PPL in regard to adequacy of their promotional activities, PPL in a note stated, "We agree that substantional educational programmes to spend a large amount on these activities due to fund constraints should be substantially enhanced. However PPL can not afford to spend a large amount on these activities".

Regarding the imbalance use of fertilisers. PPL informed the Committee, "The imbalance in fertilisers in not only due to inadequate attention to education of the farmers in regard to optimal dosage of different fertilizers nutrients farmers but there are other reasons too. Another such reason is that the phosphatic have fertilisers become very expensive for farmers".

During the course of examination of Department of Fertilisers, the Committee pointed out that the promotional activities undertaken by PSUs are too less and should be suitably enhanced keeping in view the imbalance in use of fertilisers. The Secretary, Fertilisers informed the Committee, "Fertilisers play a very very important role in ensuring the productivity in agriculture. Productivity in agriculture is crucial for the development of the nation and its industry. It goes hand in hand with rural credit mechanism, agricultural prices and other inputs. Actually in this country about 143 million hectares of land are under cultivation. Out of this, about 64 million hectares are under irrigation. High yielding varieties of seeds are covering about 74 million hectares. The cultivating families are around 90 million and there is a large number of small and marginal farmers.

Our endeavour from the Department of Fertilizers has been always to ensure that the production, the indigenous capability of fertilizers, the strength of the country is built, so that we are self-reliant in fertilisers especially in the nitrogen phosphate for which we had to depend on important raw materials. We are making all efforts towards that. We are aware that apart from the manufacturing role although this subject is with the Department of Agriculture it is equally our responsibility from the point of view of fertiliser promotion to play an active role on fertiliser education and to make the farmers conscious in the use of balance fertilisers. Our companies are engaged in commercial production".

As regards for correcting the imbalance in use of fertilisers the Secretary, Fertilisers further informed, "We are very clear about balanced use of fertiliser. Now, the farmer's purchasing power is to be increased. In a way, the small farmers are also entrepreneurs and they are engaged in the business of producing agricultural produce. What he wants is only some money as advance". "We fully share this concern but it is necessary to point out that this imbalance is arising as a result of the wide disparity in the nutrient prices and that is the only way to correct it. Fertiliser extension and farmers education have only a supplementary role here. It can assist in the education of the farmers but then the logic that is before the farmers is that of the relative prices of the different nutrients".

The Committe further pointed out that presently targets etc. relating to promotional activities did not form part of Memorandum of Understanding signed by various PSUs with the Ministry and enquired whether the Government would consider to incorporate promotional activities/farmers educational programmes in MOUs from now onwards. The Secretary, Fertiliser stated before the Committee, "On the question of MOU, I would like to make a submission. MOU is provided by the Department of Public Enterprises; it is purely on commercial terms; there is no provision in the MOU for other things. What we are doing is, we are getting the direction and guidance of this Committee. We will be issuing advice to all the companies and we will be discussing it. This is my first task. They must start in a larger way. They must come and play a part in PSUs and Cooperatives".

The Committee further pointed out that even the annual targets were not fixed for the providing activities to be undertaken by various PSUs/Cooperatives. The DOF in a note stated, "PSUs/Cooperatives under the administrative control of this Department have been advised to set targets for the promotional activities to be undertaken by them under the Farmers Education Programme at the beginning of every financial year keeping in view their specific commercial interests and the requirement of their marketing zones. They have also been advised to get these schemes and the targets for different activities approved by their respective Board of Directors before the beginning of every financial year".

From the further details furnished to the Committee it was noted that the instructions to various PSUs/ Cooperatives were issued on 27th February, 1996.

Educating the farmers

Research studies have pointed out a two—way relationship between education and other investments to improve agricultural productivity. Education—in the wide sense of the term primary education, literacy as well as extensional deucation and training—is a prerequisite qqqfor introducing modern methods of farming relying on fertilizers and new varieties of seeds.

Four basic stages of agricultural technology have been identified by Maureen Woodhall in a book on Education and Development and they are: (a) traditional farming depending on father to son tradition; (b) use of a single modern input like fertilizer, seed; (c) Several complementary inputs simultaneously; and (d) full irrigation—based farming. Each stage calls for different levels of education to farmers commencing from literacy, maintenance skills, rudimentary knowledge of chemistry and biology and ability to calculate the effects of changes in crops, climate and so on.

It is through adequately educated farmers who constitute local resources and by making available such local resources for improving agricultural productivity that the Ninth Plan target of 4.5 per cent rate of growt: in agriculture can be achieved. In such an approach, requirements for improving agricultural productivity and rural development converge and it is this model of rural development through local resource mobilizaton which is the crying need of the hour. With the present level of educational backwardness, it may be difficult to achieve the agricultural growth target. But with adequate human resource development, it will be possible to achieve to goal.

Education appears to be a prerequisite to increase the yield from other types of agricultural investment, Formal education of farmers also improves the effectiveness of agricultural productivity. The extension services will become more effective if farmers have a basic level of education. This raises the question of whether the formal and non—formal education including agricultural extension are substitutes for each other.

Tamil Nadu experience: In this connnection, it is worth referring to Tamil Nadu's effort to raise productivty through investment in human resources. In 1994—95, a sum of Rs. 76 crore was allotted for human resource development to upgrade the knowledge and skill of the persons engaged in the development of agriculture, fisheries, agricultural engineering, forestry, etc. For agricultural productivity improvement through broad—based extension activities, Rs. 41.81 crore was set apart in the State budget.

There can be productivity and social change simultaneously in the rural sector. For gaining an insight into this aspect one can look at theories of social and institutional transformation as an integrated process of economic development as Schumpeter, Adam Smith, Veblen,Max Weber have advocated. Farmer education should be regarded as one link in an integrated system of generating and transferring knowledge. Other links are research and the production system like industry, services, etc. A good system of communication will serve as an intemediary.

For quite some time now Tamil Nadu has been following though not explicitly the above model. It has been called knowledge, attitude, performance and practice (KAPP) model resulting in considerable improvement in productivity in al crops (e.g. rice productivity improved from 1,306 Kg in the fifties to 3,116 Kg in the nineties).

The local needs can be carefully identified and resources can be mobilized both locally and from various sources. On the basis of the local needs a plan will have to be carefully drawn up for this purpose. There are income generating shcemes through self—employment and wage–employment and both of them should take note of the local resource endowment and the over all development strategy. At present, it is not done adequately because of the absence of local planning. Efforts should be made to get the best out of such schemes through the development of human resources and better linkage with all development schemes.

Funds for promotional/farmers' fertilizer education programmes

The following table shows the amount spent for promotional activities by the PSUs/Cooperative vis-a-vis their annual turnover for the year 1994-95 and amount earmarked for 1995-96 :-

During the course of the evidence of the representatives of PSUs, Committe pointed out that the expenditure incurred by most of the PSUs/Cooperative (except IFFCO & KRIBHCO) was too meagre. Asked about the reasons/difficulty in not enhancing their budgets the CMD, NFL admitted before the Committee, "Sir, to be frank, the type of things which perhaps the hon. Chairman has in his mind, to that magnitude we are not going into the details".

When pointed out further that the expenditure on promotional activities should bear some relation with the turnover/profits of the respective PSUs, the witness stated, "We agree that as useful Members of the society, particularly the companies which are under the Government need to do something for the welfare of the farmers in order to improve, what is called, the use of fertilizers or efficient use of fertilizers. There is nothing wrong if a Central Government undertaking spends a part of its profit for this purpose. It may not be possible for the loss making companies to do so but the profit making compaines should take interest for the development of the farmers".

In this connection CMD, MFL submitted that MFL had suffered due to less demand of its products *Viz.* P & K fertilizers after their decontrol in 1992. He however stated that inspite of losses they were spending on promotional activities. He added, "We recognised the improtance of farmer's education and extension efforts and within our limited means we are providing it. We are also supplementing our own production because our production facilities are limited. We are supplementing it by trading activity in potassic fertilizers. We are importing MOP, a part of which we are utilizing in the manufacture of complex grade fertilizers or 17:17:17. It is higly rated in the Southern region, which is the traditional marketing zone. In addition to that, we are also selling MOP for direct application".

The witness further informed that there was need for common approach particularly the organisations dealing in complex fertilizers. Elaborating it further, he stated, "Every company likes to sell one's own product. In the field of fertilizer marketing we have seen a lot of duplication of resources & duplication of efforts. To avoid this type of wastage, they decide to explore the commonality of interest so that effort is not duplicated. The resources so economised can be put to fertilizer promotion effort. But, then it seems that this might not be feasible because everybody is trying to promote his own product in no preference to others' products. Some kind of propaganda is necessary. People have to be told why Vijay brand which is produced by MFL is preferable to others. Then, in that case the development of a common strategy becomes very difficult. There should be some self-abnegation on the part of the competitors so that they may work together for a common cause"

CMD, FACT elaborating the views of his company for allocating more funds for promotional activities stated, "From next year onwards, we will allocate more money in the Budget so that the programmes can be done with more emphasis. This is all the more needed because they will be given further impetus".

"In reply to a further query the witness stated, "Sir, it is fact that there is a commonality of interest insofar as the producers of potassium and phosphatic fertilizers are concerned. But, it is also a fact there is a lot of competition, today when there is a demand compression. Not everybody is able to place ones production in the market to the extent one would like to. Therefore, there is a lot of competition and everyone is stepping on each other's toes. So far, we had thought of some kind of synergy and exploitation of the synergy in this area and we had a wide ranging interaction with the Fertilizer Association of India. It was found that the commonalities can be exploited only to a very limited extent. However, in compliance of the direction of this Committee–you would recall that in the earlier meeting of the Committee–you had instructed about adopting coordinated approach in the promotion of fertilizers in education and extension effort".

When asked about the steps taken by PPL in raising in quantam funds for promotional activities. CMD PPL stated, "For 1995-96, we have provided Rs. 41 lakhs for promotional activities. And carlier, it was Rs. 30 lakh. So, we are slowly increasing it year after. That is still not sufficient. We are concentrating in the eastern part of our country, that is in states like Orissa, W. Bengal and Bihar. But we have not spent much amount. There is a justification for spending much more. We have constraints due to non-availability of funds".

However the CMD, PPL submitted before the Committee that funds for promotional activities should be pooled together and should be monitored through one agency in a given area or State which would avoid duplicity of efforts in regard to undertaking promotional activities.

He submitted, "However, for all the promotional activities and farmers' education, there can be a Central nodal agency which can be provided funds for promotional activities to avoid overlapping of same activities. For example, the total sale of fertilizers may be 15 million tonnes of nutrients. One that, Government levy cess of five to ten rupees PMT and distribute State-wise on the basis of needs. Otherwise, on the other hand each losing company may also not give any attention to promotional aspect whereas cash-rich company may not give attention to these activities because they are more concerned as to how to make more and more profits. Companies are paying less attention to promotional schemes whereas it is very very important from country's point of view".

"The funds so collected should be allotted to an agency in that particular State so that they carry out the promotional activities in one or two States. There are 13-15 companies which are manufacturing phosphatic fertilizers. That is the way how we can improve balanced fertilizer application. I can tell lyou very frankly that such approach has never been followed.

PPL wants to improve the promotional activities and farmers' education in Orissa, Bihar and Bengal. We are ready to spend Rs. 1 crore in a year. But my suggestion is that it should be through a consolidated fund. That fund should be utilised for the country as a whole. Otherwise, the same activities will be done by everybody. For example, I am also distributing the pamphlets to the farmers about how much quantity they sould use. The same thing is done by others. This overlapping can be reduced if it is done by one organisation".

During the course of evidence of representatives of DOF the Committee pointed out that he amount spent by PSUs for promotional activities was too low which was even agreed to by MDs of NFL, RCF, FACT and PPL Asked whether it did not call for higher allocation, the Secretary, Fertilizers stated, "I am very clear in may mind that the public sector companies have a social obligation. The Committee on Public Undertakings of the Parliament have made it very clear that these companies have a social obligation and they have so discharge it. So, a good investment is to invest in the human beings. Seventy five per cent of our farmers are marginal farmers with less than 2 hectares of land holding. They are able to cultivate barely enough for themselves. I am equally clear that the Goverment must make arrangements for creating awareness. Education is the basic thing. There is no question of saying that these companies should not invest more in this field. They will have to do it and the

Board will have to tell them about it. I cannot fix a percentage for them because they are autonomous. We are certainly going to benefit from your guidance on this and we will definitely give them a clear view. As far as I am concerned, in the quarterly review meeting, I will take up this issue.

The Ministry of Agriculture must play the lead role in it. I will request the agriculture sector to play the leadership role by coming into this field. The private sector companies also must play a very significant role because marketing is for everybody. We are giving a lot of support to the fertilizer companies. Therefore, the least that they can do is to give some allocation and increase their budgets for this purpose. If they do not do it they will be out of business".

When asked about the view of the DOF for fixing some percentage of turnover or profits, DOF in a written note stated, "Although there can thus be no linkage between the turn over or profits of a PSU/Cooperative with the expenditure on Farmers Education Programme, the Department is aware of the need for PSUs to increase their allocation in this regard".

The Committee further wanted to know whether DOF ever asked PSUs to raise funds for promotional activities. The Secretary, Fertilizer stated, "I will have a dialogue with them. We will issue a direction from the Government that they have to increase the allocation. But they have to consider it in their Board Meetings. We will review it in the quarterly review meeting".

Subsequently in a written note furnished to the Committee, DOF stated, "They have advised companies to pay more attention to promotional activities involving agricultural extension programmes. The response to our advice for greater emphasis on extension and farmers education is excepted to be reflected in the outlay for these activities in 1996-97. The instructions sent to CMD's/MD's of PSUs and cooperative on 27.2.1996 *inter-alia* include that the Government has decided to accept the above recommendation of the Standing Committee. You are therefore, advised to:

— fix specific target for the above mentioned promotional activities like educating the farmers about the need for balanced application of fertilizer nutrients, Farmers Meetings Demonstrations, Crop Melas, Soil Testing, Farmers Training, Seminars and any other activities compatible with the specific marketing needs and the requirements of your Boards of Directors before the beginning of each financial year under intimation to this Department;

— Send a half yearly progress report enumerating the actual achievements against these targets by 31st October of each year and the final report within one month of the close of each financial year to this Deparment;

— review the budget provision for promotional activities for 1996-97 to ensure that the financial provisions are commensurate with the physical targets".

In reply to a further query the Secretary, Fertilizers informed the Committee that in addition to Cooperatives/PSUs he was in touch with private sector companies for asking them to undertake activities for educating the farmers and related matters.

Land reforms

India is predominantly an agricultural country with nearly seventy per cent of her population living on agriculture and other allied activities. So land and land relations play an important role in formulating policies and programmes for country's development. In oder to ensure an equitable distribution of cultivable land and to give justice to actual tillers of land a series of land reform measures were adopted by the government during the post—independence period. The measures adopted are given below:

— Ceilings were imposed on large holdings and surplus land was distributed among the tenants

— Rent paid by the tenants was regulated by the State to reduce exploitation.

— Ownership rights were conferred on the tenants and sharecroppers in order to avoid eviction.

Through imposition of ceiling on agricultural holdings land was rationed and surplus land was distributed among the landless. In the beginning the unit of ceiling was an individual and not a family. Ceiling legislation was within the jurisdiction of the state legislature and different states enacted their ceiling legislation in different ways, Ceiling norms were evaded by the big land owners by illegally transferring the surplus land in the names of relatives, friends and even servants. The ceiling norm was reviewed and changed in 1972. This time a family of two to five members became a unit. In West Bengal the ceiling was 5 hectare per family. If the family size was more than five, for each additional member 0.5 hectare could be allotted. However, the total holding size per family should not exceed 7 hectares. This ceiling norm is followed till now. According to this norm, one member family should retain 2.5 hectares of land. As a result, a major son living separately or a divorced wife is entitled to a separate standard holding of 2.5 hectares. The present ceiling law is evaded by the land owners in a number of ways. In many cases minor sons have been recorded as major and false cases of divorce and separation have been shown on papers.

The third important objective of land reform was consolidation of holdings. However, excepting in Haryana, Punjab and Western U.P., not much progress has been made in this respect.

Although some of the land reform measures have been implemented effectively in West bengal there are still many loopholes. A considerable percentage of share croppers remain unrecorded. According to an official estimate 1.44 million share croppers in West Bengal have been recorded by the end of 1991. This is nearly 92 to 93% of the total share croppers.

Let us now discuss the nature of cropo—sharing and cost sharing system of share croppers in West Bengal According to the tenancy law (Bergman, 1984) a share—cropper should retain 50 per cent of the produce if the landowner provides plough, cattle, manure and seeds. They are entitled to 75% of the gross produce if no input cost is borne by the landowner. If the cost of material inputs is shared jointly by the share—cropper and the landowner, the share cropper is entitled to 50% of the gross produce in exchange of manual labour, the landowner is entitled to 25% is share cropper and the landowner in proportion to the cost shared by them.

When recording of tenants was done in West Bengal under "Operation Barga" movement, it was stated that the tenants could never be evicted from land and they would receive 75% share of crops produced on the leased in land and bear the entire input cost. It is true that the Operation Braga movement has increased the security of the recorded tenants to a large extent. Now a days it is not quite easy to evict them from their leased in land. However, till now, the recorded tenants do not receive 75% of the crokps produced on the Barga land.

Small scale field surveys in different parts of West Bengal show that the recorded share croppers still receive various types of crop shares, e.g. (a) 50%, (b) 40%, (c) 33.3% and (d) 75% of the gross produce. Share croppers receiving 75% of gross produce have to bear the entire input cost. The share croppers receiving 50% of the gross produce have to provide manual labour and the bullock power. The cost of material inputs (fertilizers—organic and inorganic and irrigation water) is generally shared equally by the share cropper and the landlord. There are however a few cases where the share croppers receiving 50% crop share do not provide any material input. They have to provide only manual labour and bullock power. Share croppers receiving 40% or 33.3% of gross produce supply manual labour only. In some cases, share croppers receiving 40% crop share provide manure in the form of cow dung.

A little bit of probing will show the reasons behind such a wide variety of cropsharing system. The official records state that by 1991 there were 1,44 million recorded share croppers occupying 0.45 million hectare land. On an average, the amount of land per recorded share cropper is approximately 0.31 hectare. Thus the holdings operated by the recorded share croppers are very small in size and the total amount of crops raised on such small plots is not sufficient for their need.

Most of the share—croppers, coming from the scheduled caste and thescheduled tribe communities are very poor. They are not in a position to bear all the input costs. So they have arrived at a mutual understanding with the land owners. The share croppers take a smaller share of crops in exchange of a certain percentage of costs to be shared by the owners. There are also other reasons on the part of the tenants for entering into such adjustments. One important reason may be the availability of consumption loans and other loans for meeting emergencies like marriage of daughters or medical treatment of the family members etc. Moreover in a large number of cases even the Barga loans were used for household consumption purposes and for meeting other emergencies. Such emergencies have sometimes prompted the recorded share croppers even to surrender their leased in land to the owners in exchange of a lump—sum money. Thus, although the recording of leased in land has increased the security of the tenants, it has failed to restore the stipulated amount of cropshare to the recorded share croppers.

Farming methods and practices in India have a long history, and have been evolved out of the experience of ages. They have well stood the test of time. The technological advances in the world, e.g., the use of fertilisers, insecticides, fungicides, irrigation pumps, machines, etc., have mostly taken place in the present century and are hardly sixty years old. It should cause no surprise if a country of India's size with millions of small farmers has not yet been able to adopt them as fully as has been done by some countries of the West and Japan in the East.

Agriculture policy

Government took little interest in the problems of agriculture before the mid-seventies of the 19th century. They were pre-occupied almost exclusively with problems of revenue police and judicial administration. It was the great Bengal and Assam Famine of 1866 and the experience of organising relief that forced the attention of the Government to the need for the development of agriculture as a means of averting famine and mitigating the hardships of the people. The first proposal to constitute a special Department of Agriculture at the Centre was put forward by the commission appointed in 1866, following the severe famine of that year but was turned down as premature.

Guided by the needs of Lancashire textile mills, the British Government undertook measures in 1869 to improve the production of long staple cotton in India. This could perhaps * same year the proposal for a special department was repeated by the Manchester Cotton Organization which led to a serious consideration of the subject by the Government. However, this attempt also did not achieve much success.

It was only in 1871 that the Department of Revenue, Agriculture and Commerce was created. It was recognised that provincial Departments of Agriculture must form an essential part of any scheme of agricultural development. The Department had a very brief existence of about seven years and was merged in the Home Department in 1879 for reasons of financial stringency. Its only achievement was to evolve a system for the collection of agricultural statistics and other data.

Very useful suggestions were made by the successive Famine and Irrigation Commissions for the development of agriculture. But, as observed by the Royal Commission on Agriculture: "The Government took no immediate action and the next ten years were spent mainly in conferences." It was the result of the recommendations of the report of the Framine Commission, 1880-81 that a separate Department of Revenue and Agriculture was revived in 1881. It was fully realised even in the initial stages that without a provincial agency, no programme of agricultural improvement, which emanated from the Headquarters, could be productive of tangible results, that the main responsibility for agricultural research and experiment must fall on provincial governments and all that the Centre could do was to give a general lead. The new department was directed to take up immediately the question of the form to be given to provincial department.

Provincial Departments of Agriculture were established in UP (then known as the NWP), Bombay, Bengal, Madras and C.P. between 1875 and 1905. Their functions were clearly defined by the Government of India and consisted largely of collection of statistical and economic data. There was some research notably in Bombay, and a few sporadic experiments in the cultivation of American cotton, groundnut, potatoes and fruit in some other provinces. But not much progress could be made by such efforts in the absence of a sound policy and an efficient organisation.

It was realised very early by the Secretariat that without technical advice no advance was possible. Dr. J.A. Voelcker, distinguished agricultural chemist, was brought over to India in 1889 to conduct an enquiry into the character of the soils and agricultural conditions. This is regarded as the "first serious step to frame a policy of agriculture research suited to the conditions of India." This was followed by the appointment, in 1891, of an Inspector-General of Agriculture with advisory functions. His duties were specified as "the systematic study of Indian agriculture, its conditions and remediable defects; the supervision and development of provincial agricultural departments; the establishment of improved agricultural methods and new staples and generally the direction of the agricultural policy of the government." An imperial mycologist and an entomologist were added to the department in 1901-3. Among the developments of this period mention should be made of the establishement of the Imperial Institute of Veterinary Research in 1889 and the Botanical and Zoological Surveys in 1890.

The report of the Famine Commission of 1901 inaugurated the next significant stage in the growth of agriculture departments. The Commission recommended the strengthening of the scientific staff of agricultural departments and legislation to set up mutual credit societies. During the period of Lord Curzon, these recommendations were implemented and agricultural departments were thoroughly reorganized. There was an expansion of the scientific staff of the departments and of their activities. With the setting up of the Imperial Agricultural Research Institute at Pusa and bringing together with it the scientific staff of the department under a single roof, organised agricultural research may be said to have begun in India. Directors of Agriculture were appointed in all the provinces. Circles were marked out and placed under Deputy Directors who were responsible for experimental seed and demonstration farms within their jurisdiction. Agricultural colleges were reorganised and research stations and experimental farms were also set up. The Imperial Agricultural Service was constituted in 1906. Altogether the years from 1905 to 1914 were the years of the steady growth in agricultural research and education and other services. The substantial advances made during these years by provincial departments were largely due to the stimulus and guidance of the central government and grants made by it.

After the reforms of 1919, agriculture became a transferred subject. Under the new arrangement, the central government was to look after the central agencies and institutions for research. The provincial governments could not make much headway since the resources at their disposal were limited. During this period some irrigation works were completed. Under the 1935 Reforms, the sphere of central government's responsibilities was further restricted. It was to look after the subjects of all India importance only.

A Royal Commission on Agriculture was appointed in 1926. It was required to examine and report on the prevailing conditions of agriculture. The Commission was asked to investigate, particularly, (1) the measures being taken for the promotion of agricultural and veterinary research, experiment, demonstration and education, the compilation of agricultural statistics, introduction of new and better crops and improvement in agricultural practices, dairy farming and the breeding of stock; (2) the existing methods of transport and marketing of agricultural produce and stock; (3) the methods by which agricultural operations were financed and credit afforded to agriculture; and (4) main factors affecting the rural prosperity and welfare of the agricultural population.

The recommendations of the Commission were made with a view to bringing about all, round efficiency in the field of agricultural production. The aim was to make agriculture a profitable industry rather than a mode of living. The Commission covered such subjects as fragmentation and subdivision of holdings, irrigation, improvement of livestock, rural education, cooperation, marketing, etc. One of the basic recommendations of the Commission was to change the outlook of the cultivator himself so that he may take an active interest in bringing about improvements. It suggested that "rural problem should be tackled as a whole in all its various aspects simultaneoulsy." It assigned and charged the government with specific responsibility for bringing improvements in rural life. The Commission's Report is still considered a reference publication on agricultural policy.

In accordance with the recommendations of the Royal Commission to review periodically the working of the Imperial Council of Agricultural Research which had been established on its recommendation, Sir John Russell, Director, Rothamsted Experimental Station, England, visited India in 1936. According to him, the Council had admirably discharged its primary duty of coordination and promotion of agricultural research in the field of crop production. He stressed the need for further use of existing knowledge, rather than he accumulation of more knowledge and stated that knowledge gained in the laboratory should be applied to cultivator's fields. He suggested that the burden of the Council should be lessened by asking universities to undertake all investigations of a scientific or non-technical nature.

He recommended that the results of research in agriculture should be made widely public. It had not been done in the past. He suggested that the Council should take the responsibility of putting the result of research into practice and act as a Development Commission. He further remarked that the Council's investigations should be directed to increasing the output per acre of food crops with a view to ensuring food supplies and liberating land for the growth of the supplimentary and fodder crops for the production of milk.

The achievements up to 1937 may be described as the creation of the Central and State Departments of Agriculture for agricultural research, education and extension and provision and intensification of facilities for research and education. In spite of considerable expansion in the staff and activities of agricultural departments, research and education facilities were very inadequate. There were few men for agricultural extension work. Stationed at the revenue divisions, they could hardly contact farmers and much less offer any technical advice to them. The demonstration farms maintained by the government failed to carry much conviction to the farmers as the facilities they had were considered something very different from their own farming situations. Agricultural education was not very effective in turning out scientists and practical farmers.

The village community spirit had been considerably weakened under the British rule. A void had been created in the village administration in spheres in which the community exercised control before. A powerful class of new vested interests in the form of moneylenders and landlords had been created. The landlords as a class lacked the traditions which their counterpart in Britain had developed and many of them were interested only in rent. The moneylender was armed with the traditions of English Law. All restrictions on accumulation of interest or increase in the burden of farmers' debt imposed by the community under the old village panchayat system had been thrown to the winds. The farming community groaned under the exploitative economic system in which the landlord and the moneylender figured prominently.

Agriculture could hardly prosper under such an exploitation. The discouragement to village and cottage industries destroyed the economic balance which characterised the older system. Persons displaced from these occupations added to the pressure on land which had already become disquieting.

The years that followed were those of upheaval in the Indian history. The Congress ministries took office in the states. World War II started. The country subsequently became free but was partitioned. The balance between agricultural resources and the industries based on them was upset. There * enterprising farmers of Punjab moved to the unsettled areas in UP and other states. One good effect of such a shift in their habitation has been the improvement in the standard of crop and animal husbandry in the areas where they settled. The war, partition, and the growing population aggravated the problem of food.

The Grow More Food Campaign began in 1942. Since then food production has received top priority. In respect of land reforms most states initiated action for the abolition of landlordism and intermediaries. Another notable development has been the setting up of a wide network of National Agricultural Extension Service. There has been considerable expansion in research and training programme as well. It was decided by the government in 1951 to channel the development of the total economy of the country through a regular planned course.

Gandhi had said: "India's soul lives in villages". India will perish if we don't take care of them. He advocated the model of development from bottom—upwards—to top. But the model we have followed is from top-down-to bottom. This model believes in trickle down and percolation theory of development. People were actively involved neither in the planning process nor in the implementation of various programmes, activities and schemes.

There is an interesting dialogue between the Mughal emperor, Akbar and and Birbal about the result of policies and programmes imposed on people from above.

Akbar was a benevolent and popular ruler. He felt that nobody would violate his or his state's order. Birbal was of the opinion that nobody could execute the order unless people were consulted and involved. Akbar wanted to test the validity of Birbal's argument. An order was issued that the people should pour one jug of milk each during the night in the four reservoirs dug for this purpose in the city. Next morning both of them found that the reservoirs were full with water instead of milk. The people, on enquiry, informed that they poured water into the reservoirs as they did not have milk to spare. They also wanted to send the message across to the king and his administrators that such orders should not be issued without consulting and involving them. People must be taken into confidence and should be explained in detail about the aims and objects of plans and schemes to get their participation.

With the advent of freedom, India faced many problems. As the task of immediate relief and rehabilitation of refugees was on the way to completion, the government began to think in terms of rebuilding the country and reawakening the people.

This made the government adopt planning as a way and method to deal with the complicated problems to change and transform the socio-economic life of the people. Thus, came the Five Year Plan—a model of human patience, skill and endeavour; a documented account of the resources both human and material, and suggestions for their optimum utilisation. A constructive revolution had begun in the form of a series of development schemes, national as well as State.

I Plan—mother of all Plan: In a sense, the First Five year Plan might be described as the mother of all subsequent plans.

Planning had become fashionable everywhere in the world at the end of the Second World War. In India, various government departments in Delhi, Bombay and other State capitals, had prepared plans for the development of the economy. The Indian government after taking over from the British did not discard these plans. It sifted out the mere feasible schemes and incorporated them into what came to be known as India's First Five Year Plan. However, it was merely, a priority list for government expenditure than a real plan. The objective of the First Five Year Plan was to prevent the government from squandering money and to set out in general terms the ideals of social and economic equality. Had the Plan failed, planning might well have been set aside, but the Gods favoured and two excellent monsoons made the Plan a success. Let us see what two of the Gandhian stalwarts had to say about the Plan.

R. K. Patil, the then Member of the Planning Commission took the draft of the First Five Year Plan For discussion with Vinoba. Vinoba found that the Plan as far as he was concerned was of no use to him as there was no mention of employment and food self-sufficiency. He felt that the only useful thing it contained was the "pin" and the rest could be consigned to the waste-paper basket.

A telegraphic message was sent by Nehru, the then Prime Minister to Vinoba to come to Delhi and apprise the members of the Planning Commission with his views. Vinoba replied promptly to Nehru that as per his wish he had started for Delhi, but on foot. Of course, he would have nothing to say to the members as they were highly knowledgeable and experts in their respective fields. However, in his pad-yatra from Wardha to Delhi, he would ascertain from people their opinions about their needs and priorities. On reaching Delhi he asked the learned members about the methods and ways by which they would like to achieve self-sufficiency and self-reliance in food. The reply of the global market and import our items in the global market and import grains at competitive rates from the would market. This did not satisfy Vinoba Bhave. He was of the opinion that every country had to be self-sufficient, the country would not be able to maintain its independence. He felt disenchanted with the ways of the government and felt that is was necessary to prepare the people who would bring pressure on policies and programmes of government.

J.C. Kumarappa served as a representative of the Sarva Seva Sangh in the Planning Commission Advisory

Board. Form New Delhi Railway Station, he engaged a tonga to reach the venue of the Board meeting in the South wing of Rashtrapati Bhavan. At the outer gate, a young officer commanded the driver to get off the road. When Kumarappa intervened that he had every right to use a public road, the office replied that he was clearing the road for Panditji (Nehru), the then Prime Minister. On Kumarappa's assertion that he was also attending the same meeting, he was allowed to proceed. But he had to encounter the same trouble at the subsequent gates too, though succeeding ultimately in his attempts. He strongly protested against this treatment to the military secretary warning him that he would ride on a bullock—cart to the meeting place if the meeting continued for the following day. In the meeting, when the question of road came up, Kumarappa pointed out that bullock-cart drive was as good a citizen as Prime Minister in a democracy and that he was insulted by denying him the use of a public road. Agreeing to the quality of all citizens in a democracy, Jawaharlal Nehru explained that the restriction "bullock carts not allowed" was to save them from would be accidents due to the frequency of military lorries on the road. To this Kumarappa quipped that a simple man like him would put up a board there "motor cars and lorries are not allowed," thereby restraining the source of danger rather than the possible victim". A peal of laughter rent the air in response to his ready wit and simple plan speaking.

He said: "Instead of burying Gandhi into our heart we are burying him deep into the earth." We wish our leaders and representatives would ponder over his words. He had the courage to tell Vinoba that he was 'number one thief" in India. Vinoba who was taken aback by this unexpected charge from his bosom friend asked for clarification. Kumarappa calmly told him that he was merely referring to his hoarding the lands, obtained through Bhoodan without proper arrangements for their distribution. Binoba immediately understood the truth behind his statement and thereafter expedited the distribution of lands to the needy.

It is necessary to recall in this context that the planning Commission was pushed to the background in the background in the wake of liberalization and structural reform programme. Though the Eighth Five Year Plan was approved by the National Development Council and the States' Eighth Five Year Plans were discussed and approved, the intellectual importance of the Planning Commission was reduced during the period 1991-95. This was partly because the Planning Commission did not change its thinking in keeping with the international wave and partly because the Planning Commission was critical about specific policy package of liberalization and structural reforms. There was also some difference in the perceptions of the Union Ministry of Finance and the Planning Commission on specific policy issues like the quality of intellectual input which the planning Commission used to provide to the policy-makers in the government had declined. Therefore, during the last two years of the Eighth Plan the Planning Commission was simply ignored.

The United Front government has decided to restore the intellectual status of the Planning Commission. It has reconstituted the Planning Commission with an eminent person who was Union Finance Minister as the Deputy Chairman. He took the task seriously and revived the image of the planning Commission. The Planning Commission completed the Annual Plan discussions for 1996-97 in a record time and prepared the approach paper as indicated by the Planning Commission. It may look a trivial matter to mention here that the Prime Minister Mr H.D. Deve Gowda, who is the Chairman of the Planning Commission, convened the first meeting of the full Commission on 16 August, 1996 and he saw to it that the meeting was held in Yojana Bhavan to boost the morale of its personnel. After Jawaharlal Nehru, no Prime Minister had visited Yojana Bhavan to preside over the full meeting of the Planning Commission Mr H.D. Deve Gowda not only presided over the full meeting but also provided broad guidelines for the Ninth Five Year Plan. Further, the Prime Minister had convened a meeting of the Chief Ministers in July 1996 to take them into confidence in formulating a crash programme for ensuring basic minimum services to the rural people. This meeting gave an opportunity for the Planning Commission to gauge the feelings of the State governments. The Planning Commission had requested the Chief Ministers to indicate their views on the Ninth Five Year Plan in the course of the 1996-97 Annual Plan discussions. After receiving the written views of the state governments and after several internal meetings of the Planning Commission, the approach paper was finalized.

The Ninth Plan has introduced a number of correctives to reverse many of the unsustainable trends in the programmes and projects of previous plans. It has also laid stress on

(1) maintenance and better utilization of existing assets/ capacities in the one hand and early completion of incomplete projects on the other, so that productivity of the existing assets improves and benefits realized early,

(2) approval of limited number of projects which are operationally viable and can be completed within a short period and for which adequate funds are available. And further, the aproval and monitoring process would become more scientific and rigorous, and

(3) a genuine push towards decentralization and people's participation in the planning process through institutional reforms and strengthening the Panchayati Raj and the different models of people's instirutions. The Centre and the States will work jointlly to overcome most of the deficiencies in prograamme formulaion and implementation.

All these strategies have certainly greater relevance in improving the efficiency of economic organization and ensuring social justice.

But there are two important constraints.

First, whether the public sector can provide adequate funds for planned development. Public investment as a whole, as mentioned earlier, is targeted to be no more than 33 per cent of the total investment as against 36.5 per cent realized during the VIII Plan. Fiscal and revenue deficits are still quite high and there is no possibility that they can be contained during the period of the Ninth Plan. The Planning Commission proposes to increase presumptive income tax on the basis of reliable reference list of facilities such as telephones, cars, gas and electricity connections. In addition, it also suggests to augment non-tax revenues through revision of irrigation charges and royalties on mines. It is doubtful, whether the government can tale such hard decisions. Populism is the source of fiscal crisis both in the Centre and the states and this continues unabated even when there is financial bankruptcy at many levels.

Secondly, where is the political will to realize th objectives laid down in the Ninth Plan? Most of the politicians have lost their credibility. The bureaucratic system has become ineffective to respond to the changes that have become inherent in the new environment. Even the Panchayati system is controlled by a number of petty and corrupt politicians. They are not likely to inspire confidence among the people. The NGOs who are sometimes called 'sacred cows' have lost their sacredness. Many of them are mere mercenariess. All the agents of change are more gor less ineffective to brin about any radical change either in the economy or in the social structure. The old desperation may frustrate new hopes. The onmly positive note that we can enshrine is that "if hopes were dupes, the fears might be liars.

There is massive evidence to support the fact that appropriate legal protection acts as an incentive for productive research. The Uruguay Round, which was concluded in 1994, marked the beginning of a significant transformation in the global economic and trade environment. Annex 1c of the final Act deals with the agreement on Trade-Related Aspects of Intellectual Property Rights (TRIPs). Section 5 (Part II) of the annex pertains to "Patents" under article 27. With reference to agriculture, the text states, "Members shall provide for the protection of Plant Varieties by Patents or by an effective sui generis system or by any combination thereof'. Since the Indian Patents Act (1970) excluded to put into place a sui generis system by evolving a legislation on plant variety protection (PVP) by the year AD 2000.

The 1970 Act was also inadequate in terms of covering processes but not the product patents in food, medicine, drugs and substances provided by chemical processes. It now stands amended through a presidential ordinance (31/12/94), thus ushering in a new patents regime.

The TRIPs agreement has introduced profound changes which will influence competitiveness, generation and diffusion of technological innovations and ultimately the technological development prospects of developing countries (DCs) The impact of the changes can thus be far-reaching, though at this early stage it is difficult to assess the full implications of the agreement. An attempt is made here to consider, in a preliminary manner, some possible implications of the new regimes. IPRs constitute an important element of trade negotiations. The GATT accord on TRIPs has raised a whole lot of apprehensions and engaged the attention of intellectuals, politicians, farmers and media for quite sometime now. The legal dimensions of TRIPs make it difficult to understand, and vulnerable to a host of misgivings. Some discernible patterns can be identified in areas relating to limited duration, PBR and exclusions. By and large, the low income and lower-middle income countries do not accord PBR and have shorter protection periods. Pharmaceuticals and foodstuffs are the most commonly excluded products.

Myth and reality

The debate on the implications of TRIPs began with reference to pharmaceuticals. Subsequently, myriad views have been expressed regarding the possible impact of TRIPs accord on Indian Agriculture.

Issues relating to germplasm and biotechnology are substantial and valid, but these are best pursued independently of the PBR debate. PBR is not a panacea, but can serve the farmers by increasing their access to improved seeds at reasonable prices by augmenting the efforts of public systems through private seed firms.

Farmer's education and related agricultural extension work falls within the jurisdiction of Ministry of Agriculture. However, 8 fertilizer producing companies in public sector and 2 in cooperative sector (where majority of paid up capital is held by the Government) under the administrative control of Deptt. of Fertilizers also carry-out agricultural extension work out of their own resources with emphasis on education of farmers in scientific application of fertilizers. These public. Sector Undertakings/Cooperatives are IFFCO, KRIBHCO, NFL, MFL, RCF, FACT, PPCL, PPL, FCI and HFC. Some of these PSUs/Cooperatives have also implemented Fertilizer Education Project with foreign assistance. The prominent activities undertaken by the PSUs/ Cooperative include farmer's meetings, demonstrations, crop melas/seminars, soil testing training programmes etc.

The Committee's examination of the subject has revealed that this area has not been given due importance as it should have been given by the fertilizer producing companies keeping in view the needs of the farming community of the Country. The Committee's recommendations/conclusions are set out in the succeeding paragraphs.

The committe regret to note that 10 fertilizer producing PSUs/Cooperatives under the administrative control of the DOF hardly allocate their funds to farmers education programme. For instance, during the year 1994-95, out of the total spending of about Rs. 10 crores by all units, Rs. 5 crores was spent by IFFCO and Rs. 2.28 crores by KRIBHCO thus leaving a meagre sum of less then Rs. 3 crores for remaining 7 units. Not to speak of sick units the HFC & FCI, big profit making untis like NFl are ending a meagre amount of Rs. 28 lakhs annualy. This Committee's view is a gross negligence on the part of public sector Undertakings which besides commercial functions, have to achieve social obligations. CMDs of some of the PSUs agreed to the suggestion of the Committee that there was need to enhance budget for these activities and even some percentage of their profits could be earmarked for the purpose. Secretary, Deptt. of Fertilizers was also can did in his admission before the Committee that the matter was being taken up with seriousness only after the Committee's deliberation over the issue and even though it may not be feasible to fix a percentage of the turnover or profits, cocenred PSUs as also the units in private sector would be asked to considerably raise the funds for farmers related programmes. Subsequently the Ministry has issued instructions to PSUs/Cooperatives to enhance their allocations for this purpose. The Committee would like the Ministry to pursue this matter with all concerned agencies for ensuring the implementation of their guidelines.

The facts and figures have compelled the Committee to observe that there is lack of foresightedness on the part of Government in regard to correcting the imbalance in use of NPK. The Government provides annual subsidy for urea of the order of about Rs. 3,000 crores at production stage and about Rs. 1650 crores on import and adhoc-subsidy for P & K fertilizer (around Rs. 500 crores annually). As compared to quantum of subsidy the Government allocation for the farmer's education programmes is very very low. For instance out of the total budget Rs. 26 crores for balanced and integrated use of fertilizers under Ministry of Agriculture for the purpose for the entire 8th Five Year Plan, the Government has spent only Rs. 7.25 crores during the first three years of the Plan. In Committee's view the allocation for a scheme like balanced and integrated use of fertilizer is too meagre and funds should be raised adequately, as the programme will help to educate the farmers in scientific way. This will help in correcting the imbalance in use of NPK fertilizer. Besides in the long run it will also help in reducing the subsidy element.

After goint into the details of spending by PSUs etc. on farmers' education programmes, the Committee are constrained to note that the activities undertaken by the concerned organisations are hardly adequate to meet the farmers requirements. Admittedly no targets were fixed for different types of promotional activities. It is only recently i.e. in February, 1996, when the Ministry has asked PSUs to take a cue from IFFCO'S efforts in this regard. The Committee would like the Government that like all other activities, specific targets should be fixed for all types of farmers' education programmes and these should be reviewed and monitored by the Ministry.

Admittedly the farmers'education programmes/ schemes do not form part of MOU signed by the Government with respective PSUs. The Committee would like the Government to examine this issue for getting these schemes a part of MOUs for regular monitoring.

The Committee's examination of the farmers fertilizer education programme has revealed that there is hardly any coordination between the PSUs. There is overlapping in the areas covered by the PSUs at all. The Farmer's related activities are carried out by PSUs through Farmers Service Centres/Kendras etc. In this context the Committee in their 13th Report on 'IFFCO & KRIBHCO' had pointed out that Farmer's Service Centres/Kendras were crowded in selected fertile areas. In pursuance of Committee's recommendation, the Deptt. of Fertilizer has asked IFFCO to initiate a study to take stock of existing farmers service centres set up by different PSUs/Cooperatives to identify deficit areas requiring further support for promotional activities. This study is expected to be completed by June, 1996. The Committee would like the Government/IFFCO to complete this study within the stipulated time. Needless to emphasis that action would be taken to set up new centres or upgrade the existing ones in deficit areas.

The Committee have been informed that some of the PSUs have successfully implemented foreign assisted fertilizer education projects. The important ones being

Indo-Britain Fertilizer Education project costing Rs. 22 crores (implemented by HFC) and Indo-EEC fertilizer education project costing Rs. 6 crores and implemented by FACT, RCF, NFL and PPCL.The only current foreign aided project is ODA funded Rainfed Farming Project which is being implemented by HFC/KRIBHCO. PSUs, as also the Ministry, informed the Committee that these projects were quite useful for the farmers of the related areas. Another project viz. Indo-British Fertilizer Education and Extension project (ODA funding) costing Rs. 55 crores is yet to approved by funding agency. Keeping in view of the quantum of money and the likely benefits of the projects, the Committee recommended that the matter may be pursued at the highest level in the Government to get the approval of the funding agency.

The Committee have been informed that each PSU carries out promotional activities independently and there was no scope of coordination with other agencies. Apart from PSUs/Cooperatives under Department of Fertilizers, Ministry of Agriculture and State Governments also carry out farmer's fertilizer education related programmes. Secretary, Fertilizers, informed the Committee that he would hold coordination meetings with Agriculture Secretary for achieving better results in this key area. The Committe would like the Government of coordinate the activities of all agencies for meaningful deployment of the funds and infrastructure. This step will ensure maximum benefit to farmers across the country with the funds and infrastructure at the disposal of the Government.

Some of the PSUs have suggested that it would be better if all funds are pooled together and different PSUs are given specific areas for carrying out promotional activities. The Committee find some meriut in the suggestion They, therefore, would like the Government to examine pros and cons of the suggestion before taking a decision in the matter.

During the course of examination, CMDs of some of the PSUs submitted before the Committee that any number of promotional programmes implemented would not produce results in correcting the present imbalance in fertilizer use, as long as urea price is low on account of huge subsidy and prices of decontrolled fertiliser viz. P & K continue to increase every season. Due to this farmers are tempted to use more and more urea. This situation calls for review of the existing pricing policy for fertilizers. The Committee, therefore, would like the Government to examine the pricing policy afresh and apprise the Committee about the decision taken in this regard.

Task ahead

The TRIPs agreement would require substantial changes in the patents regime of our country. Most developed countries, as they are members of the UPOV Conventions, accord protection to plant varieties. By contrast, only a handful of DCs have sui generis protection systems (e.g. Argentina, Chile, Kenya, the Republic of Korea, Uruguay and Zimbabwe). The PVP legislation proposed to be enacted is modelled on the basis of the International Union for the Protection of new Varieties of Plants (UPOV) guidelines. UPOV 1978 version allowed for the rights of plant breeders and farmers, whereas UPOV 1991 is more stringent in the sense that it disallows both. There is general consensus that we opt for UPOV 1978 and this option is available only till the UPOV 1991 is ratified by at least five member countries. But the fourth International Conference on Plant Genetic Resources, at Leipzig (Germany), has vindicated the state of the DCs. It succeeded in getting a global endorsement for farmers rights, paving the way for the member countries to enact PVP legislation in ways that best serve their respective national interests.

The "World Intellectual Property Organization WIPO) model law for developing countries on inventions" can serve as a general outline for the proposed law on PVP. Although, patent laws are inherently a national issue, it is time we join (albeit, selectively) various international conventions/treaties, so that cost of obtaining patents and international search reports can be reduced substantially. Also, keeping in view the distinct variations in cost of patenting across nations, there is a case for differential slabs of application fees for foreign applicants seeking patents in our country. Judicious provisions for compulsory licensing and non-voluntary license should be the feature of the proposed legislation to curb possible patent abuses. The proposed PVP has adequate safeguards to take care of farmers, researchers and environmental concerns. It is high time that the proposed legislation is enacted so that this unnecessary irritant in our trade relations, particularly with the DMEs is removed.

The TRIPs agreement aims at a certain minimum standard of IPR protection. Successful implementation of the TRIPs agreement has a number of prerequisites, the important ones being legal, administrative and institutional reforms, appropriate research investments, and first rate science and technology capability. Provided the IPR protection is adequate and effective (worldwide), the TRIPs accord can promote innovations, transfer of technology, foreign direct investment, use of genetic resources and environmental protection. The returns from the economic value of protection system far outweighs its costs. However, while legal protection may be a necessary condition for innovative activities and technology transfer, it is by no means a sufficient condition, given the importance of a host of other factors affecting research investment and the transfer and diffusion of technology in DCs and its ability to internalize benefits from the new rules of the game. The nation's capacity to move from technology importer to technology exporter will be the major determinant of its position in international hierarchy. Foresight demands towards quality and frontier areas.

Creation of a patent cell in the ICAR, is a step in the right direction. Having a clear-cut intellectual property policy and promoting patent literacy (similar to CSIR) among its scientists, must be the next logical step. A massive awareness programme needs to be undertaken to clear doubts regarding the process of patent application and registration, patent information services, inspection of files, determination of national need and the whole gamut of related issues.

To maximize opportunities, DCs must foster and reward entrepreneurship and evolve a regulatory environment conductive to technological innovation. An effective IP regime will provide the synergy between the private and public sector research institutions. This will then provide a basis for future growth and development, particularly in the case of India which has a large pool of scientific manpower.

Integrating environemntal considerations into development planning is not an easy task. Unless concern is backed by an ability to take ameliorative action, little can be achieved. India has been very conscious of this and has, over the past few decades, taken important steps to increase its capacity to handle environmental issues.

The initiatives have come equally from the Government, NGO's and individuals. Many collaborative and joint programmes exist today between the Government and the NGO's. Environment and development problems are complex and there cannot be generalized and simplified solutions. Answers have to be found which are ecologically, economically and socio-culturally consistent in the particular milie. Given the size and diversity of a country like India, this task becomes extremely difficult.

Expertise is requied in framing appropriate policies and legislation, in planning, in creating mechanisms for implementation, in * education and public awareness. India also needs to be above to bring its perspective to global forums and participate in evolving international treaties, protocols and conventions. Most importantly, with the increasing emphasis on decentralized decision—making and the stress on micro-planning, this capacity-building is taking on a greater urgency. Capability is required to enable decisions to be made in a decentralized manner—decisions which are not imported solutions, but are appropriate to the particular situation.

Addressing the plenary session of the UN Conference on Human Environment in Stockholm in 1972, Prime Minister Indira Gandhi and said, "Even though our industrial development is in its infancy and at its most difficult stage, we are taking various steps to deal with the incipient environmental imbalances, more so because of our concern for the human species, whic is also imperilled." It was at her initiative that a National Council Environmental Planning and Coordination (NECPC) was set up in 1972 to identify and investigate the problems of preserving or improving the human environment in the country, and to propose solution to environmental problems.

Another Empowered Committee, the Tiwari Committee, was set up in 1980 to review and recommend legislative measures and administrative machinery for ensuring environmental protection. On the recommendation of this Committee, the Department of Environment was set up in 1980 as the focal agency in the administrative structure of the Central Government for planning, promotion and coordination of environmental programmes. This department became part of the new Ministry of Environment and Forest in 1985.

The Ministry is the apex body under the Government of India for planning, promotion and coordination of environmental and forestry programmes. Its activities include conservation and survey of flora and fauna, prevention and control of pollution, afforestation and regeneration of degraded areas, impact assessment, forest conservation and research, and education and information. The National Wastelands Development Board and the Ganga Project Directorate are major components of the Ministry.

Most of the states have also set up their own Departments of Environment, Pollution Control Boards and other associated bodies. Various other ministries and departments, including those of Urban Development, Oceanography, Non-Conventional Energy Sources etc., at the state and central levels, are also concerned with different aspects of the environment. Greater coordination among these various agencies—government and non-government-would strengthen environmental efforts. State Governments are in the process of involving themselves seriously in environmental planning.

The Directory of Environmental NGOs, brought out by the World Wide Fund for Nature - India (WWF-I) in 1989, lists about 850 NGOs working in this field, but there are porbably at least four times this number. Their involvement is clearly seen. As the Secretary General of WWF-I says, "India's impressively large body of NGOs is becoming active on the environmental front because fo the increasingly clear nexus between meaningful, equitable, sustainable economic growth and the conservation of the environment...For instance, the National Environmental Awareness Campaign promoted by the Ministry has successfully encouraged many NGOs whose primary concerns are rural development, appropriate technology, civil rights, women's development, tribal welfare etc. The interaction between NGOs and State Governments is largely confined to functional matters (clearance, information, advice etc.) whereas for financial and technical support various central departments and agencies have to be relied upon. However now there is a concerted effort by the Government to use their expertise for their own programmes."

NGOs range from clubs which encourage and assist in adventure travel, exploration, and dissemination of knowledge about an ecosystem to agencies which deal with various issues like creating gainful employment, wastelands development, afforestation, rehabilitation of tribals, and with preparation of educational materials and aids. They may be as small as groups of two or three persons, or as large as organizations with an eight-thousand-strong membership.

One of the most important signs of environmental awareness in India is the rise of people's movements which are challenging existing socio-political structures and development models, and are showing alternative paths. These have led not only to action at the grassroot level, but are also helping to shape developmental policies.

The commitment of the international community to ensure food and nutrition security to every child, woman and man on our planet has been reiterated at several international conferences held during this decade. Some of them are:

1990 World Summit for Children, New York.

1992 International Conference on Nutrition (ICN,1992), Rome.

1992 UN Conference on Environment & Development (UNCED, 1992), Rio de Janeiro.

1993 World Conference on Human Rights (WCHR, 1993), Vienna.

1994 International Conference on Population & Development, Cairo.

1995 UN Conference on Social Development, Copenhangen.

1996 World Food Summit, Rome.

Despite such high level political reaffirmation of the need to achieve speedily the goal of "Food for All", over 800 million human beings now suffer from hunger and malnutrition. Hidden hunger, arising from the deficiency of the essential micronutrients is widespread. Endemic hunger is now more due to the lack of adequate income at the household level than due to the lack of food in the market. Both poverty as well as non-food factors such as environmental hygiene, sanitation and lack of safe drinking water are becoming major contributors of food insecurity at the level of communities and individuals. A majority of the food insecure live in Asia.

There is also increasing concern about the earth's capacity to produce adequate food for the growing population. The increase in human population, now mostly confined to the developing countries, coupled with enhanced purchasing power leading to greater capability to buy food and increasing urbanisation will lead to a higher growth rate in demand for food as well as more diversified food products in the coming millennium. Thus, on the one hand, there will be need for intensification and diversification of agriculture, particularly in the developing countries, on the other, the ecological foundations essential for sustainable advances in crop and animal productivity are getting eroded. This situation has led to the ringing of alarm bells by experts concerning the earth's capacity to produce adequate food to meet growing needs. Lester Brown has concluded; "Constraints imposed by the earth's natural systems, the environmental degradation of land and water resources and the diminshing backlog of yield-raising agricultural technologies are slowing the growth in world food production, raising questions about the earth's population carrying capacity. The earth's capacity to produce enough food to satisfy expanding demand is now emerging as the overriding environmental issue as the world approaches the 21st Century".

The year 1998 will mark the bicentenary of Malthus's essay on population. The onward march of science and technology, supported by appropriate public policies, has so far helped humankind to keep Malthusian forebodings on the population-food supply equation at bay. It is, however, becoming increasingly clear that without concerted national and global action to arrest environmental degradation, promote economic and gender equity and check population growth, the Malthusian spectre may still come true in the next century. The Food and Agriculture Organisation of the United Nations (FAO) therefore, organised a World Food Summit in Rome from November 13 to 17, 1996.

At this Summit, a Rome Declaration on World Food Security and a World Food Summit Plan of Action were adopted. The Declaration makes a commitment to reduce the number of undernourished people to half their present level no later than 2015. It also states:

"We will pusue participatory and sustainable food, agriculture, fisheries, forestry and rural development policies and practices in high and low potential areas which are essential to adequate and reliable food supplies".

"We will strive to ensure that food, agricultural trade and overall trade policies are conducive to fostering food security for all through a fair and market-oriented world trade system".

The Plan of Action includes the following seven commitments:

— Create an enabling political, social and economic environment designed to create the best conditions for the eradication of poverty, and for durable peace.

— Implement policies aimed at eradicating poverty and inequality and improving physical and economic access to sufficient, nutritionally adequate and safe food and its effective utilization.

— Pursue participatory and sustainable food, agriculture, fisheries, forestry and rural development policies and practices in high and low potential areas.

— Ensure that food, agricultural trade and overall trade policies are conducive to fostering food security for all.

— Prevent and be prepared for national disasters and man-made emergencies.

— Promote optimal allocation and use of public and private investments to foster human resources, sustianable food agriculture, fisheries and forestry systems, and rural development, in high and low potential areas.

— Implement, monitor and follow-up the Rome Plan of Action at all levels in cooperation with the international community.

The above plan of action integrates the principles of (a) conservation of the ecological foundations essential for sustainable advances in agricultural productivity and production, (b) sustainable production through ecotechnologies and (c) equity in acces to food through an appropriate blend of national and international action in the area of entitlements and employment. The Science Academies Summit held in Madras in July, 96, recommneded that all nations may provide an overall public policy support to action at these three levels through the enactment of a National Food and Livelihood Security Act designed to achieve the following objectives:

That every individual has the physical, economic, social and enviormental access to balanced diet that includes the necessary macro-and micronutrients, safe drinking water, sanitation, environmental hygiene, primary health care and education so as to lead a healthy and.productive life.

That food originates from efficient and environmentally benign production technologies that conserve and enhance the natural resource base of crops, animal husbandry, forestry, inland and marine fisheries.

Indian agriculture, which had hitherto been of a subsistence nature, is now poised for a take—off on the export front and is getting ready to face international competition. Our strategies for development of agriculture till recently were oriented towards ensuring food security to the population and food production itself was primarily meant for meeting the domestic demand. With the announcement of the new economic policy in 1991, the development perspective has changed and there is greater emphasis on producing for meeting the demand of the global market. The establishment of the World Trade Organization (WTO) in 1995 has further widened the sckôpe for exporting the agricultural produce.

India, by producing 186 million tonnes of food grains has achieved self—sufficiency on the food front. The credit goes to the hard toil of millions of farmers of this country who are wiling to experiment with innovations and accept new technologies of production and the dedicated agricultural scientists, extension workers and others who are directly or indirectly associated withthe implementation of the highyielding variety (HYV) programme and made the Green Revolution a success.

The agricultural sector in India has demonstrated an admirable performance over the past four decades, but still there is abundant scope to imporve for occupying the premier position in global market. This calls for a change in outlook and approach towards agriculture from the subsistence model to the commercial one. The Government of India is also considering granting status of industry to the agricultural sector. Boosting farm exports is also a priority area under the New Agricultural Policy (NAP). Considerable emphasis is there on food processing sector too. During the past few years all these factors have focused tha attention of corporate bodies, NRIs, multinational coompanies, etc on the agricultural sector, which is an encouraging and positive feature.

India has the unique advantage of diverse agro—climatic conditions which are conductive to growing a variety of tropical, subtropical and temperate crops including plantation and horticulture crops. India has a land area of 329 million hectares, of which the land available for crop production is 182 milion ha.

Approximately 128 million ha (72%) are being covered under food crops. The ranking of the country in the world in terms of production and yield of major crops.

The climatic features of the country are very congenial to the cultivation of a wide variety of horticultural crops on a commercial scale. India is the second largest producer of fruits and vegetables in the world. There is considerable scope for exports of both fruits and fresh vegetables in fresh and processed form. This sector has been assigned adequate priority in the national programme for agricultural development. The proposal is to increase the production of fruits to 60 million tonnes and vegetables to 120 million tonnes by AD 2000 to satisfy not only the domestic consumption but also export requirements. The world trade in floriculture is estimated at about $ 25 billion and increasing at 11 per cent per annum. Though India has been identified in the world market as a potential exporter for cut—flowers because of the present climatic and resource advantages, its share is very low (2%). The Government of India has set an ambitious export target of Rs. 100 crore by the end of the VIII Plan for floriculture.

In India, mushroom can be grown on commercial lines exclusively to meet the foreign market like Singapore, Malaysia, France, Germany, East Europe and West Asia. Availability of low cost technology, short gestation period of cropping, possibility of intensive indoor production, less labour deployment, etc make mushroom cultivation a profitable agro–business.

India is the only country in the world which produces four types of natural silk, viz mulberry silk, tusser silk, eri silk and muga silk because of favourable agro—climatic conditions. The important silk producing countries in the world are China, India, Japan, Russia and

Korea out of which India ranks second. The Government of India has allocated a budget of Rs. 860 crore during the VIII Plan for sericulture.

India possesses the largest cattle population (cows, buffaloes, sheep, goat, pig) and ranks third in the world in milk production. the current production of meat and poultry products (excluding eggs) in India is estimated at over two million tonnes per annum. This sector too needs a boost not only to meet our own increasing demand but also to increase our exports.

India stands sixth in egg production with 27 billion eggs per annum and 25th in broiler production with 400 million broilers per annum. The world market of processed chicken is about US $ 5 billion which is very attractive for India. Among the countries importing opoultry from India are Oman, Saudi Arabia, the Maldives, Bahrain, and Hong Kong. A few corporate sectors have also entered into this industry with foreign collaboration. Our products are going to be cheaper in the global market once the subsidies which are very high in European countries are withdrawn/reduced and increased in our country in view of the recent GATT accord. All these indicates tremendous potential and prospects for the globalization of Indian agriculture.

3

Horticulture

Horticulture development in the country continues to make steady progress in terms of increase in total production and export of the horticulture products. There is a vast potential in the country for growing large variety of horticulture crops like fruits, vegetables, mushroom, flowers, spices, cashewnut, coconut, arecanut, root and tuber crops, medicinal and aromatic plants, etc. The diversity of physiographic, climatic and soil characteristics makes it possible to grow horticultural crops throughout the year. During 1996-97 India produced 46.97 million tonnes of fruits. The vegetable production in the country during the same period rose to the level of 80.80 million tonnes. The country stands first in the production of banana, onion and cashew. Similarly, in coconut production, India has become the prime producer with an annual production of 15,000 million nuts during 1996-97.

The horticultural crops provide better alternatives for diversification of Indian -agriculture in view of higher returns accruing from them.

Realising the importance and the role of horticultural crops, plan allocation in ninth five year plan has been proposed to be at Rs.11,00,00,00 thousand.

The development programmes in horticulture cover

on-going programmes for fruits, coconut, vegetables, cashewnut, spices and plantation crops and new schemes of eighth five year plan for development of medicinal and aromatic plants, mushroom, floriculture, root and tuber crops and beekeeping, etc. Major schemes on use of plastics and infrastfucture development for post harvest handling and marketing were also continued.

The main thrust during the year has been to provide better planting/seed material using both conventional and modern methods, rejuvenation/ rehabilitation of existing plantations, installation of drip irrigation system, green house cultivation, control of pests and diseases, assistance of post harvest handling and collection and dissemination of market information. Budget allocation for the current year is Rs.3000 thousand.

Major Development Programmes

Fruits

The Central Sector Scheme on Integrated Development of Tropical, Arid and Temperate Zone Fruits was launched during eighth five year plan with an outlay of Rs.7,44,000 thousand. The expenditure under the scheme during the eighth plan was Rs.61,14,43 thousand. The outlay approved for 1998-99 is Rs.25,00,00 thousand. While during 1997-98 the programme was implemented with an outlay of Rs.17,00,000 thousand.

The programmes envisaged under this scheme include: (a) establishment of big nurseries under public sector (b) establishment of small district level nurseries under private sector (c) setting up of tissue culture units under public and private sectors (d) training of farmers (e) establishment of olive oil extraction plants (f) area expansion (g) improving productivity through rejuvenation and (h) demonstration plots.

During the eighth plan, 54 big nurseries, 421 small nurseries, 19 tissue culture units were established. Besides, 1316 demonstration plots were laid out and an area of 49,505 ha. under area expansion and 71,954 ha. under rejuvenation respectively, was covered. Moreover, 14,575 farmers were trained in various aspects of horticulture during this period. The scheme was continued during 1997-98 in accordance with the pattern existing during the eighth plan and is being continued in 1998-99 with an outlay of Rs.25,00,00 thousand for establishing 15 small and 200 big nurseries, 20 tissue culture units, besides area expansion of 25000 ha.

Spices

The Centrally Sponsored Integrated Programme for the Development of Spices is in operation in 25 States, two Union Territories, 21 State Agricultural Universities, 5 Institutes of ICAR and National Horticultural Research and Development Foundation and State Farms Corporation of India, etc. An amount of Rs.2,86,405 thousand was released during 1997-98 against the budget allocation of Rs.3,00000 thousand. The scheme is continued in the current year with an allocation of Rs.37,50,000 thousand.

During eighth plan 6.4 lakh nucleus planting material for pepper of high yielding varieties was produced, 130.9 lakh rooted cuttings were produced and distributed. 2093 pepper demonstration plots were laid in farmers' field and in 38,500 ha. area prophylactic plant protection measures against Phytophthora foot-rot disease were adopted. For ginger, turmeric and chillies sprogrammes included production of nucleus planting material of released varieties, establishment of 35,110 demonstration-cum-seed multiplication plots in farmers' fields, large scale plant protection demonstration programmes on chillies and ginger covering 59,500 ha.

and 1680 ha. respectively, distribution of 0.38 lakhs quality planting material of promising lines and establishment of 2260 demonstration plots in farmers' fields were undertaken. For seed spices, production and distribution of 27.10 tonnes of nucleus seed, distribution 8,31,000 minikits and establishment of 22,400 demonstration plots in farmers' fields were undertaken. For garlic, production of 10,000 tones of foundation seed and 200 tonnes of certified seed, establishment of 2,000 demonstration plots were achieved. For tamarind production and distribution of 12,500 nos., of tamrind grafts were undertaken. For large cardamom in Arunachal Pradesh and Sikkim, 30 units of compact area plantations, each covering 10 ha. are being established and maintained. For saffron, the programmes taken up include multiplication in two ha. area and establishment of 220 demonstration plots.

During the year 1998-99, it is proposed to produce 8.9 lakh nucleus planting material, production and distribution of 173.87 lakh rooted cuttings, establishing 2200 demonstration plots in farmers' field and adopt prophylactic plant protection measures in an area of 41,000 ha. under black pepper. As regards ginger, turmeric and chillies, it is proposed to establish 53,400 demonstration cum seed multiplication plots in farmers' field, take up large scale plant protection demonstrations on chillies and ginger covering 69,000 ha. and 2760 ha. respectively, distribution of 60,400 minikits and expansion of area by 18,800 ha. with high yielding varieties. It is targeted to produce 5.93 lakh quality planting materials of promising lines and establish 3670 demonstration plots in farmers field in respect of tree spices. It is proposed to produce and distribute 26 tonnes of nucleus seed, distribution of 146630 minikits and establish 44,330 demonstration plots of seed spices, 30 units of compact area plantation of large cardamon, each covering - 10 ha. are to be established and maintained in Arunachal Pradesh and Sikkim. It is also proposed to take up corn multiplication in 2 ha. and establish 400 demonstration plots of saffron. Besides, 13 demonstration cum progeny gardens for spices set up in North Eastern Region, each covering an area of 10 ha. are being maintained. In addition, 6925 plant protection equipment are to be distributed and a spice area of 3800 ha. shall be covered under soil conservation measures.

Coconut

The Coconut Development Board, set up under the Coconut Development Board Act, 1979 has been making concerted efforts to increase production and productivity of coconut. The Board also promotes product diversification and by product utilisation of coconut. India has now emerged as a leading producer of coconut with a production of 12,988 million nuts in 1996-97 from an area of 18.86 lakh ha.

An amount of Rs.308,369 thousand was released for implementation of various programmes of the Board during 1997-98. The approved outlay for 1998-99 is Rs.230,000 thousand. The programmes being implemented during 1998-99 are:

1. Production and distribution of planting material, including:
   - (a) Establishment of DSP farms.
   - (b) Coconut nursery attached to the DSP farms.
   - (c) Establishment of Regional Coconut Nursery.
   - (d) Seed procurement units.
   - (e) Production and distribution of superior coconut seedlings including hybrid and released varieties.

2. Area expansion under coconut.
3. Integrated farming in coconut holding for productivity improvement.
4. Scheme for Integrated Pest Management.
5. Processing and marketing activities.
6. Publicity and publication of extension activities.
7. National Information and Documentation Centre.
8. Strengthening the infrastructure and administration.

Special Scheme in Andaman and Nicobar Islands includes (a) Establishment of coconut plantation in Nicobar district for the benefit of the tribals (b) Multitier cropping system in Andaman Islands.

Cashew nut

India has the distinction of being world's largest producer of cashew nut. With a production of 4.30 lakh tonnes from an area of 5.67 lakh ha. cashew nut is major export crop. During eighth five year plan, various programmes for increasing the production and productivity of cashew nut were implemented with an' outlay of Rs.47,85,00 thousand. The scheme is being continued during 1997-98 and 1998-99.

An outlay of Rs.16,00,00 thousand has been provided for Centrally Sponsored Integrated Development Programme of Cashew during 199899. The programmes include area expansion, improving productivity through rejuvenation, replanting intensive pest control, establishing regional nurseries, organising farmers training programme and establishing model clonal gardens. The outlay for 1998-99 is Rs.20,00,000 thousand.

The programme was implemented in States of Kerala, Karnataka, Goa, Maharashtra, Tamil Nadu,

Andhra Pradesh, Orissa, Madhya Pradesh, West Bengal, Manipur, Meghalaya, Tripura and Union Territories of Pondicherry and Andaman Nicobar Islands. The scheme included the following:

Development of New Plantations with clones conforming to export qualities and Maintenance of Cashew Plantations raised in previous years.

This programme is being continued in the above mentioned States during the current year. Necessary assistance to the tune of Rs.7,22,83 thousand for inputs like planting materials, fertilizers and plant protection chemicals have been provided under this programme. Under fresh planting, an area of 25,701 ha. was covered under this programme, along with maintenance of 32,135 ha. raised in previous years. During 1998-99, an area of about 37,000 ha. is expected to be covered.

ReplantinglRejuvenation by Top Working of Old and Uneconomical Cashew Gardens

The objective of this programme is to replant/rejuvenate the old, senile, unthrifty, and unproductive cashew gardens with genuine clones. Input support has been provided under this programme as in the case of new planting in addition to compensation for removing the old trees. During 1997-98 an area of 21,373 ha. was replanted, along with the maintenance of 2355 ha. planted in 1995-96 and 1996-97 at a cost of Rs.11,170 thousand.

Adoption of Comprehensive Production Technology in Growers Orchards

This programme has its objective to consolidate and improve the productivity status of cashew by way of adoption of recommended package of practices in 'comprehensive manner by providing assistance for inputs like fertilizers, farmyard manure, and plant protection chemicals for period of three consecutive years. An area of 12978 ha. adopted for the package treatment in previous years in the States of Kerala, Karnataka, Goa, Maharashtra, Tamil Nadu, Andhra Pradesh, Orissa and West Bengal was maintained.

This is to carry out prophylactic plant protection measures against pests attacking foliage, root, stem, tender flushes and blossoms. Spraying and swabbing treatments have been provided. This programme was continued during 1997-98 in an area of 20,145 ha. at a total cost of Rs.17,955 thousands.

Generation of Planting Material - Establishment of Regional Nurseries

This programme was implemented with an objective of generating required number of clones for the coverage under new planting and replanting programmes by way of establishing Centralised Regional Nurseries in the States involved, during 1997-98. During 1997-98, 15 number of Regional Nurseries have been established, in addition to the maintenance of 13 nurseries established during last year at a total cost of Rs.4,500 thousand.

Pilot Demonstration of Clonal Cultivation -Development of Model Clonal Cashew Gardens

The main objective of this programme is to demonstrate the cultivation of cashew by adopting scientific agro-technologies and horticultural management practices for cultivators' field. During the year under report, 217 plots were established afresh along with maintenance of 304 plots laid out in the previous years at an outlay of Rs.200 thousands, in the States involved during 1997-98. Funds for inputs such as for planting materials, fertilizers, farm yard manure, plant protection chemicals and soil and moisture conservation measures have been provided for this programme.

Farmers' Training Programme

This programme is intended to expose the farmers to various technologies available and to train and motivate them to adopt the modern cultivation techniques in their fields by organising training programmes on cashew production technology. Financial support towards training allowances and instructional kit, etc. has been provided to 3230 farmers in the States of Kerala, Karnataka, Andhra Pradesh, Tamil Nadu, Goa, Maharashtra, Orissa and West Bengal at a cost of Rs.757 thousand.

In order to provide wider publicity on promotional aspects of cashew, an amount of Rs.400 thousand was incurred for publishing and distributing printed materials and literature in Regional Languages of the implementing States.

Vegetables

The production of vegetables, including potato, during 1995-96 is estimated at 715-91 lakh tonnes. The production of vegetables in the country is increasing significantly mainly due to popularisation of improved/ hybrid seeds of vegetables amongst the farmers.

A Central Sector Scheme on 'production and supply of vegetables seed' was implemented with an outlay of Rs-1,50,000 thousand during eighth plan with the aim to improve supply of foundation seeds of improved/hybrid varieties of vegetables crops, enhance productivity and increase overall production of vegetables. The scheme also provided support for popularisation of improved/ hybrid varieties through distribution of seed minikits in all States/Union Territories.

During 1997-98, about 31,000 vegetable seed minikits were distributed, 1063 quintals of foundation seed was produced by the implementing agencies. In order to further step up vegetables production in the country, an amount of Rs.20,000 thousand has been provided during 1998-99.

Root and Tuber Crops

Root and Tuber crops, including potato, have been identified as most important group of staple food in the tropical countries of the world. The production of potato along during 1996-97 was 250.65 lakh tonnes.

For promoting cultivation of Root and Tuber crops, a Central Sector Scheme on Development of Root and Tuber Crops for improving production and productivity of major crops like potato, sweet potato, yams, etc. is being implemented with an outlay of Rs.5000 thousands during 1998-99. For potato, major emphasis is being given on phased introduction and promotion of new technology called True Potato Seed (TPS) to replace use of bulky tubers, reduce cost of production, improve productivity and reduce dependence on cold storages. For other crops like sweet potato, yam, etc. the planting material of improved varieties is obtained from ICAR Institutes and is being multiplied at Bio-Centres already established under the scheme for further use to raise commercial crops by the farmers. About 2096 tuber minikits were distributed out during the year under report.

Cocoa

For increasing production and productivity of cocoa a central sector scheme for development of cocoa was implemented during eighth plan with an outlay of Rs.30,000 thousand. The scheme was continued during 1997-98 with an outlay of Rs.6000 thousand and being continued in 199899 with an allocation of Rs.7000 thousand. The scheme was implemented in Kerala, Karnataka, Tamil Nadu and Andhra Pradesh with the following programme components:

i) Establishment of 923 demonstration plots of high yielding clones in the farmers field.

ii) Production and distribution of 1.20 lakh vegetatively propagated cocoa planting materials.

iii) Providing assistance for setting up of 14 irrigation units.

iv) Providing financial assistance to co-operatives for organising marketing and processing of cocoa beans.

Medicinal and Aromatic Plants

The scheme for the development of medicinal and aromatic plants was implemented during eighth plan with an outlay of Rs.50,000 thousand. It was implemented during 1997-98 with an outlay of Rs.60,000 thousand, through 16 Agricultural

Universities and three CSIR Institutes and is being continued during 1998-99 with an outlay of Rs.20,000 thousand. The scheme provides for production of quality planting material of aromatic plants in 164 ha. for distribution, financial assistance for setting up of 7 modern distillation units, establishment of 16 herbal gardens having total area of 53 ha. for medicinal plants. Establishment of 16 nursery -centres for production and distribution of planting materials of important medicinal plants havė been achieved during the eighth plan. The component of demonstration plots in the farmers' fields has been taken up from 1995-96 through State Agriculture/Horticulture Department and 936 demonstration plots have been established. During 1998-99 demonstration programme has been stepped up significantly to cover 6000 demonstration units against 1000 units during 1997-98.

Floriculture

Floriculture is an emerging area with great potential in

the domestic as well as export markets. Flowers are traditionally grown in India in open field conditions. Major emphasis has been on growing of loose flowers like marigold, chrysanthemum, jasmine/tunberose, etc. which are in demand for garlands, venies or offering mainly for religious functions. In the recent years, there has been interest in growing modern cut flower corps like roses, gladiolus, carnation, orchid, etc, which are used in flower bouquets and for decoration. Many export oriented units have started greenhouse production of cut flowers for export and have made significant dent in European and Japan markets.

A Central Sector Scheme of commercial floriculture was launched in the eighth five year Plan with an outlay of Rs.142,900 thousand. A major component of the scheme was the establishment of model floriculture centres in public sector which are envisaged to be the focal centres for development of floriculture in the region through introduction of new technologies and providing training in different areas of floriculture development. Out of the eleven such centres, four at Srinagar in Jammu and Kashmir, Chail in Himachal Pradesh, Bangalore in Karnataka and Gangtok in Sikkim have started functioning. Remaining seven are under various stages of construction. The scheme was continued during 1997-98 with an allocation of Rs.30000 thousands. Under the area expansion programme, a total of 200 ha. was covered during this period. The scheme is continued during the current year with an allocation of Rs.10,00,00 thousand. Four additional' Model Floriculture centres have sanctioned during the year at Bihar, Delhi, Haryana and Madhya Pradesh. It is expected that the Model Floriculture Centres sanctioned during eighth plan would be fully operatinalised during the year giving necessary impetus for the growth of floriculture.

Mushroom

The Central Sector Scheme on mushroom cultivation started in eighth plan with an outlay of Rs.156,900 thousand primarily aimed at creating the infrastructure for spawn and pasteurized compost production and providing training to farmers for mushroom cultivation. During 1997-98, 6 additional spawn production and 5 additional pasteurized compost units were sanctioned, to provide training to 4900 farmers. An outlay of Rs.400,00 thousand was provided during 1997-98 for the scheme. The scheme is continued during the current year with an allocation of Rs.475,00 thousands is envisaged to train 25,100 farmers in the techniques of mushroom production.

Drip irrigation

This is a method of irrigation in which the network of plastic pipes distribution required quantity of water directly to the root zone of the plants. Its water benefits are in saving of water,

Green house

This is a method to control micro environment for crop production. This helps in faster germination, raising off season crops and high value crops in harsh weather conditions, etc. An area of 137 ha. is proposed covered under Green House by spending Rs.911,00 thousands during the current year with each beneficiary getting assistance for one unit of 500 sq. mts.

Mulching

A thin plastic film (20 to 200 microns) is spread around the plant to prevent the weed growth, conserve moisture, maintain soil texture and control soil borne diseases. During 1998-99, an amount of Rs.5300 thousand is proposed to be spent to bring an area of 1059 ha. under mulching.

Reduction in weeds and increase in yield. During 1997-98 a subsidy of 90% in case of SC/ST, small/ marginal and women farmers and 70% in case of other farmers with a ceiling of Rs.25000/ ha. was provided. An area of 45,000 ha. was covered under drip irrigation during 1997-98.

Development Programme for Use of Plastics in Agriculture

Total outlay of Rs. 250000 thousand has been made during eighth plan for taking up various programmes for popularising use of plastics including drip irrigation, green houses, plastics mulch in horticultural crops. The outlay for 199798 was Rs.81,00,00 thousand, while it is Rs.110,00,00 thousand for the current year.

New Plasticulture Application

To cover an area of 64 ha. under shading nets, 40 ha. under low tunnel, drying of spices and 500 under anti bird nets and 2500 anti hail nets, an amount of Rs.166,00 thousand has been earmarked to be spent under 1998-99.

Promotion of Bee Keeping

With a view to improving crop productivity and generating rural employment, have a major initiative was taken up for promoting bee keeping to improve crop productivity during eighth plan. The total outlay of the scheme was Rs.188,700 thousand. The scheme was continued in 1997-98 with an allocation of Rs.25,000 thousand.

The Main objectives of the scheme are:-

— To promote honeybee pollination for improving crop production

— To develop new strains of bee for enabling disease resistance and higher production.

— To encourage procurement processing and storage, etc., of honey and its products.

— To impart training to the unemployed for employment generation.

— To promote awareness and faster growth of bee keeping; and

— To develop feasible strategy for long term development of bee keeping.

The Scheme started functioning during 1994-95. The implementation of the scheme was proposed in all.the States and Union Territories. The scheme envisages implementation mainly as Central Sector Scheme through research institutions and by State Designated Agencies. The overall implementation of scheme in the States in general and some components in particular are to be looked after by State Designated Agency (SDA) identified by the State Government.

So far, Government/Union Territories have identified the SDAs. During eighth plan, funds to an extent of Rs.217,56 thousand have been sanctioned to the SDAs for production and distribution of about 1,30,000 bee colonies. For the implementation of the scheme during 1998-99, an outlay of Rs.250,00 thousand have been provided against Rs.11,200 thousand released during 1997-98. The SDAs were provided with Rs.7275 thousand during 1997-98 for the component of production and distribution of honey bee colonies.

Thirty-two projects on Research and Development aspects of bee keeping were approved at a total cost of Rs.9707 thousand, for implementation during eighth plan. 45 Institutes were identified for imparting training on different aspects of bee keeping development.

Promotional activities like Honey Festival and Exhibition were organised at district level in Bihar. Besides, the National Horticulture Board have organised national level honey festival.

Programmes of National Horticulture Board

The objectives of the National Horticulture Board include all aspects of Horticulture Development in the country. However, the main emphasis is being laid on post-harvest management and marketing. The schemes of the Board, therefore, have been launched covering various developmental aspects of horticulture industry arid can be grouped as under:

— Soft loan schemes for exploitation of commercial horticulture, post-harvest management and marketing.

— Schemes to provide support services like market information and transfer of technology.

— Scheme to induce awareness and updating the state of horticulture through innovative ideas and concepts.

Integrated Project on Management of Post Harvest Infrastructure of Horticulture Crops

With a view to reducing the post harvest losses and to increase the producers share in consumers I price, the Board took up this project in 1988-89. Under the project, assistance is provided for creation of post harvest infrastructure such as grading/packing facilities in the producing area, improved packaging such as plastic creates card board boxes, transport facilities with particular emphasis on developing cool chain including establishment of precooling units, cold storages and refrigerated transport vehicle, retail outlets, etc., for direct marketing and other aspect where post-harvest losses could be minimised. The soft loan having service charges of 4% is provided to the Cooperative/Corporate Sector, registered/voluntary organisations, Agro/ Horticulture Corporations, etc., for creation of such post-harvest infrastructure facilities to a maximum extent of Rs.1.00

crore per organisation. During the financial year 1997-98 the Board have released an amount of Rs.35714 thousand for the establishment of 19 cold storages, six precooling units, two specialised transport vehicles and eight grading/packing centres. The Board has also released an amount of Rs.30,20,634 in the form of subsidy for supply of 43776 numbers of plastic crates for the States of Himachal Pradesh, Haryana, Maharashtra, Punjab and Rajasthan for proper handling of fruits and vegetables.

Development of Marketing of Horticultural Produce Through Participation in Soft Loan

Under this scheme which is being implemented since 1993-94, soft loan assistance is provided to the beneficiaries i.e. co-operative societies, private and public limited co., farmers' association and public sector organisation for creating marketing infrastructure to boost the horticultural exports. Since, the scheme is in its implementation phase, NHB has gathered a rich experience to give a further improvement in this direction. The impact of this scheme is being visible on the horticulture scenario. The main objective of this scheme is to introduce new technology apart from strengthening infrastructural facilities with backward linkage among producers, processors and marketers. Soft loan assistance up to a maximum limit of Rs.1.00 crore (40% of total term loan as appraised by financial institution) is provided @ 4% service charges per annum with one year moratorium period to set up projects i.e. marketing, processing and export oriented units for purchase of plants and machineries.

During the year under report, 22 number of organisations have been assisted and amount of Rs.1,57,972 thousand was released.

Market Information Service of Horticultural Crops

Marketing of fruits and vegetables is an important aspect of post-harvest management of horticultural crops. Horticultural crops which are highly perishable in nature need quick disposal after harvesting. So, a sond system of marketing with latest and accurate information on prices and arrivals plays an important role in ensuring better remuneration to growers. If the accurate market information is available, then optimum planning can be made to send the consignments to the markets where prices prevail high.

National Horticulture Board is implementing this scheme since 1988 with its 33 Market Information Centres; located all over India especially in State capitals and wholesale markets called NHBNET. These market information centres collect information on prices and arrivals on fruits and vegetables from these markets on daily basis and transmit to Coordinating Cell at Delhi for compilation of national bulletins. Apart from this, these centres also prepare weekly and monthly bulletins and send it to coordinating cell for preparation and publication of monthly bulletins from Head Office.

Presently, market information is being supplied to 400 subscribers and is being published in 219 national and local newspapers, telecast through eight Doordarshan Kendras and Broadcast through 22 All India Radio Stations. Apart from these dissemination, Market Information Centres also sent daily bulletin to the Government organisations, Cooperative Societies engaged in Fruits and Vegetables Trade, Market Committees, State Horticulture and Marketing Departments, etc. NHB has also made arrangements to provide international prices on cut flowers, fresh fruits and vegetables and processed foods (weekly bulletins) of ITC Geneva for benefit of export oriented units.

An MOU with National Information Centre for implementing NIC-NET system with earth based satellite has also been signed. On implementation of this system, the prompt market information may reach even up to block level for benefiting actual producers to take quick decisions.

Introduction of New Technology and Concepts in Horticulture

Various research and development institutions/ universities are developing technologies which have been tested at laboratory scale and they are found to be advantageous in increasing productivity and enhancing quality in various ways. However, these remain unexploited on commercial scale. In order to test these technologies and concepts on commercial scale, this scheme is being implemented from 1993-94. Apart from testing proven technologies, the scheme also envisages to popularise use of improved tools and equipment for better production and marketing. The scheme also envisages, creating of awareness through Audio-Visual aids, distribution of literature, etc. During current financial year, outlay of Rs.1500 thousand is likely to be utilised fully on these activities.

Techno-Economic Feasibility Studies Surveys on Various Aspects of Horticullture

With a view to strengthening data base in horticulture, the Board is getting conducted Techno-Economic Feasibility Studies-Surveys for various States/Union Territories through empanelled consultants. The scheme is basically meant for development of database for taking up planning both for short term and long term development of horticulture. As such the studies would provide basis for formulating plans by the State Governments/Union Territories, which was lacking so far. During the year under report, the Board has released a sum of Rs.687 thousand to Bihar State Agricultural Marketing Board, Patna for conducting Techno Economic Feasibility Studies/surveys of five fruit and vegetable markets in Bihar.

Establishment of Nutritional Garden in Rural Areas

In order to increase the availability of fruits in the daily diet of masses particularly the rural ones, so as to overcome the problem of malnutrition, the Board took up this programme from 1990-91. Under the project, each household is provided up to 10 fruit plants suitable for growing in 'that particular area, near the dwelling unit/ dug well. Keeping in view the enthusiasm shown by the State Governments in implementation and standard of the rural masses, the scheme is being continued. This year, 24 lakhs fruit plants are being distributed entailing an expenditure of Rs.12,000 thousand under this scheme.

Transfer of Technology Through Training and Visits of Horticulture Growers

Most of the horticultural growers are aware of the latest agro-techniques developed at various research stations and these techniques are being adopted by progressive farmers in different areas. With a view to familiarising such technologies through visits to various centres of excellence, the Board provides financial assistance to State Governments of conducting such visits. The project was initiated during 1988-89. Assistance of Rs.50,000/- for a group of 50 farmers is being provided. Under the scheme, an outlay of Rs.1500 thousand has been provided during current financial year which is likely to be utilised fully and 1500 horticultural growers are likely to be benefited.

Integrated Horticulture Development in Rajasthan (District Sikar)

The Board is implementing a scheme Integrated

Horticulture Development in Rajasthan (District Sikar) through State Government for development of Agro Horticultural crops and arresting desertification. The project was approved for five years at a total cost of Rs.11,716 thousand, Board share being Rs.10,259 thousand. There is a budget provision of Rs.2631 thousand for covering 6,000 nos. Ber budding, need based demonstration 900 nos., block demonstration 33 nos. and training literature 700 nos. and an area 540 hectares and Board had released an amount of Rs.2631 thousand for achieving target.

Grant of Financial Assistance to Professional Organisations for the Development of Horticulture

The Board provides assistance up to Rs.20,000 thousand for organising exhibition, fair, seminar, symposia, etc., for the development of horticulture through voluntary organisations and cooperative societies, etc. The Board also provides assistance to State Governments for organising Udyan Pandit Competitions at State level. The assistance is limited up to Rs.200 thousand per competition up to maximum of Rs.500 thousand per State per year for three competitions. During the year 1997-98, the Board has released an amount of Rs.996 thousand to 33 organisations.

4

Fertilisers and Manure

The consumption of chemical fertilisers during 1997-98 was 161.88 lakh tonnes of nutrients (NPK) as against 143.08 lakh tonnes of nutrients achieved during 1996-97, showing an increase of 13%. The consumption of nitrogen, phosphate and potash in fertilizers increased by 5.8%, 31.5% and 33.3% respectively during 1997-98 over the previous year. During the year 1997-98, the consumption of both Di-Ammoniurn Phosphate (DAP) and Muriate of Potash, picked up very significantly. The consumption of DAP and MOP was 53.76 lakh tonnes and 17.29 lakh tonnes, respectively. The consumption of DAP in 1997-98 was 48% higher than the consumption in the corresponding period of the previous year. Similarly, the consumption of MOP was 44.3% higher. The consumption of DAP and MOP, which had reduced following decontrol in 1992, reached record levels during 1997-98. All chemical fertilisers except urea continue to be decontrolled.

Fertilisers prices

The price of urea has been increased from Rs.3660 per MT to Rs.4000 per MT w.e.f. 29-199. However decontrolled fertilisers are being made available to farmers at 1997-98 level.

It has been decided to maintain a bufferstock of 2 lakh tonnes of DAP and 55000 tonnes of MOP to meet emergent requirements. This would also help to meet requirements of States which have low demand and hence, sometimes find it difficult to induce suppliers to move fertilisers in small quantities.

Transport subsidy on de-controlled fertilisers

Additional transport subsidy on decontrolled fertilisers was introduced with effect from 1-4-1-997 for North - Eastern States including Sikkim and some parts of Jammu and Kashmir. From 1-10-98, it has been decided to extend the scheme to Himachal Pradesh, and hill areas of Uttar Pradesh and West Bengal.

Concession Scheme on Sale of decontrolled fertilisers

The scheme of concession on sale of decontrolled phosphatic and potassic (P & K) fertifiser to the farmers, originally introduced in Rabi 1992-93 season, is being continued during 1998-99 also. Under this scheme, concession is made available on sale of Di-Ammonium Phosphate (DAP), Muriate of Potash (MOP), Single Super Phosphate (SSP) and Complex fertilisers.

The rates of concession which are being paid to manufacturers and importers/suppliers during 199899 are substantially higher as compared to rates prevailing in earlier years. It has been decided to keep the maximum retail prices of decontrolled fertilisers at the same level as in 1997-98.

National Project on Development and Use of Bio-Fertilisers

Recognising the importance of bio-fertilisers as a cost effective and pollution free source of plant nutrients, the National Project on Development and use of bio-fertilisers is being continued with the aim of promoting and distributing bio-fertilisers. During the year 1997-98, 6 bio-fertiliser production units of State Govt. /Institutional agencies have been strengthened by releasing Rs. 80.00

lakhs as one time non-recurring grant-in-aid through State Governments.

Under this project, 4 Refreshers Training, 14 Orientation Training 21 Promotional Management Training and 42 Extension Workers Training were organised by NBDC and the 6 RBDCs during 199798. In addition to this, 1 National Training sponsored by Directorate of Extension (GOI) was also organised for various officers of State Govt. engaged in production and promotion of Bio-fertilisers in the country. During 1997-98, the centres produced 356 tonnes of various bio-fertiliser against the target of 375 tonnes. During the year 1998-99, these centres produced and marketed about 240 tonnes of Bio-fertilisers. However, approximately 10,000 MT of different Bio-fertilisers are being produced and marketed through GOI funded as well as other units in the country. Approximately 450-500 MT of Blue Green Algae (BGA) is being produced through BGA sub-centres. In order to promote Bio-fertiliser technology, 1 Refresher Training Course, 4 Orientation Courses on Bio-fertiliser Quality Control, 21 Extension Workers Trainings and 1 National Training have been organised upto October, 1998. Besides a target of 30 Biofertiliser Dealers Trainings has also been set as a new component in the ninth plan. To maintain a check on quality of bio-fertilisers sold in the country, 860 bio-fertiliser samples were received from various sources during 1997-98. for testing the quality of bio-fertilisers. During 1998-99 165 samples were tested till October, 1998. National Project on Development and Use of Bio-fertilisers is being implemented during 1998-99 at a cost of Rs.586.00 Lakhs.

Centrally Sponsored Scheme on Balanced & Integrated Use of Fertilisers

The Centrally Sponsored Scheme on Balanced and Integrated Use of Fertilisers; was continued. The components of the scheme have been modified for implementation during ninth plan period for providing focused impetus to strengthening of soil testing services in the country and production of compost from city garbage/waste.

The Scheme would continue to provide thrust and promote balanced and integrated use of chemical fertilisers in conjunction with organic manure/compost. The required nutrients for a particular crop would be recommended by soil testing laboratories after analysing soil samples for NPK and micro nutrients.

The soil testing services in the country would be modernised in existing NPK and micro nutrient testing facilities New NPK soil testing laboratories would be established in areas where presently these services are weak.

During 1997-98 central assistance amounting to Rs.355.55 lakhs was provided to States for augmentation of compost production facilities and strengthening of soil testing laboratories.

The scheme would also endeavour to seek broader participation from experts and fertiliser industry on soil testing services and compost making from city waste through organising regional and national seminars from time to time.

Fertiliser Control Order, 1985

The Fertiliser Control Order (1985) issued under Section 3 of Essential Commodities Act, 1985 regulates the prices, quality, trade and distribution of fertilisers in the country. It is implemented by State Governments through Enforcement Authorities notified by them.

Quality Control of Fertilisers

The number of notified Fertiliser Control Laboratories has

increased from 52 in 1992-93 to 62 during 1997-98. Its annual analytical capacity also increased from 94560 to 107670 samples during the corresponding period.

The percentage of Non Standard samples on All India Basis is hovering around 5.5% during last 5 years. However, it ranges from 8-10% in West Bengal, Madhya Pradesh and Uttar Pradesh, 3-6% in Orissa, Maharashtra, Haryana, Punjab, Karnataka and Tamil Nadu and around 2% or less in Gujarat, Rajasthan, Andhra Pradesh and Kerala.

Central Fertiliser Quality Control & Training Institute (CFQC & TI), Faridabad and Its Regional Fertiliser Control Laboratories (RFCLs)

The Institute and its Regional Laboratonles organise inspection and analysis of imported fertilisers at various discharge ports, random inspection of indigenous manufacturing units and their distribition network in the field and training of Enforcement Officers and Analysts of State Govts.

Total 2885 samples (both Imported and Indigeneous) have been analysed and 104 Fertiliser Ships have been inspected by the Fertiliser Inspectors of the Institute till October, 1998, out of which, variations from the stipulated specification were found in 7 ships/mostly in particle size, and moisture.

So far 10 training programmes for State Fertiliser Inspectors and Analysts have been organised, in which 115 officers have been trained and 5 more Programmes are scheduled during the year. The International Training Programme on Fertiliser Quality Control for the developing countries of Asia, Africa and Latin America is scheduled to be organised in the Institute from 5-1-99 to 23-2-99.

The Institute for the first time is providing a Central Assistance of Rs.10,000/- to State Governments For organising Orientation courses for Enforcement Officers and Rs.5000/- to Fertiliser Manufacturing Units for each Dealers Training Programme in the current year.

So far, 10 orientation courses and 15 Dealers Programmes have been organised till Nov.,98 against the target of 15 & 25 respectively and the same will be completed before March, 1999.

The Quick Testing Kit developed by the Institute for on the spot detection of adulteration in major fertilisers is being popularised in the field.

5

Agricultural Credit

The emphasis on Agricultural Credit has continued to be on progressive institutionalisation for providing timely and adequate credit to farmers for increasing agricultural production and productivity. Providing better access to institutional credit for small and marginal farmers and other weaker sections to enable them to adopt modern technology-and improved agricultural practices, has been one of the major objectives of the country's agricultural policy.

Institutional arrangements for Agricultural Credit

Agricultural Credit is disbursed through a multi-agency network consisting of Commercial Banks (CBS), Regional Rural Banks (RRBs) and Cooperatives. As on 31.3.1998, there were 46,691 rural and semi-urban branches of CBs, 14,496 branches of the 196 RRBs. In the Cooperative sector, there exists network of 91,720 Primary Agricultural Credit Societies (PACS), 364 District Central Cooperative Banks (DCCBs) with 28 State Cooperative Banks (SCBs) in the short term cooperative credit structure. In the long-term cooperative structure, there were 19 State Land Development Banks (SLDBs) with 2337 operational units as on 31.3.1998 catering to the requirement of investment credit. The coverage of villages by PACS/ARDBs is 99.7% with a membership of 94 million and 19.37 million respectively.

Flow of Credit

The flow of institutional ground level credit for agriculture and allied activities has increased from Rs.151,69,00,00 thousand in the year 1992-93 to Rs.309,76,00,00 thousand in 1997-98. The total credit flow from all agencies is expected to go up from Rs.380,54,00,00 thousand in 1998-99 to Rs.608,42,00,00 thousand in 2001-02 i.e. during the Ninth Five Year Plan period.

Policy Measures

In order to sustain agricultural growth, the Credit System is proposed to be restructured, so as to increase the flow of credit to agriculture particularly to small- and marginal farmers and also in view of doubling, up of the food production in ten years.- The following measures have been or are being taken to provide increased flow of credit to the agricultural sector:-

— The Commercial Banks have been asked to increase the flow of credit to agriculture.

— To strengthen the financial capability of NABARD, its capital base has been raised.

— Weak RRBs have been recapitalised

— Banks have been advised to set up specialised agricultural 'branches to deal with high-tech agricultural advances.

— Banks have been advised to extend cash credit facilities for meeting composite credit requirements of farmers.

— A proposal for revamping of cooperative credit structure has been initiated.

— Steps have also been initiated to amend Multi-State Cooperative Societies Act, with a view to restore autonomy in the cooperative institutions.

— The Cooperative Bank of India has been registered so as to enable the cooperative credit structure to impart greater internal mobility to its resources.

— NABARD has formulated a model scheme for issue of Kisan Credit Cards to farmers so that they may use them to readily purchase agricultural inputs such as seeds, fertilizers, pesticides, etc., and draw cash for their production needs. Instructions have been issued by RBI and NABARD to all the scheduled banks (excluding RRBs) and State Cooperative Banks/ RRBs respectively for introduction of a Kisan Credit Card Scheme on the lines of the Model Scheme at an early date.

— Action has been initiated to amend the National Cooperative Development Corporation (NCDC) Act, 1962, to diversify the activities of NCDC and to provide it operational freedom and access to resources.

A High Level Committee to examine issues relating to indebtedness among farmers in the State of Punjab and Haryana was set up in the Department. The recommendations of the Committee are under examination in consultation with RBI/NABARD, Ministry of Finance and State Governments, etc.

Central Financial Assistance

In order to strengthen the Cooperative Credit Institutions for meeting the credit requirement of the farmers, central financial assistance is released to the State Governments under various schemes.

The Central Financial Assistance under these schemes is released to the State Governments on the basis of proposals received from them. In case of Investment in Debentures of State Land Development Banks Scheme, the assistance is released in consultation with NABARD.

Comprehensive Crop Insurance Scheme (CCIS)

The existing CCIS was continued and 15 States and 2 Union Territories implemented the scheme during 1997-98. Since inception of the scheme in 1985 till Rabi 1997-98 about 64 million farmers have been covered over an area about 108 million hectare insuring a sum of Rs.19,22,86,411 thousand.

Modified Comprehensive Crop Insurance Scheme (MCCIS)

With a view to enlarging the coverage in terms of farmers, crops and risks under crop insurance it has been decided, in principle, to introduce a MCCIS from Kharif 1999 season as a permanent substitute of on-going CCIS and the Experimental Crop Insurance Scheme (ECIS). Details of the new scheme are being worked out in consultation with the Ministries/Departments concerned, the implementing agency i.e. General Insurance Corporation of India (GIC) and the States/UTs.

6

Agricultural Trade

The agricultural sector with its significant share in GDP plays a significant role in the employment generation especially in the rural sector. In the aftermath of agreement on agriculture under the aegis of W.T.O., it has significant potential as a net foreign exchange earner.

The main approach of the Government Policy has been to control trade in a manner to ensure adequate availability of essential feed items to consumers at reasonable prices and to protect farmers from foreign competition. The main objectives of export and import policy are given as under:

Exports: To maximise agricultural exports, in order to ensure remunerative prices to the farmers and boost foreign exchange earnings, keeping in view, the prime consideration of sufficient availability of essential commodities (particularly of mass consumption to the domestic consumers at reasonable prices.

Imports: To regulate imports, keeping in view, the domestic demand and supply situation, indigenous production, export potential and consideration of foreign exchange.

Export policy for 1998-99 in respect of pal agricultural commodities as contained in EXIM policy 1997-2002 is given below:

Rice: Export of both basmati and non-basmati rice is allowed freely subject to registration of contracts with APEDA.

Coarse grains: Export is allowed up to a quantitative ceiling of one lakh NIT during 1998-99.

Wheat & Wheat Products: Export of wheat is banned now, but export of wheat products, whether in bulk or in consumer packs, is allowed within an overall quantitative ceilings of one lakh tonnes; during 1998-99.

Pulses: Export is permitted against a licence but except those in consumer packs upto 5 kg.

Paddy (rice in husk): Export permitted under a licence.

Oilseeds: The export of oilseeds has been allowed for consumption purposes.

Oilmeals: Export is free without any restrictions.

Tobacco: Export is free without any restrictions for both (a) Unmanufactured and M Manufactured.

Spices: Export is free without any restrictions.

Cashew:. Export is free without any restrictions.

Horticultural & Floricultural Products: Export is free without any restrictions.

Fresh Vegetables: Export is free without any restrictions. However, export of Potato is banned.

Onion: Export is canalised through NAFED.

Export Performance: Increased export of agricultural commodities has been witnessed over the years. In the last five years, the value of agricultural exports has increased from Rs.10810.97 crore during the year 1993-94 to Rs.20052.72 crore in the, year 1997-98. The commodities like wheat, rice, groundnut, oilmeals and raw cotton (including waste) where significant increase of exports (in quantity) has taken place during the last five years.

Removal of Quantitative restriction on imports

Quantitative restrictions on imports are maintained under Article-XVIII-B of GATT Agreement. This is a GATT consistent measurement for countries having balance of payment difficulties. Ministry of Commerce, in consultation with this Department has prepared a phase out plan for removal of Quantitative restrictions spanning over five to seven years. Currently, three phases of decreasing duration have been suggested: Fy 1997-2000 (1-phase), Fy.2000-2002 (11-phase) and Fy 2002-2003 (111phase). The phase-out programme is being done on the basis of sensitivity of the particular crop from the, point of view of (1) its implications on the principal vocation of majority of our farm population and (ii) its importance as a staple item of feed. Items of critical nature like cereals, coarse grains, edible oils and oilseeds etc, are in the third phase.

Trade Division of the Department of Agriculture & Cooperation deals with the liberalisation of Import-Export Policy in respect of Agricultural Commodities in liaison with the Ministry of Commerce. The liberalisation of trade is a continuous process, the primary objective is to help maximise agricultural exports and foreign exchange earning and also ensure remunerative prices to the farmers keeping in view the domestic requirements of the commodities of mass consumption.

7

Agro-Industries and Agricultural Finance

The meaning attached to the term "Cottage Industries" has undergone changes with the progress in technology and its definition no longer restricts it to industries using manual labour and simple tools only. The use of power and machines has been admitted in the definition of the term. The basic implications which differentiate the cottage industries from large scale and heavy industries are: (1) the small scale of production, and (2) usually the worker works on his own, although the employment of wage-paid labour is not ruled out. Attempts to define the term very precisely have not been quite successful. With technological progress the concept behind cottage industries has been undergoing modifications. However, the sense in which the term is employed is commonly well understood.

Cottage industries may be divided into four broad classes, viz., handicrafts, home industries, small-scale industries and village industries. The dexterity of human hands and mainly their use in making the final product are the characteristics of handicrafts. Handicrafts, as the name indicates, always represent the best type of art for the art produced by hand can hardly be excelled.

In home industries, hand or power driven machinery may be used. But the chief characteristics of home industries is that raw materials are procurable locally and labour consists normally of family members. If there are any outsiders they are employed only as apprentices. The industry thus gets the most careful attention of the master.

Small industries are distinguishable by the place of work, the amount of capital invested and equipment used. They are carried on either in the house of the artisan or in a small workshop run by the entrepreneur. The capital invested may be theoretically large as is the case with ivory carving. But generally the capital is limited and this places restrictions on the employment of labour, the use of machinery, etc.

Hired labour may be employed both in the small-scale and village industries; but the village industries have necessarily to be located in the villages, while the small industries may even be located in the urban or semi-urban areas. The number or employees in the small industries should also not be large and may not exceed nine persons.

The importance of village and cottage industries is emphasised by the fact that India, in spite of considerable progress towards urbanisation in the recent past, still lives in villages and her national economy is predominantly agricultural. Her agriculture, even when the required degree of intensity of cultivation is achieved through the development of irrigation, use of fertilizers and above all with the assistance of an all-pervading extension service, by its very seasonal nature and overcrowding in it, would not be able to free itself from the disguised unemployment and underemployment.

The industrial development, with its concentration in towns, is no solution to the problem of unemployment in villages. The small enterprises employed about 20 million workers as against about five million workers in the factory establishments in 1966. There has been a great rise in building and other construction activities and people have found new employment opportunities in them. But this is so only during the transitional stage of economic development and the tempo of construction programmes may slow down. Therefore a more stable source of employment has to be looked for. Rural industries provide great promise in this respect.

The greatest advantage of small and cottage industries is that employment is provided in the natural setting of the workers' own place with numerous physical, moral and other benefits that go with such employment. It helps them to develop inherent talents and aptitudes in occupations congenial to them. Another important reason for employment to be found in the villages and not outside is that agriculture may not provide full employment, yet a larger labour force has to remain in villages at certain periods to provide the needed labour for cultivation, weeding, harvesting and other operations. Mechanised agriculture, to any appreciable extent, does not seem to be a practical proposition for many years to come. The introduction and encouragement of well-chosen village industries in each region of India, on grounds of availability of raw material, local talent, the ability of the industry to fit in with and adjust within a limit with the peak labour demand in agriculture, should add to rural welfare in many ways.

— It will reduce considerably unemployment and underemployment in many regions.

— It will provide useful outlet for many of the raw materials and waste material of agriculture, the transport of which, for reasons of their bulk and low value, is not economical over long distances. Such raw material will be converted into national wealth.

— The farmer and his family members will get an additional source of income which is so needed to raise their standard of living and help them tide over difficulties caused by the failure of crops.

— The country is facing an extreme shortage of foreign exchange. The restrictions on imports does not help very much to ease the problem. An all-out effort required to encourage exports. The produce of cottage industries hae fairly reasonable prospects of commanding foreign markets where there is great demand for them. The opening of cottage industries emporia in some of the European countries has already brought to light the potentialities of these products as earners of foreign exchange.

Phulkaris of Punjab, shawls, wood work and art pieces of Kashmir, are but a few items, which are much in demand in other countries and promise to fetch prices commensurate with the labour put in the production of these commodities.

— The products of small industries which employ local raw materials and talent do not call for any heavy capital investment. This suits our austere economy.

— There need not be any clash between the large and small industries. If properly organised, small industries will provide employment opportunities to enable India to achieve her cherished goal of full employment, but also act as feeders to large industries.

— A developing economy depending upon deficit financing has to face a time lag between the commencement and completion of big projects particularly when the country lacks technical know-how and equipment. During this period, the available consumption goods cannot keep pace with the rise in the purchasing power. Products of cottage and small-scale industries would come in very handy under these circumstances. In addition to making available a variety of consumer goods, they will to a great extent be free from the distribution problem. Transportation over long distances would not be necessary and a major portion of the products would be consumed near the producing centres. These readily available goods will help to mop up the newly released purchasing power and fill the necessary gap, till the investment on capital good strats producing consumer goods.

— India is wedded to a democratic form of government and is committed to a socialistic pattern of society. Like peasant farming in agriculture, cottage and small industries in the industrial sector strengthen the foundation of democracy and socialist structure of society. For this reason also, cottage and small industries have to get a place in the national economy to usher in economic democracy and the desired social order.

In view of the benefits conferred on the national economy and increase in rural welfare, cottage and small scale industries have a very strong case for rehabilitation and development. The power projects completed and nearing completion under the Five Year Plans are adding to the supply of total electricity in the country at reasonable costs.

The Government have already taken up the programmes of rural electrification. This should give further impetus to development of small industries in villages. This favourable development in the availability of cheap power in rural areas can greatly help to remove the stigma attached to cottage industries of being sweated ones with low returns. As technological progress in the form of the steam engine gave a staggering blow to the small scale production in the 19th century, the change from steam power to electric power, particularly in countries where the electric power can be produced cheaply, can help in reversing the process from large scale to small scale production in the case of a number of products on economic grounds, considerations of rural welfare and decentraliisation of economy in the interest of a democratic socialistic set up. It is just not a theoretical deducation but is in actual practice in countries like Japan and Switzerland.

The various forms of help needed by the small scale industries are described below:

— An organised extension service of technical guidance to the cottage workers in designing, use of tools and machines and production of quality goods or goods according to demand.

— The extension service has to be supported with appropriate research institutions at central, regional and state levels.

— Development of industrial cooperatives for supplies, services, finance, and marketing of products and in some instances even for production. If farming can be run on cooperative lines, there appears no reason why it cannot be done in the production of goods in certain cottage or village industries as well. For an understanding of the causes of failure of cooperative societies in the past, the findings of Sri Vishwanathan Vekumalla who surveyed some of the representative industrial cooperatives in Andhra would be of interest. These are:

(a) Societies do not have enough capital either to give full time work to members or to enable them to manage until the products are sold. Consequently the members are obliged to produce for the local market or for the local sahukar.

(b) The limited benefits conferred by the societies make the members disloyal. The artisans distrust one another.

(c) Some influential members as office beares utilise the societies' funds to further their own personal ends.

(d) The consumer, majority of whom have low incomes, care more for cheap goods rather than for quality. The member artisans face keen competition from non-members who under-sell by producing inferior stuff for the market.

(e) Instead of obtaining the cooperation of the supervising officials, the office bearers of some societies actually betray their own cause by hoodwinking them.

With cooperative education, proper training and supervision, these difficulties can be overcome but it must be clearly realised that efforts on a cooperative basis in all possible directions are necessary for the development of handicrafts and cottage industries. It is only through cooperation that these industries can reduce their costs of production and marketing.

— There should be adequate and institutional credit made available to the cottage workers for meeting the financial needs of their business.

— The State should help develop home and foreign markets for cottage goods.

— A system of quality control must be imposed on the cottage products.

— Government should give preference to cottage products in buying their requirements.

Agro industries

Nobody quite knows who first propounded the thesis that India could stamp out poverty by setting up agro-industries in a big way. The term came into vogue no more than a decade ago. But since then it has become highly fashionable. Almost everything ranging from a giant nuclear power reactor to cellophane packing is now sought to be justified on the ground that it is necessary to promote agro-industries. Most of the big business houses have already diversified into the field and others want to do so.

For the new entrepreneurs it is not merely a matter of keeping up with the established industrial Joneses. The opportunities are vast and highly attractive, considering the governmental incentives on offer. The authorities in their anxiety to industrialise the countryside have decided to extend the benefits to a large number of industries whose link agriculture is remote if at all one exists. The 155-point list of "agro-industries" issued by the Commissioner of Small-Scale Industries, for instance, includes refrigeration plants for milk and factories for the canning of fish.

The Planning Commission goes even further. It says that any enterprise which processes farm produce, supplies chemical inputs to agriculture (fertilizers, insecticides, etc.), manufactures improved agricultural equipment (hoes, bullock cart tyres, tractors, etc.), or helps raise farm output is an agro-industry. This means that the term not only covers the nation's biggest industry—cotton textiles—but also the whole range of plantations like tea, coffee and cashewnut and of course, jute.

Going only by statistics the result is somewhat ironical. They show that a much bigger segment of the Indian industry was agro-based at the time of

Independence than has been the case in recent years. In 1951 agro-industries accounted for 75 per cent of the total productive capital employed and 78 per cent of all value added by manufacturing in the orga. ised sector. By 1963, however, these percentage had fallen respectively to 34 and 53. The steep decline in these figures does not mean that agro-industries are on their way out. But it does indicate that their growth has been slow in comparison with the phenomenal expansion of other industries like steel, oil refining or electronics.

The word "agro-industries" broadly means industries manufacturing "input" for agriculture, or processing agricultural "output." Agencies supporting agriculture by designing and manufacturing inputs are termed as "agro-industrials" and those supported by agricultural products are classed as "agro-based industries."

Generally most of the industries use agricultural output as basic raw material. But the concept of agro-based industries leave out of account "industrial product". It is confined to those industries that are engaged in processing the agricultural produce either for consumption or for the use of industry. They include wheat milling, rice milling, dal-making, oil crushing, cotton ginning, khandsari, fruit beverages, and so on. Thus, the agro-industries serve at both the ends of farming.

In the first instance agro-industrials provide the essential input and in the second phase agro-based industries function as an outlet for agricultural output. The purpose of helping these industries is to make farming a profitable and commercially viable proposition; since agro-industrials directly influence the cost structure of farming and agro-based industries, they have their impact on the receipts of the farmer. Agro-industries also serve as a means for providing better employment opportunities to the labour during off season.

The concept of agro-industrial is not new. Formerly the village smith, the carpenter and cobbler used to prepare and repair the various traditional types of agricultural tools and implements. These industries were, and in some regions still are, the part and parcel of rural life. The agricultural implements are exchanged for a share in the harvest.

Likewise in its refined form modern agro-industrial manufacture, process and supply agriculture inputs either on cash basis or realise the value in instalments. The distribution of fertilizers and seeds has been taken over by the cooperatives for quite a long time now. The various agro-industrial corporations in the states seek to supply agriculture machinery on cash, credit and hire-purchase system.

The idea of "in—kind" assistance has been mooted from the simple fact that outright cash grant to the farmer for production is often misused and misdirected in consumption. Even those genuinely interested in buying implements and machinery, have faced numerous problems in purchasing them at reasonable prices. The farmer who is detached from urban life takes time in locating the supplier and picking up the operating technique. Because of "scarcity" of modern machinery, is said that a "black market" has also grown in agricultural inputs.

The purpose of establishing the agro-industrial corporations, therefore, is not only to equip the farmer with modern implements but also to train him in the operation of machines—so essential at the early stages of mechanisation, ensure proper use of funds and protect the farmer from the difficulties involved in purchasing right type of machinery and implements suitable for cultivation in his region. In India, the soil and climate conditions so sharply differ from one region to another that only regional corporations could take a better view and mould the tools according to regional requirements.

Although there has been an impressive development of large-scale industries during the two decades of planned development, India still remains predominantly a country of villages and small industries. About two crore persons are engaged in these industries, of whom nearly 90 lakhs work in the handloom industries, i.e., more than the total number of persons employed in the organised industries and mining put together.

The small-scale and village industries sector covers a wide range of traditional and modern small-scale industries including handloom, khadi, powerloom, sericulture, coir, handicrafts, village industries and mechanised small-scale industries.

This sector consists broadly of (i) traditional cottage and household industries (viz., handloom, khadi & village industries, handicrafts, sericulture and coir industry), and (ii) modern small scale industries (defined as those having investment of up to Rs. 10 lakhs in plant and machinery and Rs. 15 lakhs in the case of ancillary industries). As distinguished from modern small scale industries, the traditional cottage and household industries are located mostly in rural and semi-urban areas. A large number of these traditional industries do not use power-operated appliances and equipment. These also involve relatively lower levels of investment and technology and provide largely part-time employment. A very large number of the persons dependent on traditional industries belong to the poorer sections of the society and live below the poverty line. However, a number of these industries produce certain essential articles required by the masses and also some other items which are exported. The number of persons employed in principal traditional industries is estimated at 140 lakhs, including about 57 lakhs in the handloom industry and about 36 lakhs in sericulture. Much of this employment is neither full-time nor well remunerative. Modern small scale industries are estimated to provide full-time employment to about 28 lakh persons.

The Industrial Policy Resolution of the Government of India, 1948 recognised cottage and small scale industries as an important sector of our economy. The Cottage Industries Board and the Cottage Industries Directorate were accordingly set up. Since each of these industries have their own complexities and problems, separate Boards were also created to look after individual industries such as coir, silk and handicrafts. The Small Scale Industries Organisation was also created to take care of those small enterprises which were outside the orbit of all such Boards. For purposes of definition, it was decided that a unit which has an investment of less than Rs. 5 lakhs and employs less than 50 persons could be classed as small scale. The limit on employment has been removed since then.

In spite of the awareness of the importance of cottage and small scale industries and initiative of the organisational measures as mentioned above nothing much could be achieved during the First Plan period. Some protection was given to handloom and three or four other village industries. But a large number of the cottage industries faced strong competition from mill and factory-made goods.

In order to review the problems and programmes of such industries, a Village and Small Industries Committee was set up in 1955 under the chairmanship of Prof. D.G. Karve. The recommendations of the Committee deal with the following three objectives:

— Further technological unemployment such as occurs in traditional village industries should be avoided as far as possible.

— Employment opportunities for as large a number as possible should be created through different village and small industries.

— The basis should be prepared for an essentially decentralised society and also for progressive economic development at a fairly rapid rate.

With these objectives in view, the Committee considered that the progressive expansion and modernisation of rural industry could be best brought about by the establishment of small industries units, along with the necessary services in large villages and small towns located all over the country. Industrial expansion on the periphery of large towns could scarcely be said to reduce the concentration of industry. What was needed, therefore, was a pattern of industrial activity in which a group of villages converging on their natural industrial and urban centre, form a unit, what the Committee called "a pyramid of industry broad-based on a progressive rural economy."

The Committee also visualised the introduction of technical improvement even in the traditional village industries. It was recommended that for the future there should be a regular programme of gradual transition to better techniques.

Necessitated by the acceptance of a socialist pattern of society as the national objective and to meet the requirement of the planned economic development, a fresh statement of industrial policy was made on April 30, 1956. "The Resolution accepted the policy of supporting cottage as well as village and small scale industries by restricting the volume of production in the large scale sector by differential taxation or direct subsidies. The aim of state policy was declared as that of ensuring a decentralised sector acquiring sufficient vitality to be self-supporting and integrating its development with that of the large scale industry. The state was thus to concentrate on measures designed to improve the competitive strength of the small scale producer."

The second Five Year Plan could then take bolder steps for the development of small scale and cottage industries, as a means of achieving dispersed industrial growth on the one hand and provide better employment opportunities on the other. The Development Commissioner's Organisation for Small Scale Industries was set up at the Centre as the apex administrative machinery which has since then rendered technical assistance through a network of 15 State Institutions, Branch Institues and 36 Extension Centres already established for this purpose all over the country.

Intensive area and marketing schemes for khadi and village industries were introduced. The scheme aimed at the integrated economic development of selected contiguous areas with population ranging between 20,000 to 30,000 with a view to developing village industries as an integral part of the rural economy. The number of such intensive areas was increased from 35 in 1955-56 to 200 at the end of the Second Plan.

A provision of Rs. 10 crores was also made for setting up industrial estates. The object was to provide conditions favourable to working efficiency, maintenance of uniform standards in production and economic utilisation of materials and equipment. This was intended to enable the small scale units to have the advantage of common services and other facilities such as good site, electricity, water, gas, steam, compressed air, railway sidings, watch and ward, etc.

It was felt in 1959 that the impact of the small industries programme was more confined to the cities and towns or to areas within close proximity of the headquarters of the Institutes and Extension Centres and had not permeated the countryside. Little advance had been made by this programme into rural areas. The objective of regional and dispersed development of industries as conceived by the Second Plan had not been achieved.

In order to carry the programme to the underdeveloped areas and make the people interested in the development of small industry, an intensive development campaign programme was chalked out.

The programme was primarily to be launched in such areas (districts), which though underdeveloped, offered maximum potentialities for the development of small industries. Closest cooperation was also intended to be provided among the Central Small Industries Organisation including the Small Industries Service Insitute, the State Directorates of Industries, National Small Industries Corporation (P) Ltd. and other official and non-official institutions and agencies. The underlying idea of the campaign was to carry the development programme to the very doors of the potential entrepreneurs and apprise them of the benefits that were likely to accrue to them from taking up small scale industries.

At the end of September 1960 the scheme was in operation in 65 intensive and 18 preintensive areas. The basic unit for working out the scheme was a selected areas comprising 30-40 villages with a population of about 20,000. Warrangal district in Andhra Pradesh and Pali as well as Bhilwara districts in Rajasthan were the first to receive the benefit of this programme.

Sugar industry

In view of the significant role the sugar industry plays in the country's economy, it is desirable to have a broad study of the industry. According, an attempt has been made to examine empirically the various facets of this industry.

It may be of interest to mention here that so far as white sugar industry (NIC-206) is concerned, this forms and organised sector and as such data on it are available regularly on a uniform and continuing basis through annual industrial surveys carried out by the National Sample Survey Organisation and released regularly by the Central Statistical Organisation in their ASI (Annual Survey of Industries) reports.

As regards the data in respect of other constituent, namely, brown sugar (Khandsari) NIC-207) and jaggery (Gur), it is also available through the industrial enquiries but only in respect of those units which are covered under Factories Act. Most of the industrial units in respect of this contituent fall in the unorganised sector. The data for this constituent are thus not available annually on a uniform and continuing basis, as it is in respect of white sugar. However, it has been collected periodically and the latest data available in respect of this sector is for the year 1988-89.

Sugar industry comprises quite a significant part of the Food Group Industry and has contributed quite significantly to it. Accordingly, an attempt has been made in the study to examine the sugar industry as also the Food Group Industry for the year 1992-93, the year for which the latest data are available.

The comparative picture of both the industrial groups has been presented. The represents the various key parameters like the fixed capital, employment, output, value added and other related structural aspects of these industries.

It may be observed from the factories in the sugar industry comprise only 6.10 per cent of the total food industry but its fixed capital is as large as 39.76 per cent and invested capital 48.42 per cent—almost half of the food industry. Its wage share in the total food industry is also quite high 43.9 per cent. It employs about one-third of the persons engaged in the food manufacturing activity and contributes an equal amount (33.08%) in terms of value added to the food industry. An equally significant feature to note is that as large as 53.59% of the gross capital formation in the food industry is made in the sugar industry. This parameter itself indicates how an important role sugar industry is playing in the food industry and hence to the industrial sector in which Food Industry contributes more than 13 per cent in terms of value added—the key measure of contribution.

In view of the important role the sugar industry is playing in the entire food industry, it is felt that an examination of structural ratios and technical co-efficients like fixed/invested capital per factory, employees per factory, value added per factory, gross capital formation per factory may be quite useful for the planner and policy makers. These ratios throw important in formation and demonstrate the significant role of the sugar industry at the micro-level.

According, some of the essential structural ratios and technical co-efficients have been derived in respect of both these industries and are presented.

Reveals the importance of sugar industry at the micro level. The significant feature which emerges from the examination of these structural ratios is that invested capital per factory in sugar industry is as high as Rs. 690 lakh as compared to Rs. 93 lakh in food industry. Similar is the situation with respect to fixed capital per factory, which is about seven times higher in the sugar industry.

Same is the story with the gross capital formation—and important indicator of the growth of the industry. Here too it is nine times higher. The value added per factory in the sugar industry is more than five times than the food industry. Thus significant contribution of the sugar industry to the food industry is amply established.

The study reveals that the refined sugar factories which come under organised sector has around 30 per cent of the total 1306 sugar industrial units. It has around 99 per cent of the fixed capital and 95 per cent of the value added of the sugar industry.

Brown sugar, the other constituent of the sugar industry, however, plays a significant role, since the unorganised sector totally pertains to the units engaged in producing brown sugar and gur. Latest data in respect of the unorganised sector is available for the year 1988-99.

Summarises the position in respect of both the constituents—white and brown sugar. The key parameters like the number of industrial units, fixed/invested capital, total output, total workers and the contribution made by both the constituents measured in terms of value added are given.

The most significant feature which has emerged from the study is that the sugar industry is incurrring heavy losses. This dismal phenomenon merits urgent attention. As regards generating employment it may be seen that about 27 per cent of the employees are engaged in the brown sugar industrial units which constitute about 70 per cent of the total sugar industry. It employees only 1.39 per cent of the total fixed capital (Rs. 3198 crore and Rs. 44 crore in the white and brown sugar respectively).

A disturbing feature which has emergedf from the

study and merits special mention is that labour in the brown sugar industry is very much under-paid. It has been observed from that although labour in the brown sugar industry comprises about 27% of the labour engaged in the total sugar industry, as far as its wage share is concerned, it is only a little over 6 per cent.

The labour in the refined sugar industry receivees Rs. 95 per day, while his counterpart in the brown sugar industry receives only Rs. 35. In other words, labour in the brown sugar industry receives as low as 37 per cent of the daily wages paid to the labour in the white sugar industrial units. On the other hand rate of return on the capital in the brown sugar industry is almost double than the white sugar industry; this being 50.32% and 25.75% in the brown and refind sugar industries respectively.

It has been observed that in the units belonging to manufacturing of refined sugar, the gross okutput per factory is Rs. 25 crore at the national level. While, gross value added per factory comes to Rs. 5 crore only. The gross fixed capital per factory is Rs. 8 crore and the average employment per factory works out to 645 persons. The labour productivity at the national level in respect kof refined sugar industry works out to Rs. 4 lakh, while employees are getting Rs. 35261 as annual emoluments. Furthermore, in the units engaged in the production of indigenous sugari i.e. Bhura, Khandsari and Gur, the labour productivity is only Rs. 64984, while the employees are getting about Rs. 6531 per annum. The output-input ratio in refined sugar and khandsari units works out to 1.23 and 1.17 respectively. It is also worth mentioning that the labour share in the value added in the refined sugar units is only 50% as compared to 71% in the units engaged in the manufacturing of khandsari. The rate of return on cpital is also 51% in the units engaged in the production of indigenous sugar as cokmpared to 26% in the units engaged in the manufacturing and refining of sugar.

In the earlier sections we have made an attempt to examine the intra-and inter industrial differentials in the various key parameters in industrial sector in respect of total food industry as well as the white and brown sugar constituents of the sugar industry. In view of the non-availability of the data in respect of unorganised sector, the study had to be restricted to the organised sector of these industries for the year 1992-93, the latest data for which it is available.

However, with a view to having the total scenario of the sugar industry—we have attempted in this section to examine both the organised and unokrganised sectors of the industry. As the latest data in respect of the unorganised sector is available for the year 1988-89, the study is limited to this period only. However, it is felt, that the study of both the organised and unorganised sector of the industry do throw light on the various dimensions of the industry and help us in assessment of the growth pattern of the sugar industry and selp us in assessment of the growth pattern of the sugar industry, as also the contributions being made by the organised as well as unorganised sector.

In view of the importance of the brown sugar industry in the unorganised sector, the data in respect of refined sugar industry have been presented seperately for both the organised and unorganised sectors. This would, it is feltl, considerably facilitate the appraisal of the contribution made by the brown sugar industry in the total sugar industry.

It has been observed that 96% of the industrial units engaged in the sugar industry are in the unorganised sector. Persons employed in both the sectors are almost of the same order, although number of factories in the organised sector constitute only 4.1% of the total sugar industry. In other words the sugar industry in the organised sector which comprises primarily the white (refined) sugar constiuents of this sugar industry is highly employment oriented. It is equally highly capital oriented as well. For, it forms on 96% the total fixed capital in the sugar industry, though it has only 4 per cent industrial units. Unorganised sector of the sugar industry only contribute about 4% each of the total output and the total output and the total value.

A distriburbing feature which, however, emerges from the study is that, although labour engaged in the unorganised sector is a s hogh as 50 per cent, it receives only 4.26 per cent of the wages share. The labour in the unorganised sector is bery much underpaid and being deprived of the fair wages.

The aspect relating to production of sugarcane, area under sugarcane and yield per hectare etc. have also been examined. It has been observed that the production of sugarcane was only 57.1 million tonnes during 1950-51 and it increased to 265 million tonnes in 1995-96, an annual compound growth rate of 3.5% has been observed during the last four decade in the production of sugarcane. The area under sugarcane during 1950-51 was 1.7 million hectare which increased to 3.7 million hectare which increased to 3.7 million hectares in 1990-91 and 3.8 million hectares at present. The per capita availability of sugar has increased from 5 kg. during 1955-56 to 7.4 kg. in 1970-71. However, during 1990-91 the per capita availability of sugar has increased to about 13 kg. The annual increase in per capita availability of sugar works out to 2.8 per cent during the last three decades.

Rubber

There is big potential in the rubber sector and /cooperative can minimise the gap between production of rubber and consumption in the state. Keeping this aspect in view, NCDC is providing assistance to cooperatives for setting up rubber processing unis and to enable farmers to get a good price for the collection of latex, its conversion into value added rubber sheets for marketing. The cooperation has supported 17 rubber processing units in the state with funds of Rs.7 crore of which 11 units are in operation.

Traditionally latex is obtained from rubber plant by the farmers and is converted into rubber sheets by them. These sheets are procured by private agencies or rubber cooperatives for marketing in the area having demand for rubber. Cooperatives have been engaged in procurement of rubber sheets and are also setting up their own rubber processing units for conversion of latex into value added rubber products which have a great demand in the rubber industry. Sixty per cent of rubber production in the state is channelised through rubber cooperatives. RUBBERMARK is the state federation of these 35 rubber cooperatives. The federation provides technical guidance and input services like supply of fertilisers, insecticides and material for rubber tapping to the rubber societies. The Federation also organises marketing of rubber products on behalf of societies.

Coconut

A Central scheme for assisting cooperatives under an EEC backed Integrated Coconut Development Project at a total cost of Rs.104.76 crore is currently under implementation in Kerala through KERAFED. The NCDC has released about Rs.63 crore upto March 1995 against the total commitment of Rs. 80.79 crore. About 900 PACVs are covered under this project with participation of about 29 lkh farmers. One Oil Mill with a capacity of 200 TPD has been set up and two mills are under implementation. The unit crushed around 19800 MT of copra in 1994-95 achieving 64 per cent oil recovery.

Coir

Importance of coir has increased in the recent past since coir products are biodegradable and environmental friendly. The local consumption and export demand of coir fiber and coir based products has shown a rising trend.

Coir industry in Kerala has been marked by drudgery and unhygeinic conditions. To save the workforce from polluting working conditions and back breaking traditional methods of coir extraction, Kerala government has launched an Integrated Coir Development Project with financial assistance from NCDC. The project involves machanisation in the areas of defibering and spinning. The project envisages setting up 100 coir defibering units in northern districts of the state for extracting fibre from green jusk and 200 coir spinning units having 100 motorised ratts each, mostly in southern districts.

Motorised treadle ratts would spin superior yarn of uniform quality and of varieties required for manufacturing quality products and for export. The changeover to the motorised treadle ratts would result in additional mandays of employment and increased production on account of higher productivity.

The Integrated Coir Development Project with an estimated cost of Rs.44.8 crore took of in 1993-94. NCDC has sanctioned establishment of 171 units comprising 46 defibering units and 125 spinning units at an estimated cost of Rs.32.16 crores. Nine spining units and one defibering unit have been commissioned and kothers would be commissioned within a period of 3 to 12 months.

The NCDC has undertaken a systematic and sustained approach to create appropriate storage capacity through cooperative. With NCDC's assistance cooperatives in the state have constructed 1966 rural and 131 marketing godowns with 3 lakhs tonnes storing capacity. These infrastructural facilities have helped cooperatives to ensure timely supply of agricultural inputs in the interior areas and also to ensure better price to the farmers for their produce. In addition, 49 rural godowns with a total capacity of 11,100 MTs and two marketing godowns with 650 MTs capacity are under construction in the state.

Fisheries

There are about 2 lakh fishermen in the marine sector of Kerala. Out of them, 1.5 lakh fishermen have been covered by 291 primary level Fishermen Development Welfare Cooperative Societies. This means about 75 per cent of the marine fishermen were brought under the cooperative fold. Kerala State Cooperative Federation for Fisheries Development Ltd., (MATSYAFED) is the apex federation of these primary societies.

Since 1985-86, NCDC has been promoting and funding Integrated Fisheries Development Projects (IFDP) wherein all the activities from production to final marketing are integrated with forward and backward linkages. The main components of such projects are fishing input, infrastructure, marketing support, project management, extension training, computerisation etc. Under these projects, special emphasis is laid on training of employees, education of fishermen members of the societies and creation of infrastructure for production, storage, processing and marketing of fish. About 22.892 fishermen in the marine sector have been beneficiaries of NCDC schemes. NCDC has so far sanctioned Rs. 47.99 crore and released Rs. 3769 crore for the Integrated Fisheries Development Project Phase I, II and III implemented/being implemented by MATSYAFED.

Phase-I of IFDP was implemented in 15 villages of

Thiruvananthapuram Ernakulam and Kanpur districts covering 4577 fishermen. It has enabled a good increase of Rs.4,700 in the annual income of fishermen members. Phase-II covered 37 primaties located in six districts, Thiruvananthapuram, Kollam, Alappuzha, Thrissur, Malappuram and Kozhikode. The third phase of IFDP, which has already commenced is in its fourth year of implementation.

Integrated Cooperative Development Project (ICDP) are also being implemented in Kerala. Such projects, unlike other NCDC assisted projects which are for a specific activity, have a plus point in the sense that these provide a wholesome package of services to the rural community. The concept of ICDP is to make a comprehensive programme for integrated development of cooperatives of the agricultural and allied sectors as a whole in the district in order to enhance the volume of business of all cooperatives, whether credit societies, marketing societies, consumer societies, fisheries, handlooms etc.

The NCDC has so far assisted ICDP programmes in five districts namely Wyanad, Palakkad, Kottayam, Pathanamthitta and Idukki. Implementation of ICDP in the districts of Palakkad., Wynad and Kottayam with a total block cost of Rs.18.46 crore is over. About 500 primary agricultural credit societies, 40 marketing societies and 35 other cooperatives have benefitted from these three ICDPs. Thus, over the years NCDC has diversified its activities to cover almost all sectors of rural economy.

Timber

FAO estimates that in 1994, the world produced 3,419.9 mcum of round wood, out of which India's share was only 293.9 mcum (8.59%). Firewood and charcoal accounted for as much as 91.5% (269.2 mcum) of the

Indian Production (FAO, 1994). Although only less than 10% of the total wood production in the country is used for industrial purpopses, industrial demand has been rising sharply. Projected demands for forest products show a 22 to 183% increase from 1990 to 2000. By a long—term trend analysis of forest products in India, Rao (1992) showed that production of almost all products except pulpwood and particles and veneer sheets registered an increase in the 1980s. Industrial use of wood has been growing at the rate of 3.5 per cent per annum, according to him.

The decade from 1975–76 to 1985–86, saw Indian production of wood and wood products recording an increase of 22 to 135%. However, statistics on timber production is less revealing, perhaps as incomplete as its demand itself. Timber is normally obtained from government forests, community and private forests and farm lands. While the timber extracted from the national forests is reported in the official statistics, the timber harvested from the other sources goes unreported in the official statistics. Therefore, the epithet 'recorded production', a gross underestimate of total production is fashionable among foresters.

According to FSI, consumption of firewood exceeded recorded production by a staggering 195 mcum in 1987. All existing projections show that there is a big gap between demand and supply of industrial timber too. Total sustained yield increment of existing forests is stated to be 35 million m^3 With an additional 4–5 million m^3 from private sources, it sums up to a grand total of 40 million m^3 (Campbell, 1987). To meet the industrial needs alone (64.4 mcum in 2000 AD, according to NCA, 1976), an additional sustained yield increment of 24 mcum will be needed. Furthermore, all indicators suggest that this gap is going to grow. Presumably this wide gap between demand and sup[ply is being met from unrecorded sources like farm lands and agroforestry and other privately owned sources.

Given this huge deficit in industrial timber availability in the country, we may probably have two options. The first, is to enhance the area under plantation forests and to improve their productivity. However, given a conservative average productivity of 0.3 cum/ha for long rotation timber and roundwood species, and 3–5 cum/ha for short rotation pulp wood, this would then mean at least 30 million ha of new plantations for timber species and two million ha for pulpwood–a total for 32 million ha for industrial needs alone (Campbell, 1987). Considering the poor productivity of forest plantations and the general inhability to expand area under plantation forestry, it is impossible to achieve such gargantuan targets through the plantation forestry route.

Pisciculture

Fish Farming in Madhya Pradesh has emerged as a major economic activity adopted by a large number of farmers apart from the members of traditional fishermen community. Thanks to adoption of various development measures, the annual fish production has touched over 80 lakh tonnes while annual spawn production has reached 52 crore during last four years. The common varities of fishes found in the state are: Katla (Catla catla) Mirgal (Cirrhinus Cirrhosal), Rohu (Labeo Rohital), Magur (Clarias Betgracus), Silond (Silonia Silonidia) Bata (Labeo Batal), Bami (Mastacarnbelus Armatus), Signi (Hetero Pneustes fossils), Gunguch (Lepidocephalichthy Guntel) etc.

The state government encouraged fisheries sector as a thrust area and launched the ambitious Rajiv Gandhi Mission for Fisheries Development with the sole object to promote pisciculture, ensure economic uplift of fishermen and generate employment oportunities for them. The average per capita annual income of fishermen has shown a 30 per cent increase from Rs. 8,800 to Rs. 12,000 due to a number of well planned steps taken by the government, such as constitution of cooperative societies, training them, conducting study tours for fish farmers, renovation of village ponds, transfer of power from Fisheries Department to panchayat bodies, constructing housing units for fishermen, Group Accident Insurance Scheme for fishermen etc. In Gandhi Sagar reservoir in Mandsaur district alone, where fish production touched 3424 metric tonne, the per capita annual income of 1416 fishermen operating there has increased from Rs. 10,000 to Rs. 18,000.

The Fisheries Department has delegated adequate powers to the newly elected panchayat bodies regarding leasing out ponds and issuing licences to cooperative societies of fishermen in reservoirs. tanks or ponds. Now village panchayats can issue licence for fishing in reservoir spread in 2.5 acres, Janpad panchayat for reservoir measuring from 25 to 100 acres and district panchayat from 100 to 500 acres. The district panchayat has also been entrusted the responsibility to sanction loan and grant to fishermen's cooperative societies. There are about 51,296 tanks with 8465 hectare water area under the ownership of village panchayats.

With a view to ensuring employment to maximum number of people in fisheries sector, greater attention has been focussed on fishing on cooperative basis as a result of which 136.47 lakh man–days employment were created. There are 1416 cooperative societies of fishermen including 460 Scheduled Tribe and 164 Scheduled Caste cooperative societies. These are provided loans and grants to purchase fishing boats, fishing nets, fish seeds and other essential equipment. The annual budget of 1995—96 proposed loan of Rs. 1.50 lakh and grant of 12.60 lakh to the cooperative societies operating in different resrvoirs, tanks and rural ponds. A 25—member Adarsha Fisheries Cooperative Society of Salaiya in Chattarpur district was handed over Motisagar tank for a period of ten years. It earned a net annual income of Rs. 1.49 lakh during 1994—95 and now is in position of supplying fish seeds to other cooperative socieities.

Similarly, the 25—member cooperative society of tribal fishermen in tribal dominated Jhabua district leased out 105 hectare Charbovali tank for a long period. All members of the society were given training in fish crop cultivation and three fibreglass fishing boats and five other boats were provided to them apart from other basic facilities. The society earned 3 lakh during 1994—95 which fetched an average annual income between Rs. 6000 to Rs. 10,000 to each member.

Fish farming has received encouraging response not only from the traditional fishermen but from women entrepreneurs also. There are 17 cooperative societies of women fish farmers operating successfully. Mrs. Jyotsana Singh of Guna district has become the first women fish farmer of the state to have set up her own Chinese hatchery complex at her village Rampur. The annual spawn production of the hatchery is 25 lakh. Similarly, a sidow and mother of two children Meera Bai of Suktara village of Seoni district adopted fish cultivation in 4.5 hectare tank. She is now able to bring up her two children. She formed a group of 14 other women. Today each of them earns Rs. 700–1000 per month.

Basic infrastructural facilities for development of fisheries have been increased and a number of welfare programmes for fishermen have been launched by the state government. Special activities have been taken up under Literacy Mission to spread literacy among fishermen. A cold storage of 10 tonne capacity is under construction near Gandhi Sagar reservoir in Mandsaur district and a five—tonne capacity cold storage near Demar fish farm in Raipur is nearing completion. Insulated box and cycles have been distributed to retailers. Besides, construction of 20 fish handling sheds is underway, 250 housing units have been constructed near Gandhi Sagar, Dudhwa (Bastar district) and Tawa (Hoshangabad district) reservoirs for the fishermen operating there.

Fish farmers have not limited themselves to fish. They have also taken u other economic activities associated with pisciculture like fish—cum—duck rearing, fish—cum—poultry rearing and prawn cultivation etc. The State's fish prawn hatchery has been set up in Balaghat district. The Fisheries Development Corporation has chalked out a Rs. 4.79 crore Prawn Cultivation Project for commercial cultivation Project for commercial cultivaton and supply of prawn.

Thus pisciculture has gained momentum in the state and has become a substantial source of income for many.

Fertilizers

Application of fertilizers plays very vital role in foodgrain production. During 1986-87 fertilizer consumption was 8.64 million tonnes and the foodgrains production was 143.43 million tonnes (estimated) during 1994-95 and foodgrain production is likely to be around 186 million tonnes (estimated).

It is imperative that use of chemical fertilizers, which is a costly input, is made on soil-test based fertilizer recommendations. There are about 496 soil testing labortories, both static and mobile, functioning in the country with a total analying capacity of approximately 60 lakh soil samples per annum. With intensification of agriculture, soils have started exhibiting deficiencies in secondary and micro-nutrients. Some soil testing laboratories are being equipped with Atomic Absorption Spectrophotometers (AAS) for detecting the deficiency of micro-nutrients and advising farmers about correct requirements of these nutrients along with major plant nutrients for different crops.

Productivity of the soil is undergoing strains as per unit crop yields are stagnating and higher doses of fertilizers are not giving commensurate increase in yields. Besides, chemical fertilizers being industrial products are prone to cost increases every year, becoming unaffordable for large segments of farmers. In order to obviate the above constraints, a Centrally-sponsored scheme 'Balanced and Integrated Use of Fertilizers' is implemented to promote use of chemical fertilizers n conjuction with enhanced use of organics, compost, green manuring and bio-fertilizers. The farmers are also trained for preparing their own compost so as to reduce dependency on chemical fertilizers. Apart from this, the scheme also endeavours to convert city garbage into compost.

Organic manures that are bulky materials obtained from de-composition of renewable and natural organic waste in rural and urban areas containing small quantities of plant nutrients are essential for improving the physical properties, soil structure, water holding capacity and increase in microbial production and humus contents of the soil. it is estimated that about 275 million tonnes of rural and 6.4 million tonnes of urban compost is being produced and used in the country.

Ministry of Agriculture, Department of Agriculture and Cooperation is implementing a scheme 'National Project on Development and Use of Bio-fertilizer' with a view to produce, distribute and promote bio-fertilizers use by organising training and demonstration programmes and also quality testing of bio-fertilizers.

Unde the scheme, one national centre at Ghaziabad in Uttar Pradesh and six regional centres at Bangalore, Bhubaneswar, Hissar, Imphal, Jabalpur and Nagpur have been established The production from these centres is about 300 tonnes of bio-fertilizers during 1994-95. In addition to production, these centres have 'Culture Collection Bank' with a good number of effective and promising strains. Quality testing of bio-fertilizers has also been taken up at these centres. So far, 26 bio-fertilizer production units have been financed by the Ministry in various states for production of bio-fertilizer. During 1994-95, the production of bio-fertilizer by the units financed by the Ministry is estimated at about 2000 tonnes. In addition, blue green (BGA) centres in the states are also producing about 350-400 tonnes (estimated) of BGA for its use in wetland paddy.

The Government has issued the Fertilizer (Control) Order, 1985 under the Essential Commodities Act, 1955. This Order contains specifications of fertilizers being sold in the country, methods of sampling and analysis and provision for appoinment of enforcement agencies for regulating the trade and distribution of fertilizer quality control * laboratories in various states. In addition there is one Central`Fertilizer Quality Control and Training Institute at Faridabad with its three regional centres at Bombay, Calcutta and Madras. Total analysing capacity of these laboratories in the country is 96,500 fertilizer samples per annum. The Institue organises training programmes for State Enforcement Officers, State Fertilizer Analysis and for foreigners from developing countries. Besides, training courses for fertilizer dealers are also organised in collaboration with the state governments and the fertilizer industry. The Institute has developed a Quick Testing Kit for on the spot detection of adulteration in fertilizers in the field.

Four decades of planning and development has brought India to the frontline of fertilizer producing countries and is today the fourth largest producer of nitrogenous fertilizers in the world. There are, at present, 58 fertilizer units manufacturing a wide range of nitrogenous and complex fertilizers, including nine units producing ammonium sulphate as a by-product. Besides, there are about 80 units producing single super-phosphate. Production capacity of nitrogen has increased from a modest 85,00 tonnes in 1951-52 to 89.72 lakh tonnes as on 31 March 1995 and that of phosphatic fertilizers from 63,000 tonnes to 28.22 lakh tonnes of P^2O^5 during the same period. Against the nominal production of 16,000 tonnes of nitrogen and 11,000 tonnes of phosphate in 1951-52, the country proudced 79.45 lakh tonnes of nitrogen and 24.93 lakh tonnes of phosphate during 1994-95. Despite massive increase in the indigenous capacity production of fertilizers over the years, substantial imports, either in the form of finshed fertilizers or its raw materials and intermediates, are requied every year to meet the country's growing demand. The overall per hectare consumption of fertilizer nutrients in the country has been rising steadily and has now reached a level of about 68 kg from a mere 0.55 kg in 1950-51.

One large scale gas-based nitrogenous fertilizer plant, with an annual installed capacity of 3.34 lakh tonnes of nitrogen is presently under implementation at Shahjahanpur (UP) and likely to go on stream during 1995-96.

With a veiw to making fertilizers available to farmers at a price they could afford, the Retention Price Scheme was introduced in 1977. Its aim was to insulate farmers from the rising trend in fertilizer prices and to ensure that fertilizer consumption in the country did not suffer as its growing use was an essential component of the Green Revolution strategy of India's development. The scheme simultaneously aimed at ensuring reasonable return on investment to indigenous manufacturers and to attract further investment in this vital sector. The scheme proved its worth in terms of stimulating greater production and use of fertilizers and thereby contributing to greater agricultural production. Inspite of substantial increases in the prices of feedstocks, utilities wages etc. and consequent revision in the retention prices, the selling prices of fertilizers to farmers remained almost frozen for ten years between 1981 and 1991. Thus, while the objective of promoting increased use of fertilizer by farmers was served, this added to the quantum of subsidy borne by the Government year after year. The fertilizer subsidy bill borne by the Government went up from Rs. 375 crore in 1981-82 to Rs. 5,166 crore in 1994-95. Realising that the country could no longer afford to continue with a system which imposed a large and growing burden of fertilizer subsidy, the Government effected an increase of 30 per cent in the selling price of fertilizers in August 1991 after a gap of a decade. While this served to bring down the subsidy requirement from what it would have been in the absence of the price revision, it did not offer much relief in terms of the absolute amount of subsidy bill for the year because, inspite of 30 per cent price increase, fertilizers continued to be heavily subsidised and also because of the otherwise welcome growth in production and consumption of fertilizers.

A Joint Parliamentary Committee was set up to go into the verious aspects of fertilizer pricing and subsidy. Based on its recommendations, Government announced some major changes in the fertilizer pricing policy in August 1992. All price and distribution controls on phosphatic and potassic fertilizers were removed and the selling price of urea was reduced by 10 per cent with effect from 25 August 1992. However, the controlled price of urea was again increased by 20 per cent with effect from 10 June 1993.

To make production and marketing of phosphatic and complex fertilizers more competitive vis-avis imports in the wake of withdrawal of price and movement controls, various other corrective measures have been taken by the Government. These include: abolition of import durty on phosphoric acid-a basic raw material for phosphatic fertilizers, free availability of foreign exchange for import of raw materials and intermediates for manufacture of DAP and complex fertilizers at official exchange rates (till unification of exchange rates in March 1993) and lowering of railway freight for phosphatic and potassic fertilizers. In order to cushion the impact of increase in the prices of decontrolled fertilizers on farmers since Rabi 1992-93 season, a special subside of Rs. 1,000 per tonne on DAP and Muriate of Potash (MOP) and corresponding relief in the case of complex fertilizers was announced. From 1993-94, this special concession in the case of phosphatic fertilizers has been restricted to indigenous products only. These concessions have been extended during the current year 1995-96 also.

The farmers educatonal programmes/promotional activities are carried out by PSUs/Cooperatives through their Agro-Service Centres/Farmers Service Centres/ Kendras in their marketing areas. The following statement shows Agro-Service Centres/Krishi Vigyan Kendras/Farmers Service Centres opened by different PSUs/Cooperatives:

During the course of examination of various PSUs it came out that even though these Kendras were performing well, no specific study has been made by any of the PSU to know the impact of these Kendras in their respective areas.

Admittedly there was overlapping of activities carried out by different PSUs. Some of the PSU like PPCL submitted before the Committee that its present strength of Farmers Service Centres was not adequate.

The Standing Committee in their 13th Report on IFFCO and KRIBHCO' had pointed out that the Farmers' Service Centres/Kendras were crowded in selected fertile areas. In pursuance of the Committee's recommendation, DOF informed in September, 1995 that they had initiated a study to take stock of the existing farmers service centres set up by different PSUs/Cooperatives to identify deficit areas requiring further support for promotional activities.

The terms of reference of the study are as follows:

— List of the existing Farmers Service Centres (FSCs) run by the different PSU/Cooperative Societies may be complied alongwith relevant details like area covered etc.

— Identification of deficit areas where new FSCs could be set up.

— Estimated expenditure involved in setting up FSCs in the deficit areas of the country and the ability of different PSUs/Cooperatives to share this expenditue within their resource constraints.

— Companywise annual phasing of expenditure on setting up of new FSCs including the basis for prioritisation.

— Whether FAI could be asked to coordinate the promotional activities of differnt organisations including cooperatives and FIs?

As regards the progress in the matter, DOF informed:

> "This study has been assigned to IFFCO. It is expected that the study would be completed by the end of June, 1996, Dr. V. Kumar, Marketing Director of IFFCO is carrying out this study. Based on the findings of the study, conclusions will be drawn regarding:

(i) Adequacy of the promotional activities to be undertaken by PSUs/Multi-State Cooperatives under the Farmers Education Programme in 1996-97; and

(ii) Identification of deficit areas for setting up new farming service centre".

The Committee wanted to know whether pooling of funds/resources of PSUs for promotional activities and earmarking of areas to specific PSUs would not be a better coordinated approach for promotional activities which would also be beneficial for the farmers. DOF in a written note started:

> "Each PSU/Cooperative designs its Farmers Education Programmes in accordance with its maketing requirements. PSUs/Cooperatives concentrate their marketing activities in certain specified areas. The content of Farmers Education Programmes has to take into account the product mix of the Fertilizer Undertakings sponsoring them as well as local variations based on agro-climatic factors and farming practices. In view of this, it is preferable to allow inhibited expression to innovativeness at the field level in the design of these programmes. Earmarking of areas to specific PSUs may not necessarily result in synergies because of the difficulty in making the allotted areas co-terminus with the core marketing areas of the companies. The intensity of competition among the Undertakings particularly in respect of decontrolled fertilizers and during the time of demand depression, also detracts from the feasibility of a pooling arrangement".

The Committee also desired to know whether specific

directions from Government in the matter will not help in coordinating and increasing the promotional activities. DOF in a written note stated:

> "This Department will monitor the implementation of activities under the Farmers Education Programme to provide the necessary policy inputs, resolve conflicts and promote the application of phosphate and potassic fertilizers".

Apart from their own resources the following PSUs/ Cooperatives.

During the course of examination of PSUs which implemented these programmes, the Committe equired whether any assessment or evaluation was done by any independent agency or funding agency to know the results/impact of these projects. PSL's in their written notes informed the Committee that funding agencies had appointed independent agency to evaluate the performance of these projects. The projects were highly appreciable by the evaluation agencies.

During the evidence of the representatives of DOF the Committee wanted to know whether the DOF agreed with the views of the evaluating agencies, "We generally agree with the assessment made by evaluating agencies".

In this connection representative of DOF stated during evidence, "Sir, in each of these foreign aided projects, there has been concurrent as well as post-completion evaluation. It has been a very elaborate exercise in all the foreign funded projects. They employ consultants to undertake this exercise. As you had observed, the overall outcome, the overall evaluation has been positive. Of course, certain deficiencies have been pointed out. The Ministry has also participated in this exercise of evaluation".

However, from one of the evaluation reports regarding INDO-EEC Phase II programme, the Committee find the following lacunae:

(i) Objectives should have been more clearly defined to focus on improvements to the incomes of small and marginal farmers through raised agricultural productivity.

(ii) Capital expenditure–Particularly on construction and vehicles–should have been excluded or kept to a minimum.

(iii) Extension methodology should have been amplified and rationlized; with greater emphasis on demonstrations.

(iv) The projects should have tried to introduce more sustainable methods or soils sampling and analysis, particularly by encouraging rough-and-ready testing at farmer level.

(v) All or more social activities should have been excluded as being irrelevant to the main Project objectives".

Another project *viz.* Indo-British Fertilizer Education and Extension Project (ODA funding) costing Rs. 55 crores is yet to be approved by funding agency.

When asked by the Committee whether the Ministry pursued for the approval of the proposed Indo-British Fertilizer Projects, DOF in a written note stated:

> "ODA of UK has not agreed to consider the Indo-British Fertilizer Project for financial assistance because it does not get into their RNR Sector Strategy for India".

Underutilized resources

Underutilization may be in the intensity of land use and

agricultural productivity or the levels of utilisation of labour force. Measures ofunderutilization can be: (a) a straightforward measure of idle resources, of production capacity at a given level of technology and organization, eg fallow land, unemployment and underemployment according to atime measure; (b) misallocation of resources due to lack of knowledge of superior alternatives or distortion in the structure okf incentives; and (c) underutilization in terms of productivity. According to Prof. Brahmananda, even though aggregate capital may be adequate potentially at the macrolevel, capital in the form of wage goods capacity may be deficient. It is in the process of production of wage goods at the local level through local planning that local resource mobilization can take place and productivity can be improved and social change brought about. At the grass roots level in the rural areas, there is urgent need for improving productivity and promoting social change with better education.

Rural development refers to a number of development programmes. Earlier it was linked only with agricultural development but on the basis of the experience during the last few decades we can speak of holistic rural development which includes agriculture, rural development, rural indutries, and hollistic self—supporting development.

In order to accelerate such a holistic rural development there are three major potential areas for integration which are: (a) stepping up the existing wage employment programme in rural areas ofor capital construction in agriculture and for ecodevelopment; (b) stimulating the growth of households by intergrating them with the existing self—employment programmes like IRDP; and (c) accelerating the pace of social development.

In sum, we will emphasize that poverty alleviation programmes should be properly integratd with over—all development. No rural development is possible without wipping out p[overty or reducing it in stages. The integration of poverty alleviation objective with the over–all development strategy has to be distinguished from the issue of integrating poverty alleviation programmes with the over–all development strategy. The over—all development strategy is concerned with questions like investment priorities, choice of technique and location of projects through trickle down effects. It tries to reduce poverty. A greater and more specific role has to be given to investment in agiven resources, eg bringing down the capital output ratio to a certain level sector by sector). But integration of poverty alleviation programmes with over–all development strategy tries to ensure that poverty alleviation programmes subserve the goals of over—all development. At present, the schemes for increasing incomes and employment do not adequately take care of it. In this also there should be a greater role both for human resource development and human development.

Local Resource mobilization & local planning

Indeed at the local level, resources like land, labour and human and physical resources—physical capital to a limited extent are available. Techno—economic surveys can identify the potential resources. But will all the labour force be mobilized for gainful and productive employment? This is a more important task and accompllishing ths depends on the integration of the techno—economic approach with other aspect of the social system and development process. This is the concern of many mono—disciplines like economics, engineering, sociology, psychology, etc. All such studies have pointed out that only at the local level, the basic needs, particularly of vulnerable sections can be identified and they justify larger investment in primary education for promoting health, nutrition, rural development, family size, fertility, literacy and awareness of national culture.

It is true that rural development is in the main equivalent to the development of food and cash croops and their needed inputs—irrigation, fertilizer, seeds and other resource inputs—animal husbandry, dairying and poultry farming, fisheries, forestry and agro—industries. (Dr. Malcolm S. Adisheshiah in Bulletin of Madras Institute of Development Studies, January 1991 P.41). But such investments in agricultural developmentare bound to be more effective when there is adequate investment in human resource development, particularly in literacy and primary education. Between the I and VII Five Year Plans, there has been a decline in agriculture, forestry, animal husbandry, fisheries irrigation, rural development and village and cottage industry from Rs. 45,924.70 crore to Rs. 45,523.02 crore (ie from 54.92% to 23.62% of the total public sector outlay). But in spite of the decline in agricultural outaly, rural development culd have been quickened if only there had been more investment in human resources and human developmen. Local resource mobilization with local planning seems to be a promising vehicle for promoting rural development and alleviating poverty.

Local resource mobilization and substitution of human capital as well as physical capital is in conformity with the experience of some of the Scandinavian countries and Japan in this context. Theyhave been able to substitute the scarce resources with resource mobilizaton at the local level in rural and agricultural sectorsin particular. Such local resources cannot flow to higher levels but can improve productivity at the local level. This resource augmenting effect has the advatage of accelerating agricultural growth.

In such an effort, equity will have to be given special consideration. The disadvantaged population has to be seen not in therole ofobjects of participation but they are to be integrated as the subjects ofoperation. There should be also anb organizational structure which promotes the effective participation of the disadvantagedpopulation. The emergence of local bodies with elected representatives, one hopes, will make it possible to privide thisinfrastructure.

There should be sound planning at the three levels of District Panchayats, Panchayat Samithis and Village Panchayats.

To achieve the ambitious objectives of the Ninth Plan (1997-2002), the government has to face hard realities in mobilizing the required amount of huge resources. The Prime Minister and Chairman of the Planning Commission has called for collective efforts to raise resources of the order of Rs. 8,75,000 crore to finance the Plan. The approach paper urges that the country has to take 'difficult decisions' which, as Mr. H.D. Deve Gowda explained, would in include reduction of fiscal deficit, rational user charges for power and irrigation, disinvestment of public sector and transparent and focused subsidies. The Deputy Chairman of the Planning Commission, Prof Madhu Dandavate has rightly emphasized that the much needed public investment in various sectors could be available only if the required will is demonstrated in exploring new sources of revenues at all levels—the Centre, the States and local governments. He also noted that serious efforts are necessary to ensure better tax compliance and also to bring presumptive incomes computed from high expenditures of creamy layers under the tax net.

Insofar as disinvestment of public sector undertakings as a source of revenue mobilization is concerned, the earlier experience is not at all encouraging. The failure of the disinvestment programme in 1995-96 and all indications of its repetition in regard to the target of mopping up Rs. 5,000 crore in the current fiscal year amply shows that the Ninth Plan should not bank much on this source prior to restructuring of the PSUs.

It may be noted here that an important reason for the inefficiency of PSUs is the defective MOUs which fix responsibilities of the organisations but remain silent on the responsibilities of government and administrative ministries. This needs to be corrected and efficiency enhanced since the government has to justify the existence of this sector and make the enterprises commercially viable.

Insofar as the States' efforts are concerned, there is room fro enhancing revenue collection provided political will is mobilized, administrative machinery for taxation is properly cleaned and temptation of the government for populist spending is arrested. There is huge amount of tax arrears, under assessment of levy, tax evasion through foul means, complete absence of or unjustifiably low rates of tariffs and charges against public services rendered and inefficiently managed State PSUs running on heavy government subsidies. Bold steps to reverse the trend is urgently necessary. This also applies to the Union government by and large.

The approach paper aims at an annual rate of savings at the rate of 26.2 per cent as against the peak of 24.6 per cent in 1989-90. Since the biggest source of savings in the household sector which mobilizes around one-fifth of GDP, there is ample opportunity of raising this source through tax-related saving incentives and stability of the capital market for shares and debentures. Proper incentive pattern is also necessary for saving in physical assets which alone comprise more than 55 per cent of the total household sector savings. The savings of the private corporate sector is only 2.7 per cent which may be easily raised to three per cent of GDP through incentives and better collection. The lowest is the public sector savings which are stagnating at around Id. 7 per cent. The savings from government companies and statutory corporations have started declining since 1990-91 and presently accounts for less than three per cent of GDP. Unless the negative savings on account of government administration and departmental enterprises are checked effectively, one could nolt expect larger savings from the public sector.

At the same time, the huge amount of government subsidy on account of food and fertilizers, petroleum and petroleum products, sugar and other selective items should be withdrawn from those who have the capacity to pay at the rate of open market prices. The oil pool deficit alone has reached public destribution system would claim a whopping Rs. 2,000 crore. There is no justification of suppresssing the administered prices since its substitute is only a resort to deficit financing that would come in the way of macro-economic adjustment in the country.

The system of income taxation in India has remained utterly inequitable as millions of highly rich people go untaxed due to fear of unpopularity among politicians. Thus, the much talked about unexploited source of agricultural income tax has remained a forbidden fruit. In spite of the fact that the Green Revolution and the new agricultural strategy with all kinds of agro-mechanisation subsidy together with a price support programme for farm products have placed more and more wealth in the hands of rich farmers, no political decision has yet been taken to bring the wealthy section of farmers under the income tax net. The K.N. Raj Committee recommended long ago a progressive tax structure for agricultural incomes along with the incomes from non-agricultural sources and also from allied activities of the farm sector. Some members in the NDC while approving the Ninth Plan approach paper, urged upon mobilization of black money as a revenue raising device. Since the agricultural sector offers a golden opportunity to earners of illegal incomes to conceal black money and black wealth under the veil of untaxed farm incomes and since the gap between poverty and prosperity in the farming community has greatly widened as a result of the emergence of highly rich agriculturists, the imposition of agricultural income tax along with non-agricultural income will not only fetch huge funds to the resource-starved exhequer, but will also reduce considerably the prevailing inequality of incomes in rural areas on the one hand and mop up a large part of black money on the other. The other areas of unequal treatment lies in the complete absence of income tax among Scheduled and backward classes, where, too a large section of people has become millionaires due to business activity, government contracts, construction works and heavy development expenditure incurred in backward regions by the government in course of the five year plans, These rich people also go untaxed. In order to remove such utter discrimination, it is urgently necessary that these creamy layers be invariably brought within the income tax net.

Thus, what the foregoing discussion implies is that bold decisions and hard determination are necessary to give a proper shape to the economy after the aspirations of the Ninth Plan approach paper. While political will is a pre-condition, the States' unqualified co-operation will be the most basic factor. However, the aspirations of resource-starved States will urgently need attention particularly with respect to their autonomy and larger access to Central tax sharing which has been the main irritant in the Centre-State relationship. The Centrally-sponsored schemes which have remained only half-hearted attempts for all these years should be left to the responsibility of the States with hundred per cent resource disposal to them. The declining trend of the share of the State' Plan in the total public sector plan outlay needs to be reversed in the Ninth Plan and the decentralized planning should call for strengthening of the administrative set-up of Panchayati Raj institutions at all levels. Accountability and monitoring of activity must be ensured at every step so that development plan does not degenerate into expenditure plan. If all revenue sources are properly exploited, implementation of programmes is carried out in the right perspective and utmost care is maintained in government consumption expenses, there is no reason why the aspirations of the approach paper should not come into reality.

The Chief Minister of Tamil Nadu, India in his budget speech delivered on July 17, 1996 made the following announcement.

Feed the people who are hungary Educate the people to uplift the World

To fulfil this dream of Mahakavi Bharatiyar, this Government will launch a new "Hunger Free Area Programme" with an aim to eradicate poverty induced hunger. A number of schemes are already under implementation to alleviate poverty and to cater to the nutrition requirements of different groups of the population. Gaps in this coverage will be identified which can then be specifically targeted under the Hunger Free Area programme. Preovision has been made in the Budget for preparing a detailed strategy to implement this programme in association with Dr. M.S. Swaminathan.

Studies at MSSRF have shown that by adding a

horizontal dimension to numerous vertically structured programmes and by promoting a coalition of all concerned with ending hunger and deprivation, it is now possible to provid opportunities for a healthy and productive life for all.

The problem of food and nutrition security at the level of the individual has to be viewed in 3 dimensions. First,, inadequate purchasing power leads to calorie-protein under-nutrition. Second, the lack of the needed quantity and variety of micronutrients and vitamins in the diet leads to several nutritional disorders including blingness caused by Vitamin A deficiency. This kind of problem is referred to as "hidden hunger", a problem which affects today more than 2 billion people in the world. Third, lack of environmental hygiene and sanitation leads to a low biological absorption and retention of food, due to intestinal infection and diarrohea. Thus, both food and non-food factors assume importance in determining the nutrition secu;rity of an individual. Concurrent action at all these levels is necessary in a Hunger-Free Area Programme. The various steps involved in this process are described below:

— Identify the basic underlying reasons for chronic under and malnutrition.

— Collate information on available programmes and opportunities for the sustainable end of hunger.

— Articulate the steps needed to provide the 'missing elements' in achieving the end of hunger.

— Mobilise local level community action and commiotment for achieving the end of endemic hunger by the end of the Ninth Five Year Plan and enlist mass media support for this purpose.

— Assess the extent of (i) Financial resources required

(ii) Technical resources for technological empowerment necessary (iii) Managerial and Organisational resources needed.

— Foster the organization of a Grassroots level Coalition for Ending Hunger in each HFAP area comprising representatives of

(a) Elected representatives of the people.

(b) Government agencies.

(c) Civil society-non-governmental organizations, voluntary agencies, services organizations like Rotary clubs, Lions clubs, etc.

(d) Academia-Research, Training Instituitons and Universities.

(e) Corporate Sector.

(f) Financial Institutions and

(g) Mass Media.

The Coalition for Ending Hunger will be responsible for designing, implementing and monitoring the Hunger Free Area programme.

The challenge lies in converting HFAP from a concept into an operational programme. In such a programme, emphasis will have to be placed during the remaining years of this century on generating additional livelihood opportunities for those living below the poverty line in villages and towns. The increasing feminisation of poverty demands that priority attention be given to women and girl children. Based on these considerations, the following operational framework is suggested for a National Hunger-Free Area Programme.

This phase will relate tot he analysis of gaps and constraints. Under the Gap Analysis Programme, an inventory will be made of all the entitlements currently available to those living below the poverty line both through the Central and State Government programmes. The inventory will be suitably classified so as to differentiate social security and nutrition intervention programmes from those relating to employment generation.

Once the Entitlements Database is compiled detailed study based on random sampling techniques will be conducted in about 100 villages of a district to assess the extent to which the entitlements have actually reached the intended families. Within families, special studies will be conducted to ascertain the extent of male-female differences in access to entitlements. The gap between what the poor are entitled to and what they are actually receiving will be grouped according to gender and economic status (I.E., those having assets like land or livestock or fish pond or tress and those who do not own any productive asset).

Once the GAP Analysis is completed, a careful identification of the reasons for the gap and the contrainsts faced by the pooring getting their entitlements will be made. Such a gap and constraints analysis will be the starting how direct and imdirect opverty elimination programmes can be made to reach the unreached organisationfunctioning in the villages including under the GAP Analysis would be made together with an assessment of their effectiveness in serving as bridges between Government agencies and the poor. Discussions will be held with both voluntary organizations and men and women members of elected Panchayats and Nagarpalikas on how the gap can be ended and how the delivery systems of poverty in thier efficiency and impact.

This phase will be a strategic planning phase giving particular attention to the following:

— Steps needed to fill the gap between entitlements and actual delivery.

— Opportunities for mobilising human, financial resources in the concerned areas for improving the efficiency of delilvery of on-going programmes and for initiating new programmes to meet the unmet minimum needs of the population.

— Identification of methods of achieving synergy and convergence among all the programmes, whether governmental or non-governmental.

— Articulation of new livelihood opportunities based on both farm and non-farm occupations.

— Introduction of organisational and management methods which will ensure the oversight and effective participation of the primary stake holders in the implementation of programmes designed tto strengthen the security of their livelihoods, and

— Identification of young women and men in the concerned villages for forming a Corps of Hunger Fighters. The young hunger fighters would undertake responsibilities such as creating awareness of entitlements, improving delivery systems and promoting environmental hygiene and garbage and sewage recycling.

The hunger fighters would be given a small honorarium for meeting their travel and other expenses and for compensating them for thier time. The members of the Corps of Hunger Fighters will be drawn from those who have a social or economic stake in living in their respective villages. There will be equal number of women and men in such a corps.

As a result of the work done during phases 1 and 2, awareness of the possibilities for ending hunger and deprivation, analaysis of methods of achieving the desired goals and an implementable action plan would have emerged. The Action Programme, to be effective, must emerge from discussions with the poor families and on the basis of their suggestions. The phase will therefore be opportune to establish a broad based local level Coalition for Ending Hunger and Deprivation. Such a Coalition for Ending Hunger could consist of representatives of local self-government institutions, government agencies responsible for fighting poverty and hunger, academic community, the civil society, corporate sector, women's and youth organisations, financial institutions and the mass media. Such a coalition will assign specific tasks to each member of the coalition in the areas of awareness generation, resource mobilisation task implementation, monitoring and evaluation. The Coalition will aim to add a horizontal dimension zto vertically structured government programmes. Coalition members will also help to develop methods of achieving gender equality and eliminating social evils like dowery and alcoholism.

During ths period, HFAP will be converted from a desirable concept to anb implementable local level action plan. Intensive efforts will be made to sensitise all sections of the community to the uncommon opportunities now available for achieving a sustainable end to hunger. The poor themselves will play an active role in both the planning and implementation phase. Many of the members of the grassroots level Corps of Hunger Fighters will come from landless labour families. The Corps of Hunger Fighters will include elected members of Panchayats and Nagarpalikas, so that they are able to serve as links between the elected bodies and the people. There should be a minimum of two members of the corps drawn form every village/town, so that they are able to play a role in improving environmental hygiene and sanitation as well as the health and nutrition secutity of the families living in their village/town.

Ours is a land of the young. Nearly 400 million women and men are below the age of 21. The nation's future depends upon the opportunity they get for a productive and healthy life. Youth can be attracted and retained in farming only if farming becomes and economically rewarding. This is where ecological agriculture, which is knowledge intensive, can prove to be a double advantage.

Our society is characterised by cultural, religious, linguistic and political pluralism. Political pluralism at the level of the central government provides an opportunity for elevating issues relating to hunger elimination and poverty alleviation to a level of overriding priority, transcending political frontiers and placing them at the top of the political agenda. The Government of Tamil Nadu has taken the first bold step in this directon by deciding to initiate a cencerted attempt to eliminate poverty-induced hunger. We should work for spreading the Hunger-Free Area programme throughout the country before we enter the next century.

A common symptom of rural poverty which India shares along with other developing countries is the existence of underutilized resources, such as land, water and endemic underemployment of labour. Poverty itself is the lot of about 39 per cent of the population as against about 20 poer cent as per calculations of theearlier government. During the period 1983—84 to 1987—88, rural poverty fell from 45.6 per cent to 39 per cent while between 1987—88 and 93—94, it fell only by a further 1.7 per cent.

In 1987—88, unemployment inperson—years was

estimated to be 12.43 million in usual principal status, 15.30 million in weekly status, and 18.95 million on daily status. Even causal labour employment is 38.4 per cent among rural males and 31.4 per cent among rural females.

The above phenomenon has been interpreted from different perspectives. It is regarded as due to the fickleness of the poor and, therefore, the total literacy campaign in India seeks to encnouraged the poor to come together and improvve their lot. It can also be seen as an inherent attribute of the socio—economic structure retarding growth and perpetuating poverty. Land reforms is the answer to this situation. A third perspective is to look at it as a potential for local resource mobilization and its concomitant local—level planning. In this context , the 73rd constitutional amendment conferring constitutional status to local bodies and for greater decentralization in the country is worth noting.

It is this point of view that the present paper has adopted. It is noted that there is an enormous potential for alleviating poverty which such underutilized resources represent. Along side with the resource augmenting aspect, the mobilization of local resources also promises the simultanneous attainment of other adjectives which are apecial to rural development like greater decentralization in planning, increasing popular paraticipation and ensuring a greater degree of self—reliance on the part of local communities. Macro planning embodied in the Ninth Plan alone cannot cope with the highly particularized and the localized problems of identifying development potentialities in the rural communities. Even though the basic criteria of rural development are participation, production, distribution and consumption, participation takes on a different meaning. The disadvantaged people are not to be cast inthe role of the objects of participation, but they are to be integrated as the subjects of the operation. Both human resource development and human development are the objectives in rural development and a World Bank study has shown that there will not be adequate resources for human development if government funds alone are to be depended upon. It is imperative to use local resources and community resources will have to be mobilized. Also the interdependence between eduction, health, sanitation and other social development sectors has to be taken care of because all of them jointly promote rural development.

In this paper, we have discussed, the broad outlines of the Ninth Plan to show the resource constraints. Secondly, the interdependence between agriculture and rural development is noted and it is concluded that there is no alternative except to mobilize local resources. Reference in this context is not only to mobilization of financial resources through imposition of appropriate taxes in agriculture, but also more importantly to mobilize non–financial resources like labour, locally available material and technical expertise.

Development strategy

In the Ninth Plan, the strategy of development has to be mobelizational in the sense of reaching out to those regions or sections of people who have been bypassed in the process of development and has also to aim at the efficiency of resource use on areas and sectors which have already been developed. Supply side efficiency and technological transformations have to be interwoven withe the economic process of production potential and in this process meet the demands of those who are currentoy left out of the process of development. In working out the production potential in the agricultural sector, the approach of agroclimatic planning, which emphasizes both land and water development strategies at the subregional level, is to be vigorously pursued. This approach sets specific targets for projects like tank irrigation, watershed development, modernization and completion of canal system and diversification of cropping sequences in different agro-climatic regions of India.

For attainment of output targets in various sectors/ subsectors in the Ninth Plan, investment levels have to be increased in critical sectors like agriculture, rural development, industry, power, telecommunications, transport, etc. With increased public investment in infrastructural facilities, private and community investment is also likely to crowd in.

The trend in real investment in the agricultural sector is disturbing and has to be reversed. Fixed capital formation was 8.63 per cent of agricultural GDP in 1984-85, but is only 8.55 per cent in 1994-95 at 80/81 prices. Even if the agricultural incremental capital output ratio (ICOR) is around three, a 12 per cent rate of fixed capital formation is necessary. Increasing levels of investments in the agricultural sector have to be brought about through increased public investment in irrigation, rural government to set up a Rural Infrastructural Development Fund (RIDF) as announced in the Central Budget for 1995-96 will help in financing the ongoing rural projects in backward areas. The co-operative sector has to participate in increased investment activities in the various sector of the economy. Certain NABARD studies show the self-help co-operatives for decentralized development can generate self-sustaining employment and income but such efforts would require initial refinancing support from outside. Training, infrastructure, including roads, quality control and processing or export home demand areas in each district. The RIDF must meet this challinge, so that benefits of liberalization reach our small farmers.

Integrated watershed development projects oould neet to be closely monitored. Various soil and water conservation technologies eill need to be energetically pursued to raise productivity in the marginal and rainfed land holdings. Improved water management stragegies in irrigated and assured rainfall areas will have to be pursued. As per preliminary estimates, the share of gross irrigated area in gross cropped area is likely to be 46.4 per cent by the terminal of the Ninth Plan. Emphasis will continue to be laid on diversified agriculture and crop intensification will be propagated with crop intensity reasching the level of 1.40 by 2001-2002.

The output structure in the Ninth Plan needs to be conducive to the generation of 8-9 million employment opportunities per year. Emphasis will be laid on high employment elasticity activities like (i) animal husbandry, fisheries, horticulture, etc. (ii) sugar, fish canning and preservation; tobacco pruducts and cotton ginning. For those who are left out on the agricultural and rural growth process, the government is committed to an Employment Assurance Scheme.

In order to achieve the various output levels and to sustain the growing and well-diversified economy in the Ninth Plan, it is necessary to evolve judicious public policies towards investment and technology which can mobilise latent resources which are lying unutilised in the economy and can unleash wider processes of agricultural growth and decentralized developments linked to ;national and world markets.

The perspective plan in the Ninth Plan may, therefore, amongst other strategies have to:

— institutionalize the Accelerated Irrigation Benefit Programme for completing large and medium irrigation programme;

— operationalize the strategy of perspective planning for the water sector being worked out by the special Commission set up for this sector;

— raise fixed investment in the agricultural sector to at least 12 per cent of agricultural CDP; work out the private invesment inducing aspects of public investment in the water, land development, agricultural technology and research and agricultural markets sector;

— carry-forward the agro-climatic planning strategy;

— complete the process of agricultural economic reform, including tariff reform, removal of trade bottlenecks, rural credit reform and liberalization of the co-operative sector; and

— work out the institutional support-base for small farmers and employment for landless labourers

Farm mechanisation

The Governmental programmes have been oriented to promote the farm mechanisation and make the improved and modern agricultural machines available to the farmers throughout the country with a view to increasing the agricultural production and removing socio-economical disparity among the farmers. Farmers have been provided assistance for owning agricultural machinery including tractors. The infrastructure for human resource development on farm machinery has been expanded with a view to imparting training in the proper selection, operation, repair/maintenance and management of farm machinery. During these training programmes, emphasis has also been given on the energy conservation techniques in the use of agricultural machinery. Besides this, farm machines are tested with a view to evaluating their performance characteristics and upgrading their quality. However, despite a progressive increase in the use of agricultural machines, its sustainable benefits towards agricutural development have not been uniform in-as-much as only the improvement has mostly been in the northern states and in a few pockets/areas where irrigation facilities have been developed.

Although animal and human power continue to be the main power sources in agriculture, yet the power driven machines, namely tractors, power-tillers and combine harvestors continue to be in the frontline of farm machanisation. Fuel efficient tractors and better quality farm machines are now available in the country. Tractors are mostly sold in Haryana, Punjab, Uttar Pradesh and Madhya Pradesh and power tillers in Assam, West Bengal, Karnataka, Tamil Nadu, Kerala and Maharashtra.

During the Eighth Plan, thrust has been given to popularise the improved animal/power driven implements and small tractors with the objectives of promotion of mechanisation and to reduce the drudgrey associated with the farm operations. Water management has also been given specific attention and the water saving devices viz., sprinkler and drip irrigation system have been promoted through oilseeds, pulses and horticulture development programmes. Industrial designs, prototypes, jigs and fixtures have also been developed * . These schemes would give a fillip to the promotion of agricultural mechanisation in the country.

Farm Machinery Training and Testing Institutes set up a Budni (Madhya Pradesh), Hissar (Haryana), Garladinne (Andhra Pradesh) and Biswanath Chariali (Assam) impart on-the-job training in selection, operation, maintenance and management of farm machinery. These institutes also undertake testing of farm machinery to ascertain their performance characteristics and suggest improvement in their quality. So far over 43,000 personnel were trained and 1,160 test reports on farm machinery released. Two more institutes are likely to be set up in Rajasthan and Tamil Nadu. To suplement the efforts of these institutes five state agricultural universities have been identified for undertaking training on farm machinery and two agricultural universities for testing activities.

The Government of India and state government jointly established 17 state agro-industries corporations with the objective of streamlining input distribution and extending other agro-services to the farmers. These have significantly contributed to agricultral development, improvement of agro engineering services and promotion of agro-based industries during last two decades. Corporations in Gujarat, Haryana, Kerala, Maharashtra, Punjab and Madhya Pradesh earned estimated profits totalling Rs. 1,192.61 lakh during 1993-94. The National Productivity Performance Award for 1991-92 in the agro-industries sector was won by Punjab Agro-Industries Corporation Limited and Certificate of Merit for sustained productivity efforts was won by the Gujarat Agro-Industries Corporation Limited.

The Dangerous Machines (Regulation) Act, 1983 provides for the regulation of trade and commerce in production, supply, distribution and use of the products of any industry producing dangerous machines with a view to securing the welfare of labourers operating such machines, and for payment of compersation for the death or bodily injury suffered by any farmer/labourer while operating any such machines. The scope of the Act extends to the 'Dangerous Machines' intended to be used in agriculture and rural sectors. However, presently, only power thresher used in the agricultural production process has been brought under the purview of the Act.

Plant protection

The Government of India has adopted Integrated Pest Management (IPM) as a major thrust area and main plan of crop protection programme during Eighth plan. IPM approach is eco-friendly which aims at minimal use of hazardous chemical pesticides by employing all available alternate pest control methods and techniques such as cultural, mechanical and biological and bio-pesticides.

The Government of India has set up IPM Farmers Field Schools (FFS) for rice, cotton, sugarcane, vegetables, oilseeds and pulses etc., to impart training to farmers and extension workers. During, 1994-95, 844 farmers field schools were organised wherein 3,934 extension officers and 25,161 farmers have been trained. Besided 585 agricultural extension officers have been trained through season long training programme organised in rice, cotton and vegetables in various states.

The surveillance for pests and diseases on economically important crops was carried out by sample roving survey on an area of 5.55 lakh hectare and about 1,464 million parasites and predators were released for controlling identified pests on important crops during 1994. All the strategic areas in Thar desert were kept under continuous watch from April to October 1994 by conducting regular surveys and a few small concentration of locust hopper/adults of two grasshoppers species were detected and controlled over a total area of 327 hectare in Jaisalmer, Barmer and Jodhpur areas. As a result of timely operation swarm formation of locust has been effectively checked. To upgrade the skills of farmers and locust staff, two field training on locust control, one each at Bikaner and Palanpur were organised during November 1994.

The current legislation governing the plant quarantine rules entitled, 'The Plants, Fruits and Seeds

(Regulation of Import into India) Order, 1989 (PFS Order 1989) came into force replacing the PFS Order 1984 in the wake of New Policy on Seed Development (NPSD) effective from 1 October 1988. The inspection procedure has been simplified in order to boost the export of floriculture and other agricultural commodities under NPSD.

The National Plant Protection Training Institute, Hyderabad continued to organise training programmes on various aspects of plant protection with special emphasis on IPM. It organised 30 training courses for master trainers in which 375 persons were trained. Beside special training course has been organised for technical personnel of fertilizer industry in Integrated Pest Management technology.

The Registration Committee constituted under the Section (5) of the Insecticides Act, 1968 received a total of 3,206 applications out of which 2193 registration certificates have been granted under various sections/ subsections of the Act. With a view to promote safer and non-chemical pesticides in IPM, biocides and plant origin pesticides like Bacillus thuringiensis and Bacillus sphaericus and need based pesticides have been provisionally registered and allowed commercialisation.

In agriculture, an Evergreen Revolution is called for, signifying the sustainable use of natural resources.As the eminent scientist Dr M.S. Swaminathan says the time has come to lay emphasis on knowledge-based inputs rather than on the physical inputs only (such as fertilizers and seeds) to derive the best from the land without depletng its inner strngth. A learning revolution is to be brought about. Fortunatley, icon–based computer technoloy shows that literacy need not be a barrier in bringing about a better awareness of theecofriendly methodsof cultivation. It would beachallenge for the plannersto decentralize the knowledge based on agriculture to cover villages using computers and telecommunication links.

Modern ecofriendly practices such as biologicalpest control and post–harvest technologies) should find high priority on the S & T agenda.

It is heartening to note that the Ninth Plan approach has emphasized the importance of biocontrol agents and biogenic fertilizers.

Projects

The Agricultural Development Projects (ADPs) with the assitance from the World Bank are being implemented in the states of Bihar, Rajasthan and Tamil Nadu to enhance the long term sustainability in agricultural development and to create necessary infrastructure in the rural areas. Besides, three on-going ADPs, a project for Assam has been recently negotiated and three ADP proposals in respect of Andhra Pradesh, Maharashtra and Haryana are in the pipeline and under active consideration.

UNDP/FAO supported 'Farm Centred Agricultural Resource Management (FARM) Programme' has been started in 1994. Five on-going watersheds of NWDPRA have been selected as demonstration sites for the programme.

The Government of Denmark initially launched one Integrated Watershed Development Project in the State of Karnataka in 1990-91 to cover an area of 41,032 hectare at an outlay of Rs. 11.25 crore for five and a half years. Keeping in view the successful implementation of this project DANIDA agreed for a phase-II project which has appraised in February 1995. The second project i.e. Comprehensive Watershed Development Project, Tirunelveli, Tamil Nadu, to cover an area of 18,000 hectare with an outlay of Rs. 6.25 crore for three and a half years is in operation since 1990-91. Second Phase of this project has been negotiated and the project has become operational from 1994. Another DANIDA assisted Comprehensive Watershed Development Project is in operation from 1992-93 in Koraput district of Orissa to cover an area of 43,000 hectare at a cost of Rs. 13.25 crore. The fourth project i.e. Comprehensive Watershed Development Project in Tamil Nadu-Ramanathpuram has also become operational from 1994 to cover an area of 11,000 hectare at a cost of Rs. 13.03 crore. Appraisal of a Comprehensive Watershed Development Project in Madhya Pradesh was completed. Appraisal report of this project has been received.

European Economic Community (EEC) assisted Integrated Watershed Management Project namely, Doon Valley Integrated Watershed Management Project is in operation in Uttar Pradesh since April 1993 with an area of 1,72,155 hectare at a cost of Rs. 808.5 million for nine years. The major components are social forestry, livestock, horticulture, minor irrigation, agriculture, soil consevation, energy conservation, community participation, management and administration. South Bhagirathi (Phase II) Integrated Watershed Management Project, has started in 1989 for a period of seven years with an outlay of Rs. 141.75 million to cover an area of 48,915 hectare. Bhimtal Integrated Watershed Managment Project, UP was implemented from 1991 for a period of seven years to area of 21,582 hectare at a cost of Rs. 115 million. the major components are forestry, agriculture, soil conservation horticulture, minor irrigation, animal husbandary, pilot and administration activities.

Two KFW Germany assisted watershed development projets, one in Maharashtra at a cost of Rs. 550.75 million and another in Karnataka at a cost of 12 million DM are being implemented. During 1995-96, under Maharashtra Integrated Watershed Development Project monitoring of the progress under on-going micro-watershed project and appraisal of new micro-watershed projects will be carried out. Under Watershed

Organisation Trust (WOTR) Project training activity and identification of non-governmental organisations (NGOs) will be taken up. Under Karnataka Watershed Project field activities will be initiated.

The Project aims to develop five watershed in five districts of Karnataka (three agro-climatic zones of Karnataka state) in line of the ongoing Participatory Integrated Watershed Development Project (PIDOW). This project is to be taken up in the districts of Bidar, Gulbarga, Bijapur, Raichur and Chikmanglur of Karnataka covering a project area of 30,000 hectare (74,968 hectare of geographical area). The Project aims to develop the watershed with the active participation of the farmers by developing Sanghas as Self Help Groups with the active collaboration of NGOs in each of the district. The estimated cost of the Project is Rs. 20.73 crore for 1995 to 1998.

Promotional schemes

The Committee also enquired from M/o Agriculture about their projects/schemes on fertiliser education. The Ministry of Agriculture in a detailed note furnished to the Committee stated that they are implementing the following projects for promoting fertilisers consumption and for creating awareness about balanced and efficient use of fertilisers:

(a) Concession on sale of decontrolled fertilisers:

In order to cushion the impact of increase in prices of decontrolled P & K fertilisers, a scheme for providing concession on these fertilisers was taken up during 1992-93. Under this scheme a concession of Rs. 1000/- per tonne on DAP and on MOP and proportionately on other P & K fertilisers was provided. During 1993-94 this concession was withdrawn from imported DAP and was extended to SSP at the rate of Rs. 340/- per tonne. On other products the rate of concession remained the same. During 1992-93 and 1993-94 the scheme was implemented through respective State Governments for which detailed guidelines were issued to them. However, during 1994-95 the concession was made available directly to the manufactures on receipt of reports of sales to the farmers verified by the State Govts. The same pattern to continuing during the current year. The funds released under this scheme for sale of decontrolled fertilisers for concession to the farmers are as follows:

Year	(Rs. in crores)
1992-93	339.73
1993-94	517.34
1994-95	514.02

(b) Balanced and integrated use of fertilisers:

The objective of the scheme is to promote balance use of NPK fertilisers alongwith organic manure, compost, green manure and bio-fertilisers with added emphasis on the use of micro nutrients in high fertiliser consuming areas. The outlay for the scheme during 8th Plan is Rs. 26 crores. The scheme has the following components:

(i) Strengthening of soil, seed, fertilizer, bio-fertiliser labs.

(ii) Demonstration and Training on use of micro nutrients (other than Zinc).

(iii) Training on bio-composting.

(iv) Setting up of compost units.

(v) Awards to Panchayats and farmers on organic farming/sustainable Agriculture.

The expenditure incurred under the scheme during the 8th Plan is as follows:

Year	(Rs. in lakhs)
1992-93	150
1993-94	205
1994-95	475

(c) National project on development of fertiliser

The fertiliser consumption at present is mainly restricted to irrigated areas with very little consumption in rainfed areas. Department of Agriculture and Cooperation started a Centrally Sponsored Scheme during 1994-95 to increase the integrated use of fertilisers alongwith organic manure in rainfed areas. The outlay of the scheme during 8th Plan is Rs. 10.2 crores. The schemes has the following components:

(i) Supply of small fertiliser bags to farmers.

(ii) Demonstration on Integrated Nutrient Supply System.

(iii) Demonstration on improved methods of compost making.

(iv) Assistance for production of green manure seed.

During 1994-95 funds amounting to Rs. 129.2 lakhs were released to the State Governments.

(d) National project on development and use of bio-fertiliser: Bio-fertilisers are renewable source of nitrogen. DAC is implementing the National Project on Development and Use of Bio-fertilisers to produce, distribute and promoteuse of bio-fertilisers. The outlay for the scheme during the 8th Plan is Rs. 8 crores.

To implement this project a National Centre at

Ghaziabad and 6 Regional Centres one each at Bangalore. Bhubaneshwar, Hissar, Imphal, Jabalpur and Nagpur have been established from this, there is a provision under the scheme to extend financial support upto Rs. 13 lakhs per unit for setting up of bio-fertiliser production units and Rs. 1.5 lakhs for setting up of Blue Green Algae (BGA) Centres.

Expenditure incurred under the scheme is as follows:

Year	(Rs. in lakhs)
1992-93	125
1993-94	145
1994-95	210

(e) Technology mission on oilseeds and pulses programmes i.e. oilseed production programme (OPP) and national pulses development project (NPDP):

Under these programmes the component relating to fertilisers includes distribution of micronutrients and gypsum as source of Sulphur to the farmers at the subsidised rates. In addition distribution of rhyzobium culture and phosphate solubilizing bacteria (PSB) are also supplied to the farmers at concessional rates.

- Frontline demonstrations are being conducted by the Scientists of ICAR on judicious use of fertilisers for pulses and oilseeds and the block demonstrations are organised by the State Departments of Agriculture in which use of fertilisers is demonstrated. In addition training programmes for the benefit of farmers are also organised to educate them on balanced use of fertilizers in case of oilseeds and pulses.

(f) National watershed development project on rainfed areas (NWDPRA):

Agro-chemicals are costly and often un-available to resource-poor farmers and as such they are encouraged to adopt organic resources which are cheap, easily manageable and involve no risk factor when compared to agro-chemicals. Under the scheme on NWDPRA organic farming is being promoted through Intergrated Nutrient Management Programme for which extensive training is given to the field functionaries as well as farmers of the watershed areas.

Rural credit

The Union Finance Ministry has asked the Reserve Bank of India (RBI) to speed up the process of awarding licences to set up local area banks (LABs). There are, currently, about 45 applications pending with the apex bank for the purpose. The apex bank is in the process of finalising the licences for nine local area banks, out of which one will be in West Bengal. Already two such licences have been given, one each for Maharashtra and Karnataka.

The concept of LAB, which was mooted in the first budget of the United Front government for 1996—97, is to gear up the banking operations in the rural and backward areas. The government will thus be relieved from the pains of infusing capital subsidies to the regional banks (RRBs) in order to get rid of their heavy financial liabilities. It is hoped that the LAB will be able to replace the regional rural banks ultimately as the latter are, by and large, plagued with multifarious problems.

As per the guidelines, a local area bank can be set up after its incorporation under the Companies Act 1956, while the licence is granted by the Reserve Bank of India. Like commercial Banks, they are also governed by the

Reserve Bank of India Act of 1934. A LAB caters to a maximum of three contiguous districts. The RBI is quite discriminating in giving licence to LABs which are to provide efficient and competitive financial intermediation services in their areas of operation.

As these banks have been set up in district towns, their activities are focussed on the local customers. Their schemes are meant for agriculture and alliled activities, small—scale industrial units, Agro—industrial activities, trading activities and non–farm sector within the area of thier operation. The banks have to observe priority sector lending targets at 40 per cent of net bank credit as applicable to other commercial banks. Of this, at least 25 per cent has to be deployed for the weaker sections.

The promoter's contribution has to be atleast Rs.2 crore. The promoter/s may comprise individuals, corporate entities, trusts or societies. The head/registered office of the bank will be located at a centre within the area of operation of the bank.

Voting rights of an individual share—holder are governed by the ceiling of 10 per cent of the total voting rights as stipulated in section 12(2) of the Banking Reguation Act, 1949. It may be noted that as regards liquidity requirements and interest rates, such banks have to follow the provisions applicable to the regional banks set up under the RRB Act of 1976.

Likewise, a local area bank is subject to prudential norms, accounting policies and other policies laid down by the RBI. It is required to achieve capital adequacy of 8 per cent of the risk weighted assets from the very beginning. Similarly, norms for income recognition, assets classification and provisioning will also be applicable to it reform its very inception.

As for opening branches, LABs can be set up only in

the area of operation of LAB by complying with the branch licensing policy as it exists today. It can be said that with a good number of commercial bank branches and RRBs already operating in the rural sector, a local area bank faces great challenges. Rural and semi–urban areas form an important deposit base of commercial banks contribution around 33 per cent of their total deposits. Presently, these banks have a large network in the rural sector with hardly any competition in the mobilisation of deposits.

In case LABs perform well and create in image for themselves, they can surely give a tough time to commercial banks where inefficiency has become the order of the day. As for the RRBs, they are already unviable and perhaps the government may revive the idea of merging them with their sponsored banks. Moreover, the deregulated rates of interest on deposits may create a difficult situation with the local banks by offering better interest rates.

It is also true that around 23 per cent of the nationalised banks' advances go to rural and demi—urban areas. Nationalised banks are now setting up specialised branches for agricultural and small–scale sector. Besides, their large branch network in rural and semi—urban areas, as also their decades of experience in rural lending impart to them an added advantage. Hence, LABs have to employ effective marketing strategies for extending credit in rural areas even if they have to offer competitive interest rates. The field functionaries in rural and semi–urban branches have to be more vigilant and aware about the credit potential in agriculture and allied activities. Besides, they need to ensure adequate suppluy of credit under various government sponsored schemes.

A more comprehensive rural credit strategy can be worked out if strategy can be worked out if NABARD can be granted powers to become the lead form bank with cooperatives, RRBs and local area banks. In that case, the burden of priority sector lending can be taken off the public sector, foreign and private sector banks, along with the concept of concessional credit. Therefore, in that eventuality, banks should be given the option to lend to agriculture based industries without any mandate.

As we all know, agricultural and rural development are a continuous process and banks have to commit themselves to rural financing on a short–term and long–term basis. The focus has to shift to financing of small farmers, landless labourers, village artisans and services. LABs have to ensure that they are adequately organised to handle the task. Mass social banking has to be the aim along with observing sound tenets of banking. The creating of local area banks must not become one more futile exercise if the attitudes and approaches of banks and their staff continue to remain the same as those of commercial banks, cooperative banks and regional rural banks.

It has been estimated that the demand for agricultural credit in the country would be of the order of Rs. 1,10,900 crore by 1999—2000 A.D., while the supply of institutional credit (including bank credit from all types of banks) would be hardly around Rs. 90,000 crore. This shortfall has to be taken care of by the local area banks with full zeal and commitment for rural development. Since the service area approach is not applied to LABs, they can work with more flexibility. The percentage of agricultural credit to net bank credit has been declining over the last crouple of years. As such, LABs have to take new initiatives.

Finally, it is necessary that the local area banks do not suffer fromthe problem of lack of viability as has been the case with the regional rural banks. In April 1993 there was a demand for setting up a National Rural Bank by amalgamating all the existing regional rural banks but ultimately, the idea floated in Parliament could not fructify. Perhaps, time has now come when this experiment could be undertaken in such a way that the new national rural bank is made responsible for monitoring the RRBs and LABs so that should any problem arise in their functioning, it should be solved without any delay. There is no doubt that the new set–up of LABs does require some kind of institutional back—up for monitoring and advisory functions on a regular and continuous basis.

National Bank for Agriculture and Rural Development (NABARD) came into existence on 12 July 1982. It took over the functions of the erstwhile Agriculture Credit Department, Rural Planning and Credit Cell of the Reserve Bank of India and Agriculture Refinance and Development Corporation. Its subscribed and paid-up capital is Rs. 100 crore, contributed by the Central Government and the Reserve Bank of India in equal proportions. NABARD was established for providing credit for promotion of agriculture, small scale industries, cottage and village industries, handicrafts and other allied economic activities in rural areas with a view to promoting integrated rural development and securing prosperity of rural areas.

NABARD is an apex institution accredited with all matters concerning policy planning and operations in the field of credit for agriculture and other economic activities in the rural areas. Its functions are to: (i) serve as an apex refinancing agency for institutions providing investment and production credit for promoting various development activities in the rural areas; (ii) take measures towards institution building for improving absorptive capacity of credit delivery system including monitoring, formulation of rehabilitation schemes, restructuring of credit institutions, training of personnel, etc; (iii) coordinate rural financing activities of all institutions engaged in the developmental work at field-level and maintain liaison with Central/state governments, Reserve Bank of India and other national institutions concerned with policy formulation and also (iv) undertake monitoring and evaluation of projects refinanced by it.

NABARD's refinance is available to the state land development banks, state cooperative banks, scheduled commercial banks and regional rural banks. While the ultimate beneficiaries of investment credit can be individuals, partnership concerns, companies and state-owned corporations of cooperative societies, production credit is generally given to individuals. During 1993-94, NABARD sanctioned short term credit limits aggregating Rs. 3,451 crore to state cooperative banks for financing seasonal agricultural operations as compared to Rs. 3,316 crore sanctioned during 1992-93. NABARD also disbursed Rs. 329.6 crore as refinance assistance to Regional Rural Banks. The total disbursements of NABARD during 1993-94 to the commercial banks for various purposes was Rs. 1,029 crore.

Integrated rural development programme

Integraged Rural Development Programme envisages capital subsidy and credit assistance to identified poor families for acquiring income generating assets to come-up above the poverty line. The total term credit disbursed during 1993-94 by the banks was Rs. 1,468.44 crore as against Rs. 1,036.80 crore in 1992-93. The total number of beneficiaries assisted during 1993-94 was 25.38 lakh as against 20.68 lakh in 1992-93. Both interms of credit disbursal and the number of beneficiaries who were financed the targets were exceeded during 1993-94.

During 1994-95 (upto 30 November 1994), a sum of Rs. 617.01 crore has been disbursed by the banks to 9.90 lakh beneficiaries.

Regional Rural Banks (RRBs) had established to take the banking services to the doorsteps of rural masses especially in unbanked rural areas. These banks were to provide institutional credit to the weaker sections of the society at concessional rate of interest who had perforce been depending on private money-lenders. The banks were also intended to mobilise rural savings and channelise for supporting productive activities in the rural areas. As on 31 March 1994, 196 RRBs have been functioning in 23 states covering 398 of the 492 districts with a network of 14,547 branches. The credit support provided by these banks amounted to Rs. * 8,830.58 crore were mobilised as deposits by RRBs in 361.02 lakh accounts as on 31 March 1994. The financial position of the RRBs has been a source of continuous anxiety. The losses incurred by these banks have been increasing year after year. During 1993-94, only 25 banks had earned profits and the remainingd 171 banks had incurred losses.

The precarious fiscal position of the government, the unviability of many public sector units and eroding profitability of commercial banks have precluded large—scale new investments for agricultural projects. Industries either supplying inputs to agriculture like seed, fertilizer and implements or using agricultural produce as inputs like various food processing industries offer better prospects for foreign investment.

In the case of food processing industries, India can tap the vast potential that exists in the West European countries for exporting fruits and vegetables by setting up food processing units. The scope for improvement in research and development (R & D) will improve with the new foreign investment and new technology transfer policy. The investment scenario in the country has already started showing marks of change. Many well—known foreign companies are showing interest in investing in India and many may follow. On the whole, the policy changes will be beneficial for the development of agricultural sector and, in turn, the entire economy .

The provison of credit to the agricultural producers on right time, amount and terms had attracted the attention of the policy–markers even before Independence. Our agricultural credit system has been gravely weakened by the burden of subsidized interest rates, poor recovery of loans, high intermediation costs of co—operatives and commercial banks and debt write–offs. The poorest farmers have suffered the most. What matters most to farmers is the timely availability of credit. Our present system does nt ensure this. Estimates suggest that rural households have come to rely on informal credit markets (including money—lenders) for 60 t 70 per cent of their credit needs, even though interest rates charged are typically over 30 per cent. Increased flow of institutional credit to agriculture will require reconsideration of interest rate structure, in particular of subsidies built into the structure. Most of the commercial banks have not achieved the bench mark level of 18 per cent share of agricultural lending out of their total credit disbursement.

The resurrection of private investment in agriculture depends on the reversal of trends in investment and upkeep of public infrastructure, the maintenance of remunerative prices for agricultural produce, encouraging processing of agricultural waste, the phasing out of domestic trade and marketing restrictions and the scaling down of preferential protection to the industrial sector. Private investment will also respond to the opening up of agricultural export opportunities arising from the new exchange rate regime and necessary accompanying measures to lift controls on export of agricultural products.

Globalization will benefit the Indian economy in several ways. With Indian producers becoming internationally competitive, there will not be any complaint abut recession because tha eholw world will constitute a market for Indian products. This will incidentally ensure a massive increase in exports which is the key to globalization, faster economic growth and self–reliance in the Indian context. The Government of India's drive towards globalization—linking the economy organically with the world economy—has been motivated by three principal expectations. First, the entry of foreign competitors into India's domestic market will stimulate local producers to minimize their cost of production; secondly, with reduced local costs and free access to imports, India's exports can be rapidly expanded; and thirdly, with freedom of access to foreign investment, the economy will benefit from an inflow of both financial resources and advanced technology. These factors are, presumably, aslo expected to transform Indian agriculture and elevate its growth rate.

Small Industries development

Technical advice and assistance to small scale manufacturers is provided by the Small Industries Development Organisation through its network of 16 service institutes, 16 branch institutes, 58 extension, production and training centres. The organisation also provides common service and tool room facilities in workshops attached to small industries, service institutes and extension centres. It conducts courses in management and technical disciplines. During 1974-75, it provided technical assistance to 1,02,684 entrepreneurs and visited 70,965 factories for spot guidance.

Two new centres namely the Central Insititute of Tool Design, Hyderabad, and The Institute for Design of Electrical Measuring Instruments, Bombay, have started providing technical guidance and training for entrepreneurs.

The National Small Industries Corporation, which was set up in 1955, operates the scheme of procuring machinery for small-scale manufacturers on a hire-purchase basis on concessional terms. The value of machines delivered under this scheme during the period April-October 1974 was Rs. 5.69 crores as against Rs. 3.25 crores during the corresponding period of the previous year. It also assists the small-scale sector in processing orders from government departments and agencies. The value of stores purchased by the Directorate General of Supply and Disposals from April to November 1974 was about Rs. 37 crores. The Prototype Development and Training Centres set up with American, West German and Japanese assistance at Rajkot, Okhla (Delhi) and Howrah impart training to persons engaged in small-scale industries.

Hitherto the emphasis was minly on agro-based industries. The growth of these industries was no doubt important for providing a ready market to the agricultural outputs, to create employment opportunities in view of seasonal nature of agriculture and to stabilise the farmer's income. Several specialised agencies such as the State Finance Corporations, Small Scale Reserve Bank, and the various technical guidance and assistance schemes of the Central Government, State Governments, Reserve Bank and State Bank of India were directed mainly to sustain the growth of small scale and cottage industries.

It was, however, realised at a later stage that the institutional at the "output" end is only one part of the game. Indian agriculture does not face any serious problem from the demand side. It is with the improvement in the technique of production that the cost of farming can be reduced and the productivity of the land can be improved in order to meet ever growing demand of agricultural outpout from direct consumers as well as from industries. The institutional set-up was, therefore, geared up to discover means for improving the technique of agricultural production and also to manufacture agriculture machinery.

At the highest level various agricultural research centres, headed by Indian Council of Agriculture Research, are performing important functions in the development and distribution of scientific knowledge of agriculture. There is also the Indian Society of Agriculture Engineers which provides a wealth of information for the application of science and technology to farming. At the village level cooperative societies are propagating and, where possible, implementing, the programmes of the research centres.

Cooperative societies and various official organisations have performed important functions but because of their limitations, these agencies could not meet the requirements of mechanised agriculture which has recetly gained importance for improving agricultural productivity.

Agro-industrial corporations

Thus with a view to meeting the rapidly growing demand of farmers for standard agricultural machinery equipment, e.g., tractors, power tillers, power threshers, seed-cum-fertilisers, drills, power sprayers and dusters, diesel and electric pump-sets, on cash or hire-purchase basis, the State Agro-Industrial Corporations have been established by the Government.

These corporation have been established in almost all the states. They are performing multifarious activities connected with not only the supply of agricultural machinery but also providing credit for the purpose. Some of them have ambitious programmes of designing and assembling tractors and manufacturing various tools and implements. But in fairness to the Corporations it must be recorded that none of them is more than three years old. What is more, some of them have the right ideas. In Gujarat, for instance, the AIC has decided to accord priority to the setting up of new cold storage plants in Banaskantha and Balsar, Onion dehydration plants at Jamnagar and Bhavnagar and hydrogenated oil unit in the Saurashtra region. In West Bengal, the AIC will supply diesel pumping sets to poor farmers owning two to five acres of land on payment of Rs. 70 cash down, the balance of the price–Rs. 3,500–being recoverable in easy instanlments. In Tamil Nadu the AIC is not only going into the processing and marketing of farm produce but will also set up factories for the servicing and repair of the 1,000 new tractors which are sold in the state every year.

It is evidnt that the growth of agro-industries cannot reverse the process of urbanisation. Most of the plants for processing farm products or "waste" materials released by the existing agro-based industries like textiles must be established near the consuming centres if they are to pave their way. All that can be done in the circumstances is to establish new industrial units, both big and small, in district towns and away from the major cities. Any effort to confine the new agro-industries to the rural or semi-urban areas is bound to hinder their growth and will in the end be self-defeating.

Since there are quite a number of common problems which these institutions are likely to face, it might be worthwhile to establish a Central Agro-Industrial Corporation of India to coordinate the work of these state institutions. Besides coordinating the working of the state corporations, the central organisation can be entrusted with research and development of technology. Centralisation of research will eliminate waste and duplication. The State Corporations will, however, continue to collect data rom their regional offices to make them available to the central organisation. It will also be the task of the cental agency to arrange the production of different components of machinery and implements in different areas according to the local facilities available on the "comparative cost" basis. The proposed corporation can also serve as an effective agency in arranging the colllection of technical knowledge from abroad and distribution of imported machinery.

The massive expenditure that the Government has incurred on agricultural development has in one way or another gone to prop up a new rich class by passing millions of small farmers and landless labourers. There are growing indications of discontent among those who have found the cost of acquiring modern equipment and agricultural inputs soaring, on the one hand, and official and somehow getting channelled away from them, on the other.

The Government's decision to establish 500 pilot agro-service centres in the country is a step in the right direction. The programme is being jointly sponsored by the Ministry of Agriculture and the Ministry of Industrial Development and is designed to provide a wide range of services from custom-hiring of tractors and other farm equiptment and repair and maintenance of agricultural machinery to soil testing, crop spraying, water anaylsis and land and field services such as levelling and contour surveying. The scheme is intended to provide employment in the rural area as well as to accelerate the process of modernisation in the villages. It is particularly aimed at providing help to the small farmers and the weaker sections of the rural community in the relatively backward areas. The rapid increase in the use of tractors, pumps, mechanical threshers and other machines, not to speak of community radios, transistors and other personal gadgetry, has created a demand for easily available repair and maintenance facilities on a wide scale. Then agro-service centres can perform a valuable function provided they are suitably staffed and have the requisite managerial competence. The Government has negotiated World Bank assistance for tractor-cum-groundwater development projects in Punjab, Haryana and Tamil Nadu. Agro-service centres could be established alongside these programmes for a start.

As far as mechanical equipment like tractors and pumps are concerned, it would be most' desirable for the country to standardise on a few broad categories (not necessarily makes) so that problems of maintenance and the stocking of parts and components are not needlessly complicated by type differences. Little thought appears to have been given to this matter so far. But it is obviously something that calls for an early policy consideration.

The DOF has informed the Committee that the Fertilizer Projects implemented/being implemented by the Public Sector fertilizer companies/cooperatives are being executed by the respective companies in coordination with Department of Fertilizer. Close liaison is maintained with the agriculture departments of the State and district level during the implementation of the project.

During the course of examination, the Committee wanted to know from the representatives of NFL/RCF/PPCL/FACT etc. about the system of coordination with other Public Sector Undertakings/Cooperatives/State agencies which are undertaking farmers education/promotional/training programmes, the NFL in a written note had informed: "Each Public Sector Undertaking undertakes its own set of Farmers Education/Promotional Training Programmes. Department of Fertilizers co-ordinates with various Public Sector Undertaking/Cooperatives/State Agencies. NFL coordinates with the State Agricultural Department and State Agricultural Universities for implementation of its own programmes".

RCF/FACT have stated that they have got close liaison with State Agricultural Department from Taluka level to State level in their primary market, i.c. Maharashtra, Karnataka & Andhra Pradesh and in secondary market from district level to State level. They have close association with all Agricultural Universities in all the States.

PPCL in a written note has informed the Committee, "PPCL, is having co-ordination with other PSU's/Cooperatives/States Agencies which are undertaking farmers education/promotional/training programmes under a common forum like the Fertilizer Association of India and its Regional Offices, Deptt. of Fertilizers, State Deptt. of Agriculture in their meetings, individual meetings, House Journals etc".

PPL on the other hand has informed the Committee in a written note: "In the present system, each PSU carries out its promotional programmes independently. Hence, the above do not require any coordination with the other PSUs/Cooperatives/State Agencies".

Whereas MFL has stated in a written note, "No joint effort is made with other Public Sector Undertakings for carrying out Educational Programmes. During the current year FAI has coordinated with all fertilizer industries to carry out a common logo and message for the promotion of balanced fertilizer use. MFL fully participated in the scheme to bring out mass media materials with a common logo and message in regional languages".

During the course of examination of representatives of NFL and MD, NFL also stated before the Committee, "I like to submit in this connection, although we do not have a formal coordinating agency to undertake this work in a real manner, in the States and district headquarters, Deputy Commissioners and Collectors also advise us on this matter".

Explaining further the CMD, MFL informed the Committee, "Primarily, this is a State function. There is an organisation at structure in the State Government which goes down to the village level and which is involved in the extension effort, maintenance of nutrient balance,etc. Restoration of nutrients balance is one of the priority areas. Likewise, the effort at the Central level is coordinated by the Agriculture Ministry. They have thei field and research organisation and they have an elaborate arrangement to get the required feedback. All this is done by the Ministry of Agriculture. As you have rightly observed, fertiliser manufacturers have only a peripheral interest in this. They have to market their products and promote the application of fertilisers. They have also to contribute their mite to this national effort of balanced fertilisation which is primarily the responsibility of the State Government and is overseen by the Ministry of Agriculture".

In this connection DOF in a written note stated, "A district is the basic geographic unit for development, administration, coordination dovetailing of development programmes of different departments and agencies is best done by the district administrations at the local level.

The field functionaries of companies/cooperatives are being instructed to work in close cooperation with the district authorities, which are amply qualified to coordinate the promotional activities of various agencies".

During the course of examination of the representative of DOF, the Secretary, Fertilizers also stated, "As a nodal Agency, Agriculture Ministry is responsible for this. I will have a meeting with Agriculture Secretary".

When asked further whether there was any coordination problem, the witness stated, "There is no such problem here in our case".

8

Development of Agriculture

Freedom from hunger was Gandhiji's priority number one for Independent India. To attain this objective, what we need now is an environmentally sustainable and socially equitable green revolution in our agriculture as it provides livelihood to 70 per cent population of the country. Just prior to our Independence, undivided India witnessed one of the most serious famines of this century–the great Bengal famine. Gandhiji speaking in Noakhali in 1946 said, "to the hungry God is bread" and "it is the duty of Independent India to ensure that every individual is enabled to earn his or her daily bread". Gandhiji's emphasis was on "food for all with human dignity". He did not want a nation of beggars or the entitlement to food being considered a charity. Thus, he asked us to desist from adopting a patronage approach towards the poor and hungry. Our first Prime Minister, Jawaharlal Nehru, responded to this call and announced in 1948 "everything else can wait but not agriculture".

We are now in the 50th year of our Independence. According to official statistics, about 200 million children, women and men will go to bed undernourished tonight. We have however successfully avoided famines during the last 50 years through a multipronged strategy consisting of (a) increased food production, (b) building grain reserves, (c) operating an extensive public distribution system, (d) protective social security measures like food for work, nutritious noon meal and employment guarantee, and (e) land reform and asset creation measures. The continued persistence of endemic hunger is now largely the result of inadequate purchasing power arising from inadequate opportunities for skilled employment.

Famines were frequent towards the part of the 19th century, when the combined population of India, Bangladesh and Pakistan was only 290 million. Our population alone is now more than thrice this number. Hence, we have every reason to be grateful for the spectacular success of the Government of India's famine avoidance and containment strategy. The time is now ripe to take the final steps essential for the total elimination of hunger. Hunger elimination is easier to achieve than poverty eradication. The poor spend a large share of their daily income on food and hence the elimination of hunger is the first step towards the alleviation of poverty. The opportunity for a productive and healthy life for every individual depends very much on the success of our hunger elimination strategy.

Economic regenration attempted in successive Five Year Plans has made agriculture a pride of national economy. This sector, today, provides livelihood to about 65 per cent of labour force, contributes nearly 29 per cent of Gross Domistic Product and accounts for a sizeable share of total value of the country's exports. It supplies bulk of wage goods required by non-agricultural sector and raw material for a large section of industry. Per capita net availability of foodgrains went up to a level of 468.5 grams per day in 1992 as compared to that of 395 grsams in early fifties. In 1994, it has, however, been provisionally estimated lower at 463.8 grams per day. In terms of gross fertilizer consumption, India ranks fourth in the world after USA, the erstwhile USSRand China. The country has the largest area in the world under pulse crops while in the field of cotton, India is the first to evolve a cotton hybrid.

Compound growth rate in agricultural production during the period 1949-50 to 1993-94 is 2.63 per cent per annum. Production of foodgrains increased significantly from 549.2 lakh tonnes in 1949-50 to 1,821 lakh tonnes in 1993-94. Cropping pattern is more diversified and cultivation of commercial crops has received new impetus in line with domestic demands and export requirements. During post-green revolution period i.e., 1967-68 to 1992-93, growth rate in agricultural production was assessed at around 2.84 per cent per annum. Production of foodgrains during this period increased from 950.5 lakh tonnes to 1,795 lakh tonnes. Cropping pattern has undergone perceptible changes and non-traditional crops like summer moong, soyabean, summer groundnut, sunflower, etc., are gradually gaining importance. In order to utilise scarce resources optimally, a short duration varieties have been introduced to use the residual moisture available from post-kharif and post-rabi cultivation.

The index of agricultural production, base TE 1981-82=100, which registered an increase of 21.4 per cent in 1988-89 and 2.1 per cent in 1989-90 over the previous year showed further increase of 3.8 per cent in 1990-91 due to increase recorded in the production of rice, wheat, pulses, oilseeds, jute and mesta, sugarcane and other commercial crops. During 1991-92, it, however, recorded a fall of two per cent due to fall in the production of various foodgrains but again registered an increase of 4.1 per centg due to increase in production of wheat coarse, cereals, pulses, ground-nut, cotton etc., during 1992-93 and again registered an increase of 2.8 per cent during 1993-94. The index of foodgrains production during 1993-94 at 148.9 showed an increase of 2.6 per cent over the previous year's production index of 145.1 Foodgrains production during 1992-93 increased by about 116 lakh tonnes over previous year's production primarily due to favourable weather conditions during the growth period of the crop. Availability of edible oils including vanaspati ha also increased significantly and its production in 1987 was 9,47,153 mt. The country has been able to sustain and improve availability of basic consumption articles and has thus, raised the standard of living.

There are three main crop seasons, namely, kharif, rabi and summer. Major kharif crops are rice, jowar, bajra, maize, cotton, sugarcane, sesame, soyabean and groundnut. Major rabi crops are wheat, jowar, barley, gram, linseed, rapeseed and mustard. Rice, maize and groundnut are grown in summer season also.

Land utilisation statistics are available for 92.8 per cent of total geographical area of 3,287.3 lakh hectare. According to land use statistics available from states, area under forests had increased from 404.8 lakh hectare in 1950-51 to 680.2 lakh hectare in 1992-92. Net sown area increased from 1,187.5 lakh to 1,414.1 lakh hectare during the same period. Broad cropping pattern indicates that though foodgrains, their relative share came down from 76.7 per cent during 1950-51 to 67.2 per cent during 1991-92.

Overall economic growth in terms of Gross Domestic Product (GDP) at constant factor cost improved from 0.8% in 1991-92 to 6.3% in 1994-95 and 7% in 1995-96 aided by a growth rate of 2.4% by agriculture and allied sectors, 11.7% by industry and construction sector and 7% by services. Overall economic growth during the first four year of the 8th Plan (1992-97) averaged 5.9% per annum compared with the planned target of 5.6%.

The domestic savings rate measured in terms of gross domestic savings as a proportion of GDP at current market prices increased from an average rate of 21.3% in 1992-93 and 1993-94 to 24.4% in 1994-95. The rate of domestic investment measured in terms of gross domestic capital formation as a proportion of GDP at current market prices increased from 21.6% in 1993-94 to 25.2% in 1994-95.

Industrial production which was virtually stagnant in 1991-92 increased by 9.4% and 12.1% in 1995-96 supported by a growth rate of 6.9% in mining, 13.6% in manufacturing and 8.1% in electricity generation. As per the latest information available, industrial growth deceleration to 8.5% in April-June 1996 due to deceleration of growth rates in all the sub-sectors (3.6% in mining, 10.4% manufacturing and 2.2% in electricity generation). As per growth rates by use-based classification, capital goods sector recorded a growth rate of 14.2%, intermediate goods 11.9%, consumer durables 11.1% and consumer non-durables 8.6% in April-June 1996. However, the growth rate of basic goods sub-sector having a weight of 39.4% in the overall industrial production was only 4% in April-June 1996.

Seven infrastructural sectors, namely, electricity, coal, steel, cement, crude oil and petroleum product & fertilizer with a combined weight of 31% in the Index of Industrial Production (IIP) recorded a growth rate of 7.8% in 1995-96. But their growth rate decelerated to 3.2% in April-August 1996 due to poor performance of electricity generation (growth rate of only 2.4%) and crude oil production (decline of production by 10.4%).

The outlook of agricultural production in 1996-97 is excellent with foodgrains output likely to reach 197 million tonnes compared with 185 million tonnes in 1995-96. This is primarily due to this year's rainfall distribution being the best in the past five years. The late withdrawal of monsoon has further ensured bright prospects for rabi production this year. The estimate of foodgrains production in 1995-96 has been scaled down to 185 million tonnes representing a sharp decline of nearly 6 million tonnes over the preceeding year. The shortfall was substantial (about 3 million tonnes) in wheat output, besides short-fall of production of rice and coarse cereals. Consequently wheat procurement dropped steeply to 8.2 million tonnes compared to 12.3 million tonnes in the preceding year. Public stock (Central Pool) of foodgrains was about 22.1 million tonnes as on September 1, 1996.

Challenge of hunger

The life and vitality of human beings depend crucially on certain vitamins and minerals that help in the efficient functioning of the brain, immune system, reproduction and energy metabolism. The body needs only small amounts of these nutrients, but it cannot synthesize them. They must be provided through diet. Deficiencies of even the small amounts required cause learning disabilities, impair work capacity and bring illness and death. Micronutrient malnutrition (silent hunger) is most devastating for pre—school children and pregnant women but is also debilitating for all ages. And it is debilitating the national economy as well. The most important and well studied micro-nutrient deficiencies are vitamin A, Iodine and Iron. Virtually every developing country has deficiencies in the micro nutrients large enough to constitute a public health problem. Many developing countries have multiple deficiencies. Taken together micronutrient deficiencies affect a far greater number of people in the world than Protein-Energy malnutrition. 1.6 billion people live in areas where soils lack sufficient iodine, 655 million suffer from goitre, 26 million have had brain damage and 5.7 million cretinism. Two billion pre-school children suffer from iron deficinet anaemia. 254 million pre-school children are affected by subclinical, severe and moderate deficiencies of Vitamin A.

In India, 167 millions are exposed to the risk of Iodine deficiency of which 54 million have goitre. Surveys conducted by DGHS indicate that 186 districts are IDD endemic area with goitre rates over 10 per cent. As regards Iron deficiency anaemia, multicentre study conducted by ICMR reveal that 87.5 per cent were anaemic. Deficiency of Vitamin A has long been known to be the largest preventable cause of blindness.

The main intervention strategies against micronutrient malnutrition are:

— Diet supplementation of vulnerable population.

— Dietary improvements.

— Fortification of common foods.

The richest sources of micronutrients are green leafy vegetable and fruits. India is rich in vegetable crops, some of which have good carotene content. Future programmes with respect to horticultural products must be directed towards identifying and propagating high micro-nutrient concentration varieties. People know when they are hungry but they have no natural hunger for vitamin. A, Iron, Iodine and other micronutrients. They do not know they need them and they often do not know what foods provide them.

Deficiency in soil nutrients reflect in the plants grown in the soil. One—half of all soils in all developing countries are deficient or low in available micronutrients. Soil depletion of S, Fe, Mn, Zn and Cu are due to intensive and indiscriminate irrigation and heavy use of high analysis chemical fertilisers. This gets reflected in the plants grown in these soils. Hence, in the national soil health care programme, we should ensure that both the macro-and micro-nutrient needs of soils are addressed.

The grim crisis, including a farmers' strike, over wheat procurement in Punjab and Haryana despite a hefty 25 per cent increase in purchase prices in a single year highlights the deep trouble brewing in our food economy. Already, the wheat buffer stock has plummeted to an alarming 2.7 million tonnes (mt), well below the recommended minimum of 3.7 mt, down from 12.9 mt just two years ago. Everything that the government has dome in the 1990s—from exporting grain when world prices are low, and importing when high, to raising procurement and issue prices unconscionably—speaks of gross mismanagement. If this continues, we could soon have Pakistan-style food riots. Already, the spectre of starvation and severe undernourishment stalks parts of Orissa, Maharashtra, Madhya Pradesh and Rajasthan. Our creaking public distribution system and its "targeted" variant, is in danger of collapsing. And yet there is irresponsible talk in policy circles of "unshackling" non-basmati rice exports and aligning domestic input and output prices with international levels.

That our food security should have been so badly undermined despite nine consecutive good monsoons speaks of a deep policy malaise and official callousness. The nineties have seen, for the first time in nearly four decades, foodgrain output growth lagging behind populaltion growth. Output growth has decelerated to less than half the 3.5 per cent rate of the 1980s. The slowdown is particularly severe in the case of rice and wheat, where the states that hold the key to marketable surpluses—and account for 80 per cent-plus of procurement—have witnessed a fall in growth rates to just 0.9 and 1.6 per cent, i.e. well below the population growth rate of 1.9 per cent. In our largest grain-producing state, paddy and wheat yields have fallen by 12 and 10 per cent respectively since 1992. Meanwhile, the output of "coarse" Meanwhile, the output of "coarse" cereals and pulses continues to shrink, eroding the food base of the poor, even as real farm wages decline.

Evidently, 30 years after it was launched, the Green Revolution has run its course or exhausted its potential, especially in the agriculturally most advanced areas. Northwestern India and parts of Andhra and Tamil Nadu show a clear trend of yields and output falling despite significant additions of inputs such as chemical fertiliser. Although eastern India has done relatively better, it simply can not compensate for the decline in the granary-states. In India as a whole, there are steeply falling returns to investment and inputs. As land is increasingly diverted to non-foodgrain uses, grain availability is further threatened. Given declining public investment in agriculture,—all this spells serious food insecurity.

Why has this happened? There are several reasons. First and foremost, the Green Revolution has come up against ecological and natural resources barriers. Its classic "package of practices" —high-yield (really high-response) seeds, big doses of irrigation, fertilisers and pesticides—backed by loans and guaranteed prices, is simply not sustainable in a natural-resources-poor society. In Punjab, 85 per cent of land has no more groundwater left to exploit. In Haryana, water-logging and salinity affect nearly a third of all land. In UP and Andhra, an overdose of chemicals is playing havoc with soil fertility. Farmers, who have oversaturated and killed lands with toxic chemicals, are now turning to nitrogen-fixing *dhancha* plants.

Secondly, unbalanced fertiliser use—encouraged by the Rs. 9,300 crore subsidy for urea—is playing havoc with soil health. The nitrogen-phosphorus-potassium ratio has changed to 8.5:6.6:1 in place of the optimal 4:2:1. (In UP, it is a dangerous 30:6:1). There is a severe and growing scarcity of micronutrients like zinc, copper, iron and manganese. A National Academy of Agricultural Sciences report warms of grave danger if micronutrients are not replenished and green-manuring not practised. Fertiliser overuse has been economically counterproductive too. Thus, fertiliser consumption has increased eight times over the past 25 years, but foodgrains output has not even doubled.

Third, the Green revolution's genetic breakthrough was largely limited to wheat and rice, which official policy favoured, while ignoring "coarse" grains)in reality, highly nutritious millets consumed by the poor). The result has been growing monocultures of rice and wheat, and loss of biodiversity. This also means inappropriate land-use: Punjab and Haryana, whose climate is unconducive to rice, have become its major producers. The Gangetic plains have turned into an environmentally unsustainable rice-wheat cropping system. Another consequence is sub-optimal use of water, and overuse of power, neither of which we can afford: the capital cost of major irrigation today is of the order of Rs. 50-80,000 per hectare. Servicing this annually alone would wipe out all profit from agriculture if the farmer were to bear the cost. He doesn't. The state does.

Fourth, in the nineties, the government deliberately changed its earlier policy of trying to keep food prices low. Following the premise that high output prices, and subsidised inputs would attract more investment and make agriculture competitive, it more than doubled the fertiliser subsidy. The idea was to "globalise" domestic prices for a specific crop spurt investment into its cultivation, but the aggregate supply response to an across-the-board increase in output prices is very weak. Hence prices have risen, but investment, yield and output have not.

These processes/factors have resulted in a first-rate agrarian crisis. This crisis cannot be resolved by adding inputs, or promoting better fertiliser/pesticide use—i.e. more of the same. Dying land which has less then two per cent organic matter left in it cannot be revived by chemical means. There is no way that our electrical system can support the current 10-12 per cent annual increase in power consumption which water-intensive agriculture demands.

A paradigm shift is on order. we need a "Doubly Green revolution", which judiciously uses advances in plant genetics and biotechnology, but is simultaneously resource conserving and environmentally sound. This means a transition from high-energy, chemical-and water-intensive agriculture to low-input, low-chemical, more organic, waterconserving farming. It means altering the direction of breeding towards sturdy, drought-and-pest-resistant seeds based on indigenous genetic material and away from rice and wheat to millets, pulses and grasses. It means moving away from monocultures to plural agri-silvi-pastoral systems which recycle biomass. It means conserving energy. It means moving from big to small farmers.

Fortunately, we have a highly evolved agricultural research-and-extension system with the resources to undertake this transition. We must strengthen it, and discourage capital-and energy-intensive seed-breeding based on exogenous material. We must abandon the chimerical goal of "globalisation" and look at our own needs, endowments and knowledge systems. Such a paradigm shift alone can resolve today agrarian crisis.

New Delhi: If you live in the cities of India what you mostly hear about is what you haven't got but should be trying to: a better job perhaps your own flat, a new vehicle, or may be a credit card or a cell phone.

Only now and again your eye may fall on newspaper stories about the wheat shortage or, if you are listening hard enough loud the rising prices and terrible shortage of atta in the market. You don't have to be a professional economist to tell that something must be very wrong if there is a foodgrain shortage after being repeatedly told that the country actually exports wheat, and also after hearing the Prime Minister's back-thumping sermon about India's self-sufficiency at the World Food Summit in Rome last month.

A couple of shocking statistics, recently released by the National Council of Applied Economic Research (NCAER) provide a horrific, if more accurate picture of where we are. The first figure is that 39 per cent of India's population of nearly one billion remains under the poverty line, a number that hasn't changed in a decade. In real terms this means that a very large number of Indians have an earning capacity of Rs. 5 or less a day, and are lucky to scratch up a meal of a couple of *chappatis*. According to another survey by the NCAER, 37 per cent of the country's rural population is landless and therefore unable to grow their own crop to fend off hunger.

The second figure, less published but available from international agencies, is that foodgrain production has been declining despite good monsoons—overall from 191 million tonne in 1994-95 to 185 million tonne in 1995-96 and in the case of wheat, from 65.5 million tonne to 62.6 million tonne in the same period. Unsurprisingly, the worst production shortfalls are in the politically volatile states of Uttar Pradesh and Bihar. Yet the naked face of hunger continues to be masked by the hypocrisy that India is an foodgrain exporter.

Still, there are plenty of Indians who want to know not merely how the government is in a position to export several million tonnes of wheat when there isn't enough to feed to the hungry, and then, to start importing two million tonnes to fill the ration shops when a widespread scarcity arises and prices begin to shoot up. A leader in The Economic Times last week argues that the government, the largest hoarder of foodgrains in the country, "is releasing large quantities in the country but not large enough quantities". It makes a strong claim for wheat imports to be put under Open General Licence amidst widespread speculation that the wheat shortage may be a repeat of last year's sugar scam and that the politicians could be back in the import-export business.

Even, if that is not the case, the situation is morally as indefensible as the problem of Indian children in labour—anywhere between 30 to 90 million depending on how you define "labour"—that the Supreme Court recently sought to curtail through stringent penalties. Surely the main reason why millions of our children are in bondage is to escape hunger?

Apart from the rising population, agro-economists put forward a number of reasons for falling production in foodgrains, among them soil exhaustion and the large number of landless that are concentrated in the states of UP, Bihar and eastern India. What they do not spell out is the endemic political instability and corruption in these states, and the interminable cycle of fodder scams and casts wars, that are pushing the poor deeper into the poverty trap. Economic reports do not point out that the agriculture ministry for many years has been managed by ministers like Devi Lal and Balram Jakhar, who only represent the narrow interests of wealthy landed farmers like themselves, and have no truck with the poor landless peasant. Devi Lal is chiefly remembered today for turning his ministerial bungalow and the Ashoka Hotel into a farmer's retreat while Balram Jakhar is the only ember of the PV Narsimha Rao's government involved inboth the *hawala* and *gawala* scams. It cost men like Jakahar nothing to proclaim that India should export pulses apart from wheat, knowing full well that production of pulses was dropping faster than that of wheat. The Deve Gowda government is heir to the same hypocrisy. The Prime Minister wants to impress the world about India's prestige as a wheat exporter but can do nothing about the gnawing pangs of hunger at home. Persisting shortages of food and soaring pricelines are not the result of natural causes alone. They are crises created by the men at the top.

Thirty years ago the Kalahandi region of Orissa had suffered a severe drought causing nearly a thousand deaths due to starvation and related diseases. The number of reported cases of starvation deaths in the current drought in the same area of Western Orissa may not exceed a dozen so far, but the magnitude of the crisis remains almost the same. Vulnerability of the people of this rainshadow area to crop loss and its consequences has hardly changed. Despite the visits of every Prime Minister of India, from Mrs Indira Gandhi to Mr H.D. Deve Gowda, to sypathise with the people and announce new projects, the basic conditions of poverty and underdevelopment have not changed.

Every 10 years there has been a severe drought and every third or fifth year has been a hard-hitting year of agricultural failure. Distress migration in mass scale, sale of household possessions and cattle and, condition of near starvation have been recurring in this region. In fact, as many as 26 out of Orissa's 30 districts have experienced over 50 per cent have experienced over 50 per cent crop loss this year and have been declared drought affected. The Kalahandi experience is a clear indictment of India's development path whether before or after liberalisation.

Failure of rains in the critical post-sowing months of June and July led to crop failure in this region. During My-October 1996 the recorded rainfall was only 632 mm against the average of 1217 mm. It is the erratic nature of the rainfall rather than its absence which upsets the farming process most of the time. The sprouts of paddy as usual dried up in June-July last year. While the traditional sources of water supply have disappeared new irrigation facilities have not sprung up. The worst affected districts of Bolangir and Nuapada (until recently a part of Kalahandi) are strewn with rivers and rivulets which overflow during the rainy season. They carry water into Mahanadi whose basin suffers from floods in the coastral area of Orissa practically every year.

Earlier people had their community tanks, bunds and small barrages to block river water. Slowly the affluent families and government established their control over these lands and used them for other purposes. Over the years community tanks went dry due to lack of public care. Currently only a small portion of cultivable land is irrigated by a few small reservoirs and lift irrigation projects.

During the past two decades the drinking water supply has considerably improved with the installation of tube wells. Even then visitors would see streams of women going to rivers to collect pots of water strained through sand as river water in this region tastes sweeter than underground water. People of the area have been demanding a number of small reservoirs from rivers and streams which would save rain water and tanks in specific spots in the area. this should be supplemented by deep borewells in some places. Lifting water from rivers and tanks through pumps should also be systematically arranged. In fact, an organisation called Sahavagi Vikas Abhijan has made a panchayat-wise study of the irrigation proposals made by the people.

In six blocks of Kalahandi-Nuapara region, which are chronically droughtprone, it has suggested 795 such projects, which would cost approximately Rs. 1,540 crore with a command area of nearly 1,15,000 hectares.

Very little has been done to chalk out a long-term strategy demanded by the people. The much trotted KBK (Longterm Action Plan for Kalahandi Bolangir Koraput region), formulated on the initiative of the PMO in 1993, put all the existing schemes and their allocations together for a five-year period amounting to nearly Rs. 5,000 crore. It is a point of ridicule in the eyes of the public and also the administration since it neither provides additional resources nor addresses the basic causes of the recurring crisis.

There has been some awakening—however marginal it may be among the people. In recent weeks there have been block office gheraos and rasta roko campaigns by people in some places demanding long-term measures to prevent recurrence of drought. Hopefully, the newly elected panchayat leaders will join the stream of awareness growing among the people of the region to carry on a new struggle for the basic human right to a livelihood. Experience shows that when people assert their right to control and utilise their resources then state and capital wake up to negotiate with them.

The term Green Revolution was coined by Dr. William Gadd of USA in 1968, when our farmers brought about a quantum jump in wheat production by taking to semi-dwarf, non-lodging varieties with great enthusiasm and when similar progress appeared feasible in rice. Punjab took the lead because of the scientific and educational backstopping given by the Punjab Agricultural University on the one hand and on the other, by the presence of the essential pre-requisites for progress such as land consolidation and leveling, rural communication, rural electrification and above all, owner cultivation.

Twenty eight years after the term "Green Revolution" was coined, we are in a position to draw a balance sheet and chalk out a strategy for the future. Apart from erasing the "begging bowl" image of India, the most important gain has been the saving of forests and land, thanks to the productivity improvement associated with high yielding varieties. This year, Indian farmers harvested over 60 million tonnes of wheat, as compared to 6 million tonnes at the time of our Independence in 1947. Punjab farmers have raised the average yield of wheat to over 40 quintals per hectare. Likewise, Tamil Nadu farmers have raised the average yield of rice to over 50 quintals per hectare. If the yield improvement associated with the Green Revolution in wheat and rice had not taken place, we will need another 70 million hectares to produce the wheat and rice we now harvest. Thus, the productivity inmprovement associated with the Green Revolution is best described as forest and land saving agriculture. The productivity improvement has taken place not only in wheat and rice but also in relation to milk and eggs. Only in the case of pulses, we are lagging behind.

The population of India is growing at a rate of 1.8 per cent per year. If this trend continues, our population will double itself in less than 40 years. Only Kerala, Tamil Nadu, Goa and Mizoram have so far achieved a demographic transition to low birth and death rates. Besides population increase, improved purchasing power among the poor will enhance the demand for food, since undernutrition and poverty go together. In contrast, per capita availability of arable land is shrinking. Water efficiency is still on the whole low and water disputes are growing. In addition to the gradual decline in per capita availability of land and water, various forms of biotic and abiotic stresses are spreading. There is still a widespread mismatch between production and post-harvest technologies. In perishable commotities like fruits, vegetables, flowers, meat and other animal products, this mismatch is often severe, affecting the inyterests of both producers and consumers. This is why foreign experts frequently refer to the setting in of a fatigue of the Green Revolution. Lester Brown and Hal Kane in their book "Full House" released last year predict that at the current rate of population growth and environmental degradation coupled with an improvement in the consumption capacity of the poor, India will have to import annually over 40 million tonnes of food grains by the year 2030. This is four times the quantity we imported in 1966 i.e. before the onset of the Green Revolution. We should examine this issue seriously and should not allow complacency overtake the farm sector, just because we now have over 30 million tonnes of food grains available with Government.

Industrial countries are responsible for much of the global environmental problems such as potential changes in temperature, precipitation, sea level and incidence of ultraviolet-B radiation. While further agricultural intensification in industrialised countries will be ecologically disastrous, the failure to achieve agricultural intensification and diversification in developing countries where farming provides most of the jobs will be socially disastrous. This is because, agriculture including crop and animal husbandary, forestry and agro-forestry, fisheries and agro-industries provides livelihood to over 70 per cent of our population. The smaller the farm, the greater is the need for higher marketable surplus for increasing income. Eleven million new livelihoods will have to be created every year in India and these have to come largely from the farm and rural industries sectors. Importing food and other agricultural commodities will hence have the same impact as importing unemployment. Thus, what we need now is an environmentally sustainable and socially equitable green revolution or what may be termed as ever-green revolution.

Those who advocate going back to the old methods of farming ignore the fact that just a century ago when the population of undivided India was 281 million, famines claimed 30 million lives between 1870 and 1900. The famine eradication strategy of India comprising the following steps is perhaps the most important achievement of independent India:

— Enhanced production and productivity.

— Better distribution through the public distribution system.

— Adequate grain reserves.

— Purchasing power enhancement through various employment generation and guarantee schemes.

— Special intervention programmes for children, pregnant and nursing mothers and old and infirm persons.

While famines have been prevented, widespread under-nutrition prevails among the economically under privileged. Since non-food factors like health care, environmental hygiene and literacy play an important role in promoting sustainable food security of the level of the individual, we should redefine security.

Steps for achieveing sustainable food security are as under:

First sustained physical access to food will involve a transition from chemical and machnery intensive to ecological farming technologies.

Second, the emphasis on economic access underlines the need for promoting sustainable livelihoods through multiple income-earning opportunities.

Third, environmental access involves on the one hand attention to soil health care, water harvesting management and the conservation of forest and biodiversity, and on the other to sanitation, environment hygiene, primary health care and primary education.

If the political vision to implement this mission is forthcoming, population stabilisation can be more readily achieved. The prediction of Margins de Condorcet made in 1975 that population will stabilise itself, if children are born for happiness and not just for existence, will then come true.

The emphasis on the individual is important, since the household is not often a homogenous unit. Women and girl children tend to suffer more from under-nutrition than men and boys. UNDP's 1995 Human Development Report contains distressing data on the growing feminisation of poverty. To give operational content to such a concept of food security, we should initiate a Hunger-Free Area Programme (HFAP) consisting of the following components:

— Ensuring sustainable availability of food production over population growth through the development and dissemination of ecotechnologies, supported by appropriate packages of services and public policies. Ecotechnology involves the blending of the ecological prudence and technologies of the past, with the best in frontier technologies, particularly biotechnology, information technology, space technology, renewablre energy technology and management technology. Without ecotechnological empowerment, farm men and women will not be able to produce more food and other agricultural commodities on an environmentally sustainable basis from less land, water and energy resources.

— Sustain the productivity of the natural resource base, by conserving and improving the ecological foundations essential for continuous advances in crop and animal productivity.

— Ensure adequacy of household incomes through promotional social security, such as accessing assets, employment and organisational and marketing empowerment. Agricultural programmes should concurrently aim at more food, more jobs and more income. Integrated attention to farm and non-farm employment and value-addition to primary agricultural commodities will be necessary to enhance income and rural livelihood security.

— Provide entitlement to food through protective social security measures to the vulnerable groups, such as employment guarantee and food for nutrition programmes.

— Introduce a National Food and Livelihood Security Act for the purpose of paying integrated attention to:

  Conservation of lands, water, forests, biodiversity and the protection of the atmosphere.

  Enchancing productivity through ecotechnologies.

  Improving distribution in order to eliminate endemic hunger.

  Maintenance of adequate food security reserves.

  Strengthneing the techno-infrastructure for better post-harvest technology and expanding the coverage of sanitary and phytosanitary measures, and

Efficient research, education, extension, marketing systems both to take full advantage of emerging opportunities in international trade and to ensure that research and extension designed to promote public good receive adequate support.

Agricultural Growth

The rate of agricultural growth of the order of around 3.2 per cent per annum during the fifties was derived from acreage increases to the extent of 70 per cent. In the sixties, the rate of growth which was only 2.1 per cent in this sector and did not neutralize even the rate of increase of population in that decade, could be derived from acreage increase to the extent of 30 per cent only. The scope for any further increase in acreage for increasing agricultural peoduction has exhausted in the seventies and the entire increase in farm production had to come from improvement in per acre productivity. This has required high level of capital–intensive effort in the development of the agricultural sector.

According to a competent study, the capital output ratio in Indian agriculture has already touched the figure of four and is close to the same scale as is required in industry. For the same reason, the fact has to be reckoned with that absorption of labour in agriculture through a significant rise in yields on land has tended to be a comparatively limited and expensive process and this process alone cannot be relied upon to solve the growing unemployment problem. The running controversy on priorities as between agriculture and industry, in particular heavy industry, is thus futile and misleading in the context of the realities of Indian economic situation and its growth prospects. The idea that India enjoys a comparative advantage in agricultural output inIndia is now crucially dependent on growth of inputs from industry.

The need is thus not to fforeclose available resources in the economy for the so called development needs of the agricultural sector but to mop up a substained part of the surpluses and incremental incomes generating in the agricultural sector to meet the investment requirements of infrastructural development, including heavy and intermediate goods industries,to inputs for agriculture at a rapid and accelerating pace.

If much credit is taken for achieving self—sufficiency in food grains relative to effective domestic demand, there is now much brave talk of making India one of the few "grain powers" in the world even while large number of Indian people still do not have access to adequate food. Agriculture in India will have to go a long way yet before it can feed the Indian people. It is too early to talk of India becoming a "grain power." But the official policy has already veered to the postion that the government would not come in the way of the farmers exporting their produce and these exports would not be banned "merely" for bringing supplies and prices down for the domestic consumers. The upshot has been that while good grains have been exported, two million tonnes of wheat are being imported in the current year, 1996—97 to meet even the effective demand in the domestic market. The danger inherent in this position is not imaginary.

The widening disparities in incomes and levels of living combined with growing concentration of land and the swelling ranks of landless rural labourers are manifest. It is not amiss either to consider the pricing of agricultural produce, more especially food grains—the primary wage goods—and examine its influence on the general price trend and structure of relative prices in the Indian economy. The Agricultural Prices Commission, to start with, recommended a particular set of prices based on its studies of the cost of production, fair return to the farmer and fair prices for the consumer.

It has been a practice, by and large, to improve upon the prices recommended by the APC in order to provide additional incentives to the surplus farmers to increase production for the market. After the launching of the so—called economic reforms in 1991, however, the baalance between the claims of the surplus farmer and the consumer has been tilting sharply in favour of the former and the inflationary impact of "incentive prices" for good grains and other agricultural produce has been ignored. Subsidised farming by way of what are called "incentive prices" for farm produce and subsidised inputs for agriculture like chemical fertilizers, private irrigation facilities like tubewells and pumpsets, power andcomparative soft—term credit, was conceived in the wake of the disastrous drought years of 1964-65 as the means of stimulating agricultural production for the market and securing control over a substantial part of the marketable surpluses so produced.

There were probably compelling reasons under the given ownership pattern in cultivable land for adopting this strategy when shortages of agricultural commodities, especially of food grains, ad emerged as an endemic problem of the economy—its stability and further growth. But the concomitant of this development has been the growing commercialization of agriculture and emergence within it to prominence of that segment of farmers with their commercial interests which produce and control agricultural surpluses. In the course of time, however, as shortage in cereals or other crops are overcome relative, of course, to effective market demand at the present low-level of purchasing power in the economy, the system of subsidised production and marketing in agriculture has become in essence a mechanism to ensure to the surplus producer a monopoly to all the gains arising from incrreases in production and productivity.

Among the vast numbers of Indian farmers, only a small fraction, and more than 10 per cent of the total, commanding the best cultivable land produces for the market on any scale. They also monopolise the subsidised supply of inputs and credit and benefits of infrastructural facilities such as irrigation and power created by public investment.

The official planners have been very brave, indeed foolhardy, to scale up from 3.5 per cent to 4.5 per cent, reportedly under political pressure, the agricultural growth rate target for the Ninth Plan. This may please the powerful lobby of rich farmers and pander to their high growth ambitions. But it casts grave doubts on the veracity and credibility of the planning exercise, especially so when the sharp set-back to agricultural production in 1995-96, a good monsoon year, should have made the planners doubly cautious in their approach to the ticklish problems and uncertain prospects of Indian agriculture.

Disturbing trends

The disturbing indications that really must hot be ignored cavalierly are that the Green Revolution in irrigated areas based on viable farmers and subsidized inputs especially chemical fertilizers, may have touched the plateau. Also to reckon with is the shrinking social base of farming, with small and marginal farmers being squeezed out and the big gentlemen farmers with large land holdings and access to modern inputs and technologies furiously developing a nexus with urban business corporations, including multinational corporations. The agricultural growth target of 4.5 per cent for the Ninth Five Year Plan may, in this context, make some sense only if it is projected not for the total production or food security for the people of India, especially half the population suffering from poverty, hunger and malnutrition, but for marketable surpluses to meet effective demand, that is demand backed by purchasing power for agricultural products, including food grains, in the domestic and the global markets.

The performance of Indian agriculture after gaining political independence has been impressive and should not be derided as has been done by the votaries of the market-oriented growth of industry as well as agriculture. Food production quadrupled between 1951 and 1991. There was also significant growth of what are known as case crops to augment supplies for a wide variety of processing industries. This success was achieved with positive intervention of the Indian State, including large public investment in irrigation, research and development and, supplies of subsidized inputs like quality seeds, fertilizers and power. This was combined with judicious support prices for agricultural produce, especially food grains. Since the launching of the so-called economic reform policies in 1991 to bring about what is loftily claimed to be the structural adjustment of the Indian economy, the position of Indian agriculture has changed ominously. The fluctuations in agriculture production have become sharper. There is shift away from food grains to cash crops. Within the food crops, production of rice and wheat has been given generous price and other incentives. The production of coarse cereals, pulses and grains has tended to decline. With the per capita availability of cereals declining, the poor have been hit hard by their rising prices. The nature and content of agricultural growth has not even been properly comprehended, let alone tackled in the approach paper on the Ninth Plan.

New strategy in the sixties

A marked feature of agricultural policy or what is known as the new agricultural strategy launched in the mid-sixties was a decisive shift of emphasis from institutional reform to technological improvement. This found expression in the organization of modern inputs for viable farming. Expansion of irrigation, especially on private account, and supply of chemical fertilizers, pesticide and quality seeds registerd a relatively big advance and helped to enhance production and productivity of farmers with addess to these facilities. Since the farmers with marketable surpluses were at the same time assured of rising levels of incentive-procurement prices, the govenment was able, side to mop up adequate qualities of agricultural produce, especially of food grains, for current consumption well as building up of the buffer stocks.

The problem of feeding the urban population and the growing non-agricultural force was acute in the fifties and the sixties. This was indeed the biggest stumbling block in the way of overall economic stability and growth. Reliance on aided imports of food grains necessarily imposed sever strains, economic and political. It may well be claimed that Indian agriculture has by now developed to a point where it is in a position to meet effective demand for food grains in the Indian market. In this sense, the agrarian crisis as it manifested itself till the mid-seventies can be said to have been resolved. But the question now to be faced is the further growth of agriculture, its content and direction.

It is not without significance either that land reforms are no longer projected in official policy as an essential prerequisite for overcoming bottlenecks to higher production and productivity in agriculture. They are at best treated as desirable purely from the social justice angle. The talk of land reforms which the political leaders indulge in from time to time is, is therefore more of a populist gesture that carries little conviction in the political power system.

The prospect of growth in agriculture in 1996-97 appears to be excellent and the year is likely to end up with foodgrains production of over 191.2 million tonnes as against 185 million tonnes in the preceding year. In commercial crops, particularly oilseeds, and cotton, significant increase in output is quite certain. The only area of concern, however, is the continued slow growth in production of pulses. Overall, the agriculture production is likely to record a growth rate of about 3 per cent in 1996-97.

1996 was the ninth successive normal monsoon year. Country wide seasonal rainfall was 103 per cent of the long—term average which was better than that of last year. The monsoon arrived almost on time and covered the entire country by June 30, two weeks earlier than the normal date. By the end of the Monsoon season (June-September),32 out of 35 meterological sub-division and 81 per cent of districts covering 91 per cent area of the country had received normal to excess rainfall. The comparative performance of the monsoon for the past ten years, 1987 to 1996. The district-wise distribution of rainfall for the past 10 years.

The spatial and temporal rainfall distribution over the country was very satisfactory except over Orrissa and Vidarbha where rainfall was marginally deficient or scanty in some districts. In the later part of June, Rajasthan and Haryana experienced floods. In third week of July, floods also occured in north Bengal and Bihar. Excessive rain due to cyclonic storm caused extensive damage twice in Andhra Pradesh, first in June and then again in early November.

Total rainfall, its spatial and temporal distribution and its impact on the production of Kharif cereals, can be seen from the rice area and production weighted rainfall index constructed for each State and aggregated over All India. Cereals production weighted cumulative rainfall indices for the entire season are computed by assigning weights based on share in the production of kharif cereals. A comparative picture of temporal distribution of rainfall during the sout-west monsoon season of 1996 as compared to 1995 and 1994.

Rabi prospects also depend to some extent on post monsoon rainfall. The cumulative rainfall during the post sout-west monsoon season 1996 (1 October to 31 December) was excess or normal in 25 meteorological sub-divisions as against 16 subdivisions during the corresponding period last year. Performance of the post-monsoon rainfall for the past 6 years.

The main states or division which received deficient or scanty rainfall during the post monsoon period are Gangetic West Bengal, Sub-Himalayan West Bengal and Sikkim, Orissa, Bihar Plateau, Jammu & Kashmir, Himachal Pradesh, Punjab, Haryana, Chandigarh, Delhi, Hills of West Uttar Pradesh and East Madhya Pradesh.

The total live storage position in 63 important reservoirs in different part of the country by the end of September, 1996 as monitored by the Central Water Commission was much better this year. It was 97.7 Thousand Million Cubic Meters (TMC) at the end of September, 1996 as against 90.1 TMC during the corresponding period of 1995. Comperative position of storage level at the end of September, 1996.

Agriculture production performance in the last five years together with the prospects for 1996-97.

Foodgrains account for about 63 per cent of

country's agricultural output and hence even a marginal decline in foodgrains production has a 'ripple effect' on rest of the economy. Despite a near normal monsoon in 1995, the foodgrains output of 185 million tonnes in 1995-96 was lower by over 6 million tonnes. This was mainly on account of decrease in production of wheat, kharif rice, bajra and pulses. The most unexpected development was the late realisation in 1996 that the wheat harvest was just about 62.6 million tonnes, lower by about 3 million tonnes over the preceding year. The reasons for decline in production of rabi foodgrain crops i.e. wheat conditions at the grain filling stage of the crop in February/March, 1996. This was a serious set back and its late realisation did cause some distortions in wheat availability. Wheat prices rose to unprecedented heights by November, 1996, promoting the Government to release larger quantities from FCI's public stocks besides taking recourse to imports. Kharif 1996 foodgrains output is likely to be 103.2 million tonnes as against only 98.2 million tonnes in 1995. If Rabi crops prospects turn out to be normal, 1996-97 foodgrains output is likely to be 191.2 million tonnes which would be close to the record production of 191.5 million tonnes achieved in 1994-95. The annual growth rate in foodgrain production in recent past.

Per hectare yield rates of rice and wheat rose significantly during seventies and eighties. Consequently, both these foodgrains registered over 3 over per cent annual growth in production between 1980-81 to 1995-96, which was significantly higher than the annual population growth of 2.14 per cent during eighties. The low annual growth of 1.2 per cent in production of pulses since 1980-81 did, however, looking at the first seven years of this decade (1990-91 to 1996-97), the annual rate of growth of foodgrains was only 1.7 per cent which is lower than the current population growth. If this trend continues it could become a matter of grave concern.

Rice production reached a record level of 81.8 million tonnes in 1995 However, production in 1995-96 was down to 79.6 million tonnes. Production in Kharif, 1996 is estimated to be 70.6 million tonnes compared to 70.1 million tonnes in Kharif, 1995. Some adverse impact on rabi/summer rice during 1996-97 on account of the deficient/scanty rains, particularly in Orissa and West Bengal and also on account of cyclonic strom in Andhra Pradesh, has been reported. Despite this, if 1996 Rabi rice output remains at 1994-95 or 1995 or 1995-96 level of around 9 million tonnes, the total output of rice may be 79.6 million tonnes in 1996-97.

Wheat output of 62.6 million tonnes in 1995-96 was 3.2 million tonnes lower over 1994-95 output of 65.8 million tonnes. Due to sudden rise in temperature at the grain filling stage of the crop in February/March, 1996, there was an unexpected decline in its productivity in major wheat growing States except Haryana and Rajasthan. Service incidence of yellow rust was also reported on wheat variety HD-2329 which is largely grown in Punjab. 1996-97 target of wheat output is 65 million tonnes. The weather parameter of temperature was initially low, which is considered beneficial for the crop growth. However, delayed winter rains in the wheat growing area have resulted in moisture stress conditions. If the rainfall/temperature conditions are normal in the Rabi season, the production of wheat may be relatively better and could be expected at around 64.50 million tonnes in 1996-97. Wheat is becoming important even in rice consuming areas and increasingly subsituting for coarse cereals as urbanisation and incomes rise. The ratio of wheat production to rice production has steadily increased from one third in 1950-51 and 1960-61 to about one half in 1970-71 and further to four fifth in 1995-96.

The area under coarse grains (bajra, maize, jowar, ragi, small millets and barley) continues to show a declining trend and stagnation in production. Coarse grains are mostly grown by small and marginal farmers in areas largely characterised by low and erratic rainfall. The coarse grains are grown mostly in Maharashtra, Rajasthan, Madhya Pradesh, Uttar Pradesh, Andhra Pradesh, Tamil Nadu and Bihar. In 1995-96, the production of all the coarse cereal crops except bajra was relatively better than 1994-95. The production of bajra in 1995-96 suffered badly in the major States of Rajashtan, Gujarat, Haryana and Maharashtra and was 5.39 million tonnes i.e. substantially lower by 24.7 per cent over the production level of 7.16 million tonnes achieved in 1994-95. Despite this, the production of coarse cereals is estimated to be 29.1 million tonnes in 1995-96. As the rainfall and weather situation, particularly during the monsoon period, has been quite favorable in the major coarse cereal growing States, the production prospects have improved and the coarse cereal out is expected to be about 33.05 million tonnes in 1996-97.

Pulses production in the country has been stagnating around 8-14 million tonnes for the last 40 years. Per capital availability of pulses has come down from 69 grams in 1961 to about 39 grams in 1996. Production fluctuates from year to year depending on the performance of monsoon. The practice of inter cropping and mixed cropping is also more prevalent in pulses, which are grown as secondary crops. The production of pulses, which crossed 14 million tonnes in 1995-96. This was due to the substantial fall in production of gram to 5.02 million tonnes in 1995-96 from a level of 6.44 million tonnes in the preceding year. This shortfall was, however, offset to some extent by higher production achieved in Tur and other pulses in 1995-96. As a result of better monsoon rainfall, the production of pulses is expected to be higher and may be around 14 million tonnes in 1996-97.

The production of commercial crops like sugarcane (283 million tonnes), oilseeds (22.4 million tonnes) cotton (13.1 million bales) have been of a record level in 1995-96. As per the present assessment, the production prospects of these crops are better in 1996-97 and the production may go up further.

Sugarcan production reached a record level of 275.54 million tonnes in 1994-95 surpassing its earlier record level of 254 million tonnes of 1991-92. Again, a record production of 283 million tonnes of sugarcane has been estimated for 1995-96. Current production prospects of sugarcane are also quite good and is expected to be about 274 million tonnes in 1996-97.

Sugar production reached an all time record level of about 164 lakh tonnes in sugar year 1995-96 (October, 1995 to September, 1996), recording a substantial jump over the precedng years of record production of 146 lakh tonnes. Two years of record output of sugar has resulted in accumulation of sizable stocks, and industry is striving to export more, depending upon whether the global prices are favorable. The Statutory Minimum Price (SMP) for sugarcane for 1995-96 was fixed at Rs. 42.50 per quintal linked to a basic recovery of 8.5 per cent and for the 1996-97 season it has been fixed at Rs. 45.90 per quintal.

The sugar industry continues to function under a regulatory system where licences have to be sought for establishing new capacity or expanding the existing installed capacity. There is also a dual price control system under which 40 per cent of output is pre-empted for use of the government for PDS, at an ex-factory price which is fixed for each of 16 Zones. The balance 60 per cent output, factories are free to sell at the market price except that the quantity for free sale is regaulated by precscribing monthly quantities that each units can sell as non-levy sugar.

During the financial year 1995-96, the releases for PDS ranged from 3.27 to 4.03 lakh tonnes per month. Similarly, the releases for freesale sugar were kept high between 6.25 to 8.30 lakh MTs per month so as to ensure that freesale market price of sugar remained at a reasonable level. The stock holding limits and turnover period of sugar and khandasari were enhanced to 1000 quintals and 30 days from 1st October, 1996 from 500 quintals and 15 days respectively to promote increased availability of sugar in the market.

During the 1995-96 sugar season, about 8.87 lakh tonnes of sugar was exported. Sugar export has been decanalized and manufacturing units are now permitted to pack sugar in 50 kg. packages for export purposes and from 5th November, 1996, also in small consumer packs of 1, 2 and 5 kgs. for indigenous use. These packages can be made from any foodgrade packaging material.

Among the nine oilseed crop grown in the country, groundnut and rapeseed/mustard together for 62 per cent of total oilseeds production. Soyabean and sunflower have to late emerged as the oilseed crops having major growth potential. The other oilseed crops include seasamum, castorseed, nigerseed, safflower linseed. Oilseeds production was 18.61 million tonnes in 1990-91 and has since touched a level of 22.42 million tonnes in 1995-96. The production in 1996-97 is likely to be 24.11 million tonnes.

Cotton production is estimated at 130.9 lakh bales of 170 kgs. each in 1995-96, and increase of 10.1 per cent over the production of 118.9 lakh bales in 1994-95. Due to increase both in area coverage and its productivity, the production of cotton is likely to go up further in 1996-97 an is expected to be around 143 lakh bales.

Production of Jute and Mesta continued to stagnate. Production which had reached a record level during

1995-86, registered a sharp decline and hovered around 6.78 to 10.29 million bales thereafter. Production in 1995-96 is expected to be 8.90 million bales, and may rise marginally to 9.19 million bales in 1996-97.

Crop production

Agricultural crop production in 1996—97 is expected to show good recovery from the slower growth in 1995—96. Growth is projected at 3 per cent after a fall of 0.4 per cent in 1995—96. The sharp decline in foodgrains production by 3.4 per cent, which was responsible for the slow growth in 1995—96, is expected to be reversed by an increased of 3.3 per cent in 1996—97. Foodgrains production is expected to recovery is primarily due to coarse cereals, as well as an anticipated rise in wheat production which suffered a sharp setback in 1995—96.

As the agricultureal year runs from July to June, the estimates for 1995—96 were only firmed up after the end of the financial year. A large downward revision (of 3 million tonnes) was made in the estimate of wheat production for 1995—96. The revision was unexpected and unexplained, because average rainfall in 1995—96 was quite normal. The revision, late in calendar year 1996, also created severe problems for the management of the food economy.

Commercial crop production has done extremely well in 1996—97 with oilseeds and cotton expected to reach record levels of 24.1 million tonnes and 14.3 million tonnes, respectively. Jute and mesta have also shown a growth of 3.4 per cent this year. Sugarcane output is, however, unlikely to maintain the record level of 283 million tonnes attained in 1995—96.

Industrial production (as measured by the index of industrial production–IIP), grew by 9.8 per cent in the first seven months of 1996—97, 1.9 percentage points slower than the 11.7 per cent growth in the in the corresponding period of 1995—96. The good performance of industrial production in 1996—97 is due entirely to the manufacturing sector, which has maintained its high growth.

The slowing of industrial production is clearly attributable to the dramatic fall in the rate of growth of electricity production and a slowing of growth in the mining sector mainly because of the 10 per cent decline in crude oil production. During the first seven months of 1996—97, electricity production (as measured by the index) has grown by only 3.4 per cent compared to the 10.1 per cent growth in the corresponding period of 1995—96. It is somewhat surprising that manufacturing sector growth has been barely affected by the slow growth in electricity production. One possibility is that captive electricity generation, which is increasingly used as a back—up to public supply, has substituted for the lack of generation by electricity boards. The high growth of diesel imports, about 22 per cent by volume in the first seven months of 1996—97 (with total refinery throughput growing in the normal range of around 4 per cent), is consistent with this hypothesis. At present, electricity statistics incorporate little or no data on captive power generation.

Another noteworthy aspect of industrial growth this year is the acceleration in the rate of growth of capital goods production to 16.6 per cent in the first seven months of this year from 15 per cent in the first seven months of last year. This has off—set the decline in the rate of growth of consumer goods and basic goos. In contrast, capital goods imports have declined by 6 per cent in the first seven months of 1996—97. This shows the increased competitiveness of the domestic capital goods industry. The overall performance of the core and infrastructure sectors during the first 8 months of 1996—97 (April—November) has been poor.

Six industries namely, electricity generation, coal, steel, crude oil, petroleum products and cement, with a combined weight of 28.8 per cent in the Index of Industrial Production (IIP), averaged a growth of 4.1 per cent in April—November, 1996, less than half the 8.9 per cent, in April—November, 1995. The deceleration in the growth rate of these infrastructure industries is mainly due to a decline in crude oil production and power generation. Hydro power generation declined by 7.7 per cent, and thermal power generation grew by only 6.4 per cent in the April—November, 1996 as compared to 14.6 per cent in the April—March, 1995—96. Coal, cement and refineries' throughput have grown faster in April—November, 1996—97 compared to the corresponding period of 1995—96. Growth of sectors such as railways, ports and telecommunications, which do not appear in the IIP, also slowed. The rate of growth of railways' revenue earning goods traffic decelerated marginally from 7 per cent during 1995—96 to 6.3 per cent for April–November 1996. Growth of cargo handled at major ports and new telephone connections provided decelerated more sharply to 4.7 per cent in April—November, 1996 (from 9.1 per cent in 1995—96) and 8.3 per cent in April—November, 1996 (from 23.3 per cent in 1995–96), respectively. The slower growth in cargo handled by ports in probably the result of a deceleration in the growth of external trade. The telecomunications slowdown, however, suggests that the pace of implementation of telecommunications reform needs to be accelerated and its scope widened to include Department of Telecommunications as a service provider. Given the parlous financial state of many public utilities, particularly the State Electricity Boards, the possibility of crises worsens with each passing year. The new government has repeatedly stressed its firm determination to reform the infrastructure and energy sectors. In line with this commitment, a number of policy decisions have been taken and new initiatives launched.

The second International Crop Science Congress, held in New Delhi from November 17 to 24, has displayed the International scientific community's will to solve the mankind's basic problem of hunger and to lay the foundation for a vibrant, yet ecologically sustainable, agriculture to meet future needs. The world's largest assembly of crop scientists, over 1500 from nearly 70 countries, emphasised that the modern biotechnology, coupled with traditional wisdom, can mould future to suit the interest of the human society. Though new challenges will keep cropping up, the science would perhaps not only be able to deal with them but might indeed convert them into opportunities for the good of humanity.

The optimism would, however, hold true only if it is matched by political will to raise farm productivity as also to distribute its gains equitably. New technology accompanied by appropriate marketing policies and international cooperation holds the key to ensuring foods security in the years to come.

Deliberations of the mega scientific event, organised jointly by the National Academy of Agricultural Sciences (NAAS) and the Indian Council of Agricultural research (ICAR), once again confirmed the widely held notion that while the scientists would be able to cope with humanity's needs they may become helpless to cope with its greed. The world renowned agricultural expert, Dr. M.S. Swaminathan, who chaired the Congress, did not mince words in passing on this message. He said: "Whether in agriculture or aquaculture, we must curb the greed revolution and promote an ever-green revolution capable of bringing about continuous advances in terrestrial and aquatic productivity without harm to the environmental capital stocks of land, water forests, biological diversity, oceans and climate upon which such advances depend."

The theme of the Congress, "Crop productivity and sustainability—shaping the future"—was highly appropriate and topical for several reasons. Despite phenomenal growth in food production, nearly one-fifth of the world population is still malnourished and hungry. The impact of the green revolution is waning and concerns of productivity decline in major crop production systems are being expressed globally, diminishing per capita availability of land and water resources, expanding biotic and abiotic stresses and natural resources, including land, forest and environment, are fast degrading. This calls for greater resolve to ensure synergism among productivity, profitability and sustainability of major cropping systems. Moreover, for safeguarding food and nutritional security at the household level, crop intensification and diversification are needed on an ecologically sustainable basis.

Let us now concentrate on another important aspect, e.g. the impact of Operation Barja on production. During 1972—73 to 1978—80 the foodgrain production in West Bengal grew at a rate of 1.7% as against 2.5% for India as a whole. During the decade of eighties, i.e. the post operation Barga period, the growth of food grain production in West Bengal was 3% as against India's 2.4% (Sengupta 1993). During this period West Bengal has also seen an increase in oilseeds and potato production. Although a large part of this increase may be the field of agriculture, the role of land reform in boosting agriculture cannot be totally denied. There are studies which show that the productivity of share cropped land is higher for recorded than for unrecorded share croppers (Chandra 1993).

A micro level survey conducted by Chaudhuri and Pal (1993) reveals that the productivity of self cultivated owned land is higher than that of land under share cropping arrangement (both recorded and unrecorded). The study also reveals that the use of input e.g. chemical fertilizers and high yielding variety (HYV) of seeds ar also lower in tenant operated plots. One possible reason is the poverty of the tenants which makes them incapable of purchasing fertilizer and necessary irrigation water for cultivation of HYV crops. Moreover there may be reluctance on the part of the share—croppers to invest more on a leased in plot whose output will have to be shared with the owner.

So far as the distribution of vested land is concerned, West Bengal has performed very well. At the end of 1991, 0.37 million hectares of land were distributed among 2.0 million families. In West Bengal, the two schemes, i.e. the distribution of surplus land and recording of Barga cover nearly 40% of the rural households. Most of the holdings are rainfed and hence it is not possible to raise Rabi or Boro crops on the plot. The scarcity of irrigation water affects the recorded share croppers equally. Another important problem of the owners of vested land is the scarcity of bullock power to till land. These people have to hire bullock and carts from their landlords and this may, in some cases, lead to exploitation by landlords.

The problems discussed so far may be eased by establishing cooperatives for agricultural inputs specially irrigation and bullock power. One obstacle to the formation of such cooperatives is fragmentation of land. The consolidation of holdings has not been done in most of the states.

At present the owners of adjacent holding may form groups for investing in shallow tubewells, pumpsets, bullocks and carts. In order to utilize a pair of bullocks an average of 4 to 5 acres of land is required. So formation of cooperatives is the easiest way of utilising the bullock power most economically. Tractors may also b purchased and maintained on a cooperative basis. For the success of cooperative movement special attention should be given to the consollidation of fragmented holdings.

The owners of marginal plots and also the poor share croppers should be trained properly to start various off—farm activity, e.g. cottage industries, animal husbandary, pisciculture etc. These off—farm activities will be their secondary sources of income. Loans and subsidies should also be made available to this group for starting such off—farm activities. All these will go a long way to make the land reform measures a success.

Food consumption

Against the per capita net availability of 501.9 gms of cereals the estimated consumption of cereals was of the order of 394 gms i.e. 78.6 per cent of the net availability. similarly in the case of pulses, per capita consumption was 28.05 gms. i.e. 75.8 per cent of net availability. Inequality in the consumption of foods among different income groups gets masked in the overall consumption estimates. Among the poor, nearly 80 per cent of consumption expenditure goes for food items. Recent surveys indicate:

— Percapita cereal consumption has declined over the years resulting in the aggregate energy intake of 1859 k.cal per capita as against 2200 k.cal recommended.

— 47.7 per cent of households have calorie inadequacy and 19.8 per cent of households have protein inadequacy. 19.5 per cent of households have both calorie and protein inadequacy.

— The exetent of moderate and severe growth retardation in preschool children varied from 34 per cent in Kerala to 72 per cent in Gujarat.

— 47 per cent of adults have body mass index value below 18.5 indicating large scale prevalance of chronic energy deficiency in the community.

— Haemoglobin levels among pregnant mothers reveal that as many as 87.5 per cent of mothers were anaemic.

— About 30 per cent of infants born had low birth weight.

— 167 million people are considered to be at risk for iodine deficiency disorders and 54 million have goitre.

— Preventable blindness due to Vitamin A deficiency still large.

Looking back the distance travelled and counting on various milestones towards food security, the country can be proud of some of the achievements so far. Yet the final milestone looks to be a long march. Shrinking arable land resources, soil degradation and depletion of nutrients from the soil, poor water management and unsustainable use of ground water, loss of momentum in the growth of food output, inefficient biological utilisation of the nutrients consumed due to poor environment and growing population are some of the problems the country faces in the march towards the final milestone of a hunger-free nation. The over-exploitation of the aquifer is also leading to the leaching of high levels of arsenic from natural underground sources into thousands of village wells in West Bengal. As estimated 200,000 people already have arsenic-induced skin lesions. It is estimated that there are about 20 million species of poants, out of which 50,000 are edible. However, we are not using more than 200 plants as food, 80 per cent of our food supply however comes only from about eight species. We are today laying much emphgasis on developing new varieties of these few plants. We should enlarge the food basket by including the excluded. Many nutritious grains fall under the classification "coarse grains". It is time we start referring to them as "nutritious grains". They are rich in micronutrients like Fe and Ca.

The momentum of growth witnessed in 1995—96 with a GDP growth of over 7 per cent, has been maintained in 1996—97, thus providing increasing evidence that the growth potential has improved as a result of the reforms initiated in 1991. With the growing participation of virtually the entire spectrum of political opinion inthe reform process, there is a good prospect that a higher growth rate would become a permanent feature of the economy.

The initial spurt of reforms from 1991—92 to 1993—94 was very successful by all accounts, resulting in a jump in economic growth to 7.2 per cent in 1994—95 (in terms of GDP at factor cost). Since 1994—95, however, there was a marked slow down in the pace of reforms. Nevertheless, GDP grew by 7.1 per cent in 1995—96. The slackening of reforms preceding and during the election period may have been responsible for some loss of momentum, but this has been revived with a series of measures in recent months.

Economic growth in 1996—97 is estimated by CSO to be around 6.8 per cent (GDP at factor cost). Thus, the Eighth Plan is likely to end with an average growth of 6.5 per cent per annum, 0.9 per cent point higher than the target rate of 5.6 per cent, and 0.5 per cent point higher than the actual achievement of the Seventh Plan. More important for the future is the fact that the average growth during the latest three years is 7 per cent, probably placing India among the top ten performers in the world during this period.

As the final year of the Eighth Plan draws to a close, a comparison of some salient dimensions of some salilent dimensions of economic performance between the Eighth Plan period and its predecessor reveals the following:

— Overall economic growth has been faster;

— The manufacturing sector has grown almost 2 per cent points faster per year in the Eighth Plan period;

— Agriculture and allied sectors have grown at about 3.5 per cent per annum in both periods;

— Both exports and imports have grown significantly faster in the Eighth Plan period;

— The balance of payments has strengthened considerably, with trade and current account deficits declining as ratios of GDP, while exports and imports have grown rapidly both in value terms as well as in proportion to GDP.

— The Central Government's fiscal deficit as a proportion of GDP has declined significantly;

— The average rate of gross domestic savings has risen substantially from 20.6 per cent of GDP in the Seventh Plan period to 23.9 per cent in the first four years of the Eighth Plan;

— With the exception of telecommunications, the rate of growth of net output (value added) of infrastructure sectors has slowed;

— The average rate of inflation has risen somewhat, though remaining below double digits.

Total gross domestic saving reached a new peak of 25.6 per cent of GDP in 1995—96, exceeding its previous peak of 24.9 per cent of GDP in 1994–95. This seems to vindicate the reform strategy of encouraging savings by expanding saving and investment opportunities, rather than giving special incentives.

Gross domestic investment (adjusted), as a proportion of GDP at current prices, rose even faster than gross domestic saving in 1995—96 to a high of 27.4 per cent from 26 per cent in the previous year. Gross domestic investment in real terms, as a proportion of GDP at constant prices, reached a new peak of 27.1 per cent, exceeding the previous peak of 25.9 per cent in 1990—91. Gross fixed capital formation which is even more important for productivity and growth, reached a new peak of 24.1 per cent of GDP in 1995—96. Private sector investment appears to have responded vigorously to the policy of promoting competition, removing policy distortions and hurdles, and improving access to factors of production (e.g. technology, capital).

Estimates of savings and investment in 1996—97 are not yet available. Indicators are mixed. On the one hand, domestic capital goods production is buoyent and disbursement of financial institutions are significantly higher, on the other hand, capital goods imports have declined, non—oil imports are lower in the first nine months of the year, corporate demand for credit appears slack, and sanctions of financial institutions are substantially lower.

The economy in 1996—97 so far presents a mixed picture in other dimensions as well. Although overall economic growth remains high at 6.8 per cent, and agriculture has rebounded, the growth of manufacturing value added has slowed and the performance of key infrastructure sectors, especially power and crude oil, is weak. The annual rate of inflation (point to point) has risen back to average long—term levels and export growth has decelerated markedly in recent months. Despite the slowdown in exports, a combination of sluggish imports and reasonably buoyant inflows of invisibles and capital flows have led to a build—up of foreign exchange reserves by over $ 2.5 billion.

Agriculture and Indian economy

The Economic Survey–1996—97 is a balanced appraisal of the past performance of the economy, attributing the gains to the policy of economic reform and liberalisaton, pursued during the last five years and presents a picture of cautious optimism for the future. While attributing the past gains to the policy of liberalisation, the Survey asserts that the policy would need to be pursued with greater vigour in future to carry the economy to higher growth path. It attributes "the loss of momentum" in the economy to "the marked slow down in the pace of reforms preceding and during the election period", but adds "this has been revived with a series of measures in recent months."

The Survey says "the initial spurt of reforms from 1991—92 t 1993—94 was very successful on all accounts, resulting in a jump in economic growth in 1994—95 to 7.2 per cent." It says GDP grew by 7.1 per cent in 1995—96 despite the slowdown in the momentum of reform and adds, econmic growth in 1996—97 is estimated by the CSO to be around 6.8 per cent (GDP at factor cost). The Eight Plan, it says is thus likely to end with an average growth of 6.5 per cent per annum, 0.9 per cent higher than the target rate of 5.6 per cent and 0.5 per cent point higher than the actual achievement of the Seventh

Plan. More important for the future is the fact that the average growth during the latest three years is 7 per cent, probably placing India among the top ten performers in the world during the period." However, when it comes to a review of sectoral performance that he Survey is compelled to be more realistic. It says "the economy in 1996–97 so far presents a mixed picture." Although, it says "overall economic growth remains high at 6.8 per cent, and agriculture has rebounded, the growth of manufacturing value added has slowed and the performance of key infrastructure sectors, especially power and crude oil, is weak. The annual rate of inflation (point to point) has risen t actual long—term levels and export growth has decelerated markedly in recent months."

On agriculture, the Survey says "production in 1996—97 is expected to show good recovery from the slower growth in 1995—96. The growth is projected at 3 per cent after a fall of 0.4 per cent in 1995–96. The sharp decline in foodgrains production by 3.4 per cent, which was responsible for the slow growth in 1995–96, is expected to be reversed by; an increase of 3.3 per cent in 1996—97. Foodgrains production is expected to recover to 191.2 million tonnes, only marginally lower than the level of production in 1994—95. The recovery is primarily due to coarse cereals, as well as anticipated rise in wheat production, which suffered a sharp setback in 1995—96." Commercial crop production has done extremely well in 1996—97 with oilseeds and cotton expected to reach record levels of 24.1 and 14.1 million tonnes respectively.

In the previous chapter, we described the situation as it prevailed in 1960-61. We shall now proceed to take a brief review of the progress made during the past decade. The last year for which some data are available is 1968-69. Therefore, in the following review, we shall cover the period from 1960-61 to 1968-69.

National Income again offers a useful summary measure to judge the performance of the economy in a given period. The particular measure of national income we shall use is specifically termed Net National Product at Factor Cost. We shall briefly refer to it as NNP. We have earlier mentioned that the NNP was Rs. 13,308 crores in 1960-61. It increased to Rs. 28,800 crores in 1968-69 was 216.4. The NNP increased annually by about 6 percentage points during 1961-62 and 1962-63; by almost 17 percentage points in 1963-64; by 26 percentage points in the next two years; by 23 percentage points in 1966-67; by 32 percentage points in 1967-68; and finally, by 6 percentage points in 1968-69. Over the eight years from 1960-61 to 1968-69, the NNP more than doubled.

This is a spectacular performance if it were all real. Unfortunately it is not all real. During the eight years from 1960-61 to 1968-69, the prices of commodities have almost doubled. This means that a rupee in 1968-69 does not mean the same thing as it did in 1960-61. Hence, to judge the real increase in NNP, we should ask what would the NNP be if the prices had remained unchanged. In other words, we should value the NNP in subsequent years at prices as they prevailed in 1960-61. We shall refer to this as Net National Product at Constant (1960-61) Prices. From such a series, it becomes clear that the NNP increased by only 26.5 per cent in eight years and not by 116.4 per cnet as appeared earlier. Thus the real increase in the NNP is only 26.5 per cent in eight years; the balance of apparent increase is a reflection of the increase in prices.

The growth in the NNP has not been steady. This is because agricultural production, which constitutes almost half of the total, is still liable to wide fluctuations from year to year. The real increase in the NNP by 6 percentage points in 1963-64 and again by 8 percentage points in 1964-65 was because of the good agricultural season in those two years. This was followed by two very bad years and the NNP actually declined in 1965-66 and remained at the same low level in 1966-67. Fortunately, the year 1967-68 turned out to be a very good year and the NNP jumped by 10 percentage points. The year 1968-69 was also a good year and the NNP is estimated to have advanced by another 2 percentage points.

Thus the anunal fluctuations in agricultural production explain the unsteady growth of the NNP. But in a period as long as 8 to 10 years, one must take good years along with bad years and reckon the fact that the real increase in NNP in eight years was only 26.5 per cent which is a compound growth rate of less than 3 per cent per annum.

The growth in the NNP must be placed alongside the growth in population. The population of the Indian Union in 1961 was 434 million. We shall know what it is when the census is taken this year. However, in the meanwhile, the population is estimated to have been growing at the annual rate of 2.5 per cent. Clearly, therefore, a growth of NNP at an annual rate of no more than 3 per cent is barely sufficient to keep pace with the growth in population; it leaves little margin to make a net improvement in the economic condition of the people. This becomes clear if we divide the NNP by the estimated population each year to get the NNP per capita. If this is done, it becomes clear that the per capita NNP increased from Rs. 306.7 in 1960-61 to just Rs. 321.3 in 1967-68 and Rs. 319.4 in 1968-69. This is an increase at best of only 4.5 per cent in eight years which is about half a per cent per annum. This summarises the performance of the economy during the past decade.

As mentioned earlier, per capita private consumer expenditure gives a more direct measure of the well-being or standard of living of a people. We have seen that the per capita private consumer expenditure was Rs. 276.3 in 1960-61. In are given the relevant data for the subsequent years. In order to assess the real changes in the per capita consumer expenditure in subsequent years at constant (1960-61) prices for the years from 1960-61 to 1968-69.

It will be seen that the per capita consumer expenditure increased from Rs. 276.3 in 1960-61 to Rs. 285.5 (at 1960-61 prices) in 1968-69. The per capita consumer expenditure shows a sudden increase (Rs. 296.0) in 1964-65 and then a sudden fall (Rs. 269.8 and Rs. 271.8) in the following two years. This is a reflection of the bumper agricultural production in 1964-65 and poor production in the following two years. The average per capita consumption during the three years 1964-65, 1965-66 and 1966-67 was Rs. 279.2 per annum. It seems more likely that the real consumption was maintained more or less at this level by carrying some of the large stocks of 1964-65 into the next two years rather than allowing it to fluctuate along with fluctuations in agricultural production. For the same reason, we should smoothen out the fluctuations in the first three years as also in the last two years. When this is done, the estimates of per capita consumer expenditure in the nine years appear as shown in. They seem more reasonable and plausible.

The upshot of the whole exercise is that the per capita consumer expenditure rose from Rs. 276.3 in 1960-61 to Rs. 289.6 in 1968-69, that is by 4.8 per cent in eight years or by about half a per cent per annum. It is obvious that it could not have risen by any more because, we have seen as the per capita income rose at best by 4.5 per cent in the eight years.

Incidentally, we may note that the per capita consumer expenditure seems to have increased a little more than has the per capita national income. The reasons seem to be firstly that the large increase in national income registered in the last two years has been mainly on account of the large increase in the production of foodgrains in these years and secondly that the net domestic capital formation as a proportion of the net domestic expenditure has gone down sharply in these two years.

This brings us to the next point namely how are these small gains of development distributed between different sections of the population–between the rural and urban populations and between the richer and poorer sections of these populations? More specifically, we ask: The average consumer expenditure in the country rose by 4.8 per cent in real terms (that is at constant prices) in the eight years from 1960-61 and 1968-69. Did this happen equally in the case of the rural and urban populations and equally in the case of the richer and poorer sections of these populations? These questions are crucial while assessing whether anything is happening to the poor of this country; whether their lot has improved materially as a result of the economic development of the past decade. If the per capita consumption in the country has risen by no more than 4.8 per cent in eight years, it is obvious that little noticeable could have happened in the nature of alleviation of poverty unless the poorer sections have profited proportionately more than the average and much more so than the rich. Did this happen during the past decade? We shall examine the facts.

Rural-urban differential

As mentioned earlier, the National Sample Survey (NSS) offers estimates of private consumer expenditure in rural and urban areas separately. In we give the NSS estimates of per capita consumer expenditure for the rural and urban populations for the years 1960-61 and 1967-68. In order to make the estimates for 1967-68 comparable with those for 1960-61, the estimates for 1967-68 must be expressed at prices prevailing in 1960-61. This is done in the second line of the Table.

As earlier mentioned, the NSS estimate of per capita private consumer expenditure for 1960-61 (Rs. 278.8) is in close agreement with the corresponding official estimate (Rs. 276.3); the NSS estimate is higher than the official estimate by less than one per cent (0.9 per cent). However, the NSS estimate of per capita private consumer expenditure for 1967-68 at 1960-61 prices (Rs. 256.2) is much below the corresponding official estimate (Rs. 287.0). Indeed the NSS estimate is short of the official estimate by as much as 10.7 per cent.

It seems that the NSS estimate of per capita private consumer expenditure for 1967-68 is an underestimate. This becomes clear if we compare it with the NSS estimate for 1960-61. It will be seen that, compared at constant 1960-61 prices, the NSS estimate for 1967-68 (Rs. 256.2) is below the NSS estimate for 1960-61 (Rs. 278.8) by as much as 8.1 per cent. Hence, if we rely on the NSS estimates, it would appear that the per capita consumption declined by as much as 8.1 per cent during the seven years from 1960-61 to 1967-68. This appears unlikely. Hence, we must conclude that the NSS estimate of per capita consumer expenditure in 1967-68 is in fact an underestimate.

We shall later examine the reasons for and the nature of this underestimation. For the present, we propose to revise the NSS estimates of rural and urban per capita consumer expenditure, both in 1960-61 and 1967-68, in order to bring them in accord with the official estimates of per capita national consumption in those years. It will be noticed that the revision is only slight for 1960-61 but is very considerable for 1967-68.

From the estimates of per capita rural and urban consumer expenditure thus revised, it will be seen that the per capita national consumer expenditure increased from Rs.276.3 in 1960-61 to Rs. 287.0 in 1967-68 that is by 3.9 per cent. In the same period, the per capita rural consumer expenditure increased from Rs. 258.8 to Rs. 268.6 that is by 3.8 per cent, while the per capita urban consumer expenditure increased from Rs. 356.4 to Rs. 364.9 that is by 2.4 per cent. Thus it seems that the average consumption in the rural area has improved a little more, though only slightly, than the average consumptions in urban area. Consequently, the rural-urban difference has been reduced a little. For instance, in 1960-61, the per capita urban consumption (Rs. 356.4) was 37.7 per cent higher than the per capita rural consumptions (Rs. 258.8). In 1967-68, the per capita urban consumption (Rs. 364.9) was only 35.9 per cent higher than the per capita rural consumption. We shall later examine the process through which the rural-urban difference has been thus reduced, even if only slightly.

Agriculture and Indian budget

It is rarely that a Finance Minister gets encomiums from various sectoins of the society for his budget proposals. But Mr. P. Chidambaram has managed to achieve such kudos with his budget proposals for 1997–98. The capital market, the corporate sector as well as the ordinary salaried class have al welcomed his proposals, as Mr. Chidambaram has tried to give something to all of them in the hope that they will all be enthused to help him raise more resources to be ploughed back into the economy.

Of course, the former Finance Minister, Dr. Manmohan Singh, who was the architect of initiating the current economic reforms policy in 1991, has said that the euphoria over the budget proposals may not last if the present government was unable to muster a consensus for resolving certain contentious macro—economic issues.

But even he is forced to admit that the most significant element of Mr. Chidambaram's budget is that India has not given up on reforms. Dr. Singh has also appreciated the direction of reform in indirect taxes and restructuring of customs duty proposed in the budget.

Mr. Chidambaram's task was not an easy one. He happens to be the Finance Minister in a coalition government formed by 13 parties and supported by a major party from outside. Even in the best of times, no Finance Minister can be have his way entirely while farming the budget proposals, as he has to take the entire Cabinet along. So Mr. Chidambaram's situation can be better appreciated.

Moreover he was presenting the budget at a time when the picture on the industrial fronts as well as on exports was not rosy. The capital market has been down for months (the sensitive index of the Mumbai stock exchange touched a three—year low last december). Industry in general had its misgiving on many crucial issues. The morale was rather low all round.

In a situation like this, Mr. Chidambaram had to do something which will psychologically lift the morale of various groups. This boosting up of the psychological morale is what he has done successfully through some bold proposals in the 1997–98 budget.

Now to analyse some of the major proposals contained in the budget. Mr. Chidambaram outlines his approach and says that "a good tax policy should aim at moderate rates, a widex tax base, simpler procedural rules and securing greater compliance. Households and the corporate sector are our best savers; we must reward them."

With this objective in mind, he has rationalised the personal income–tax structure, keeping the rate at the lowest slab at 10 per cent and the highest at 30 per cent (as against 15 per cent and 40 per cent respectively so far). He has also increased the standard deduction to Rs. 20,000 and has proposed that senior citizens having income upto Rs. 1,00,000 would not have to pay any tax. Thus with one stroke he has earned the gratitude of 12 million people who are assessed to income tax now.

To broaden the net wider, he has proposed that in future those who satisfy any of the two following economic criteria—ownership of a four–wheeler vehicle, a telephone, a house or have undertaken foreign travel in the previous year—should voluntarily file their tax returns. No one can seriously object to this proposals; but in attempting to widen the tax base, one hopes the government will ensure that unnecessary harassment is avoided.

Of course, the Finance Minister has introduced a voluntary disclosure scheme to harness black money. The measure has naturally created some controversy and entical questions have been raised. It remains to be seen how far the present scheme—which is different from similar schemes introduced earlier—is successful.

After trying to win the confidence of the individual tax payer, Mr. Chidambaram turns his attention next to the corporate sector. By abolishing the 7.5 per cent surcharge on corporate tax and reducing the rate of taxation for domestic companies to 35 per cent and for foreign companies to 48 per cent, he has conceded one of the long–term demands of industry.

His proposal in the 1996–97 budget for a Minimum Alternate tax (MAT) had some sections of industry u in arms. By now exempting export profits from MAT and bringing about modifications in the application of MAT, he has assuaged the feelings created by his last year's proposal.

Another major concession Mr. Chidambaram has given is the abolition of tax on corporate dividends in the hands of the shareholders. This single proposal, along with abolition o fthe surcharge on corporate tax and MAT modifications, has been such a morale booster for the capital market that the Mumbai stock sensitive index gained over 400 points in two trading days after the presentation of the budget.

Other proposals specifically aimed at improving the sentiment of the stock markets include acceptance in principle of buy–back of share by companies subject to certain conditions and the one–time permission to stockbrokers to corporatise their businesses without attracting tax on capital gains. Companies raising funds from the capital market will be required to give an annual statement disclosing the end—use of such funds. This is intended to restore the faith of small investors in stocks.

With regard to indirect taxes also, Mr. Chidambaram has taken some bold measures which have all been welcomed by industry in general. He has outlined that the goal was to achieve the average level of tariffs prevalent in ASEAN countries by the turn of the century. This will give time to Indian industry adjust to these changes. With that objective in mind, he has reduced the peak rate of customs duty from 50 per cent to 40 per cent.

He has reduced the duty on capital goods from 25 to 20 per cent and added that over the next two to three years, these rates would need to be further adjusted to conform to levels prevalent in other developing Asian countries.

Duties have been reduced on raw materials used by steel, chemical and textile industries. Stating that "if there is one science that will dominate the 21st century, it is the information technology and if there is one industry in which India can emerge as a world leader, it is the information technology," Mr. Chidambaram has given a number of concessions to encourage this industry.

Tourism is a major foreign exchange earner and there are specific proposals to boost investment in this sector. Coupled with the abolition of surcharge on corporate tax, one should see some surge in investment in this industry.

Like in customs duty, the Fnance Minister has given across the board concessions in central excise also. Last July, he said, he had promised that within three years "we shall have a four—rate tax structure." With this objective in view, he has introduced three rates—8 per cent, 13 per cent and 18 per cent. Jute industry has been given a special treatment, as he has exempted all jute and jute products from excise duty, Excise duty has been cut in respect of several items of mass consumption.

The 1997—98 Union Budget has broken new grounds in terms of carrying forward the liberalisation process and tax reforms by attempting to impart growth impulses to the economy. The Budget initiatives are important for more reasons than one presumably because the macro economic parameters of the economy were onthe downswing throughout most of the last year of the Eighth Plan (1997—98) with inflation rearing its head, trends in industrial production and foreign trade remaining none too ecouraging and capital markets coasting on thin trading for even blue chip companies. The 1997—98 Budget, as such, was expected to address these serious maladies so as to ensure that the economic activity gathered momentum and also to herals hope for realising the seven per cent growth target set for the Ninth Plan for which 1997–98 Budget is the inaugural year.

The Finance Minister Mr. P. Chidambaram did not dash hopes on all these things as the Budget he presented was a deft exercise in attempting to satisfy every constituency—be it salaried class, trade and industry, investors, both domestic and foreign and instiitutionals. In a master stroke, the Finance Minister attempted to rope in only one segment under the tax net and that is the services sector which is now contributing 40 per cent to the GDP. The logic is that "services" are products as much as "manufactured goods" and it was historic underestimation of this segment that had led to the neglect of any attempt to bring this into the tax net. But the credit for bringing services under the tax net must redound to the glory of the reform architect Dr. Manmohan Singh who initiated a modest but momentous beginning by introducing services tax on telephones and stock brokerage. Later, it was extended t advertising, courier and radio paging. From nowhere, the services tax fetched Rs. 970 crore for the exchequer in the fiscal year 1996—97.

It is but natural that the 1997—98 Union Budget should extend the services tax to some more aeas. The Finance Minister did not hesitate to do so and in his second budget after assuming office in July 1996, Mr. P. Chidambaram has confined his tax mobilisation effort to mop up Rs. 1205 crore only by bringing a few more services under the tax net and revising postal rates. The Budget for 1997—98 extends the service tax to cover a host of well–known services embracing transportation of goods by road, consulting engineers, custom house, steamer and clearing and forwarding agents, air travel agents, tour operators and car rental agencies, out—door caterers, pandal contractors and mandap keepers and man—power recruitment agencies. While the proposals on service tax are estimated to yield a revenue of Rs. 1200 crore in a full year, in the next fiscal year, a credit of Rs.

900 crore alone is being taken into account. The remaineder Rs. 305 crore for next year is being realised by revision of tariffs for some postal services, the proceeds of which would be for the development of postal services and in partially bridging the deficit on the numerous services being provided by the Postal Department.

A particularly noteworthy feature of the 1997—98 Budget is that it has given away massive customs tax relief amounting to Rs. 2625 crore and the reason for that as provided by the Finance Minister was that "our goal must be to achieve rapid and broad-based growth." While Mr. P. Chidambaram reduced the peak rate of customs duty from 50 to 40 per cent in a bid to align the country's tariff structure with international standards, he also reduced customs duty on capital goods from 20 to 15 per cent. Some of the intermediate inputs which witnessed cuts include steel industry inputs, cold rolled coils of iron andsteel, duty on ships brought for breaking, organic and inorganic chemicals, dyes, pigments, paints and varnishes, glues, enzymes and modified starches.

In tune with the tenet of emerging cooperative federalism, which is the hall—mark of the 13—party coalition government at the Centre, the Budget has accepted the alternative devolution formula seeking to bring in all taxes collected bythe Centre into a single divisible pool and apportion 29 per cent to the States as recommended by the Tenth Finance Commission.

The Budget of 1997—98 is a veritable bag of sops for Indian corporates and tax—payers as duty was cut across—the—board. In personal income tax, the existing rates of 15, 30 and 40 per cent is proposed to be replaced by 10, 20 and 30 per cent. The rate would be 10 per cent in the slab of Rs. 40,000 to Rs. 60,000, 20 per cent in the slab of Rs. 60,000 to Rs. 15,000 and 30 per cent for all income above Rs. 150,000. The limit on standard deductions has been raised to Rs. 20,000 which would apply uniformly to all salaried tax payers. In widening the tax net, the Budget proposed an amendment of Section 139 of the I.T. Act by which residents of large metropolises who satisfy economic criteria such as ownership of a four–wheel vehicle, telephone, flats and undertaking foreign travel in the previous year should voluntarily file their tax returns. Failure to do so would entail a simple notice from the I.T. Department. Yet another related scheme announced in the Budget pertains to the Voluntary Disclosure Scheme (VDS). Following the mandate of the National Development Council (NDC), the Minister announced the VDS to tap black money for productive purposes by which any disclosed income would be taxed at the revised highest rate of 30 per cent, the states would receive 77.5 of the proceeds on this score while the balance would be spent on bolstering the Basic Minimum Services. The scheme would start on a date to be notified by the Finance Minister and end on December 31, 1997. Some category of people would not be liable to secure immunity under this scheme and they include those held for offences under the Drugs and Psychotropic Substances, Arms Act, ordinarily punishable under the IPC and the Anti—Corruption Act.

An era of planning thus started in 1951, when the First Five Year Plan was launched. This was followed by the Second Five Year Plan (1955-56) and the Third Five Year Plan (1960-61). All these developments, from the Grow More Food Campaign in 1942 to the planned economy, are discussed separately. On the whole, the country lacked any well-defined policy of agriculture up to the end of Second Five Year Plan. Many improvements have taken place since then.

Cooperative farming, declared at one stage as the ultimate form of organisation for agricultural production, did not receive wide acceptance and that accounts for lack of any serious effort or enthusiastic response to its implementation. To achieve social justice, ceiling on the size of holdings is being imposed but there is considerable confusion in matters of detail and execution. Adequate investigations are lacking to justify the measure economically. There is good cultivable land which is lying waste in some states not because the ownership rights are vested in persons who are not able to farm it themselves but also because they do not lease it out for fear of losing their title to it. To the extent such land is brought under cultivation, the measure may prove beneficial. But where the holdings are pushed down below a certain minimum size, it is not easy to predict the effect on agricultural efficiency and production.

Quite often the emphasis on increasing the production of foodgrains has led to a fall in the production of commercial crops, leading to shortage of such products. In turn a cry is raised to increase the production of cash crops. Such an action can hardly be called a policy. Not much thought was given to preparing the estimates of cost-benefit ratio in undertaking programmes of large-scale irrigation and land reclamation. Therefore, emhasis has been changing from major to minor irrigation projects and vice versa; similarly from land reclamation to raising the standard and intensity of cultivation on land already under the plough.

These instances make it clear that hardly any well-defined policy existed and much less was pursued. A sound policy calls for precise and detailed information on cost-benefit relationships of various developmental projects, efficiency standards, and farms in various size groups in different farming type regions. First, it is necessary to have a census of agricultural resources, surveys on land use, investigations on factors inhibiting agricultural efficiency regionwise and the demand projections for the current and future needs in respect of food, cash crops, and export. Then taking the country and regions as units, sound plans need to be drawn up for land use, agricultural production, and needed supplies. To support the fulfilment of these targets, ancillary measures need be taken, namely, land reclamation, assistance in raising the intensity of cultivation, credit support, educational programmes, irrigation, etc. All such measures, for successful implementation, need a watchdog in the form of adequate farm management and agricultural economics research to guide and evaluate simultaneously the execution of the programmes in order to make them efficient and effective and to stop those measures which, on experience, have a retrograde effect.

No doubt, steps have been taken towards the direction suggested above, the major lacunae in them may be listed as follows:

— The carrying out of developmental activities on a piecemeal basis with the result that full benefits expected from such programmes have not been obtained. In UP, tube-wells, for example, were dug but could not be commissioned for lack of energisation.

— The budgetary provision for efforts in various directions were made on the basis of administrative divisions and not on a properly estimated requirement of expenditure with the consequence that the efforts were too thinly spread and proved almost futile. The early Grow More Food Campaign is an appropriate example of this.

— The approach where an investment could be most

effective from the point of view of natural factors like land, climate or economic factors like demand, particularly in the case of livestock products, has been conspicuous by its absence.

— Duplication and overlapping has often led to futility of efforts which cold never be enough according to needs and urgency.

If we examine any one of the policy measures on prices of foodgrains, production, distribution, land tenure, irrigation, land reclamation and settlement, we will see that each one has some woeful tale to tell. In the functions of the Ministry of Community Development and Cooperation and the Ministry of Agriculture, there was a considerable overlapping till they were recently merged. Between them and even within the same ministry there is duplication of positions. This leads not only to wastage of scarce funds but also to confusion in working.

A number of committees have from time to time gone into the problem of agricultural administration and machinery. All of them have helped to expand agricultural organisation. Mention may be made of the Patel Committee (1945-46) as a result of whose recommendations the Directorate of Economics and Statistics became a separate unit of the Ministry; the enquiry by N. Gopalsawami Ayyanger (1949), which recommended the creation of the Bureau of Natural Resources and Agriculture with a coordinating minister for the Ministries of Agriculture, Food and works; the W.R. Natu Enquiry 1951; and more recently the enquiry Mr. Keifer (1965). Full-scale general enquiries have also been made of the machinery of the Government of India leading to proposals for its reorganisation by Richard Tottenham in 1945, by Shri R.A. Gopalsawami in 1952 and Dr. Appleby in 1954. It may also be mentioned here that the Food Grains Policy Committee, 1947, the Grow More Food Committee 1952 and the Balwantrai Mehta Committee, 1957 also have made recommendations for the reorganisation of the machinery of agricultural administration at different levels. The desire for administrative improvement has been continuous, the suggestions for reform numerous, but the practical results of the enquiries have been rather disappointing. Piecemeal changes and adjustments have been made from time to time. There has been some bureau shuffling off and on but no thorough reorganisation that could assure the efficient functioning of the machinery for accelerating development.

Agricultural production board

In order to streamline agricultural production in the country, an Agricultural Board was constituted in 1963. The main function of the Board was to bring about expenditious implementation of the programme for the development of agriculture including animal husbandry, forestry and fisheries. The working of the board was recently reviewed and the Minister of Food, Agriculture, Community Development and Cooperation is its Chairman and the Minister of State in the Ministry of Finance, and the Member Agriculture, Planning Commission, are its members. The function and powers of the board are : (i) to secure effective and continuous coordination between the Centre and the states, in matters relating to the formulation and execution of development programmes; (ii) to review the progress of development programmes, ensure efficient arrangements for supplies and services, locate difficulties, if any, and endeavour to remove them; and (iii) to take such other measures as would ensure speedy and effective implementation of the development programmes at the Centre and in the states. The decisions of the Board will be treated as the decisions of the Government of India as long as they are within the plan provisions and within the framework of the approved budget provisions of the ministries concerned.

The Ministry of Agriculture was reorganised in 1964 on the initiative of the then Minister of Food and Agriculture who had found it a poor instrument for carrying out a dynamic and forward-looking policy aimed at making the country self-sufficient and even surplus in the foodgrains and assuring the prosperity of the farming population. The reorganisation was aimed at making the Ministry "function more effectively and to enable it more actively to associate itself with the implementation of development schemes by the states." It attempted (i) a redistribution of subjects and responsibilities among the various units of the Ministry so as to make the assignments of the units compact and specific; (ii) to assign to scientific and technical officers of the Ministry executive functions and operational responsibilities for planning, implementation and supervision of programmes, in addition to their advisory functions, to secure through "better administrative machinery"; and (iii) closer and more continuous contact between the Central and State Governments in the implementation of agricultural plan schemes and to improve Centre-State relations.

The apex of the structure of administration consists of the Minister of Food and Agriculture, who is a senior member of the Cabinet, and Ministers of State and Deputy Ministers who constitute the political executive. The Secretary of the Ministry is the official head of the Ministry and the principal adviser to the Minister. The Department of Agriculture which is one of the three departments included in the Ministry is organised in eight wings, and has besides five specialised offices, a number of supervisory and operational agencies and some cells and units for certain specific purposes.

The eight wings of the department are: (1) Production; (2) Forestry; (3) Fisheries; (4) Inputs (F) (Fertilisers); (5) Inputs (M) (Machinery); (6) Land problems; (7) Special development programmes; and (8) Coordination. The specialised of offices are: (1) The Indian Council of Agricultural Research; (2) The Directorate General of State Farms; (3) Agricultural Prices Commission; (4) The Directorate of Extension; and (5) The Directorate of Economics and Statistics.

Lastly, reference may be made to the numerous subordinate and attached offices of the Department which operate various programmes of the Ministry, expert committees and other agencies. The more important attached offices are the Directorate of Plant Protection, the Office of the Agricultural Marketing Advisor, the National Seeds Corporation, the Warehousing Corporation, etc.

Committees, both official and unofficial, expert or representative of interests, have been established to advise the Ministry on many important matters. Fifteen of these have been listed as functioning at present. These are Panel of Economists, Panel of Experts on Agricultural * Demonstration and finally Panel of Farmers to advise the Agricultural Prices Commission.

The other agencies falling in this category are: Committee for the Improvement of Agricultural Statistics; National Committee on the Preparation of Farm Management; Manual for the use of Extension Workers; Study Group on Wild Life and Wild Life Products; Indian Board for Wild Life; Central Forestry Commission; Board for Agricultural Machinery and Implements; Standing Committe of Experts on Manures and Fertilisers; National F.A.O. Liaison Committee; Central Council of Gosamvardhana; Central Variety Release Committee; Central Board of Fisheries; and Central Fisheries Research Committee.

The areas covered by these boards and committees are of vital importance to the development of agriculture and it is necessary, therefore, that they should be active bodies manned by competent personnel.

The Planning Commission's role in agricultural administration needs to be examined. It is directly and intimately connected with agricultural development at all stages from policy formulation and planning to plan implementation and evaluation. The Planning Commission's concurrence is required for the ministry's policies and programmes in detail. In fixing the targets of production, in making financial allocations in the five year plan and in the annual plans, in negotiations with the states, the Planning Commission plays a leading, if not dominant role. The working relations between the Planning Commission and the Ministry have not been always smooth and are not infrequently marked by friction.

Planning and agriculture :

Planning in India derives its objectives and social promises from Directive principles of State Policy enshrined in the Constitution. Public and private sectors are viewed as complementary. Private sector covers not only organised industry but also small scale industries, agriculture, trade and a great deal of activity in housing, construction and other fields. Individual effort and private initiative are considered necessary and desirable in national endeavour on development with optimkum of voluntary cooperation. Although in the past, economic planning did envisage a growing public sector with massive investments in basic and heavy industries, now the emphasis on the public sector is less pronounced and the current thnking on planning in the country, in general, is that it should increasingly be of an indicative nature.

Planning Commission was set up in 1950 to prepare the blue-print of development, taking an overall view of the needs and resources of the country.

The First Plan (1951-56) had a two fold objective to correct the disequilibrium in economy caused by the Second World War and partition of the country and also to initiate simultaneously a process of all-round balanced development. This was ensure increase in the national income and steady improvement in living standards. Keeping in view large-scale imports of foodgrains in 1951 and inflationary pressure on economy, the Plan accorded the highest priority to agriculture including irrigation and power projects. About 44.6 per cent of the total outlay of Rs. 2,069 crore in the public sector (later raised to Rs. 2,378 crore) was allotted for its development. The Plan also aimed at increasing the rate of investment from five to about seven per cent national income.

In 1954, Parliament decleared that the broad objectives of economic policy should be to achieve a 'socialistic pattern of society' under which the basic criteria for determining the lines of advance would be social gain and greater equality in income and wealth and not private profit. The Second Five Year Plan (1956-57 to 1960-61), therefore, sought to promote a pattern of development which sould ultimatley lead to the establishment of a socialistic pattern of society in India. In particular, it stressed that the benefits of economic development should accrue more to the relatively less privileged sections of society and there should be a progressive reduction in the concentration of incomes, wealth and economic power.

The main aims of the Second Plan were: (i) an increase of 25 per cent in the national income; (ii) rapid industrialisation with particular emphasis on the development of basic and heavy industries; (iii) large expansion of employment opportunities; and (iv) reduction of inequalities in income and wealth and more even distribution of economic power. The Plan also aimed at increasing the rate of investment from about seven per cent of the national income to 11 per cent 1960-61. The Plan laid special stress on industrialisation, increased production of iron and steel, heavy chemicals including nitrogenous fertilizers and development of heavy engineering and machine-building industry.

The Third Plan (1961-62 to 1965-66) aimed at securing a marked advance towards self-sustaining growth. Its immediate objectives were to: (i) secure an increase in the national income of over five per cent annum and at the same time ensure a pattern of investment which could sustain this rate of growth during subsequent Plan periods; (ii) achieve self-sufficiency in foodgrains and increase agricultural production to meet the requirements of industry and exports; (iii) expand basic industries like steel, chemicals, fuel and power and to establish machine-building capacity, so that the requirements of further industrialisation could be met within a period of 10 years or so mainly from the country's own resources; (iv) utilise fully the manpower resources of the country and ensure substantial expansion in employment opportunities; and (v) establish progresively greater equality of opportunity and bring about reduction in disparities of income and wealth and a more even distribution of economic power. The Plan aimed at increasing the national income by about 30 per cent from Rs. 14,500 crore in 1960-61 to about Rs. 19,000 crore by 1965-66 (at 1960-61 prices) and per capita income by about 17 per cent from Rs. 330 to Rs. 385 during the same period.

The situation created by the Indo-Pakistan conflict in 1965, two successive years of severe drought, devaluation of the currency, general rise in prices and erosion of resources available for Plan purposes delayed finalisation of the Fourth Five Year Plan. Instead, between 1966 and 1969, three Annual Plans were formulated within the framework of the draft outline of the Fourth Plan. They took into account the conditions prevailing at that time. The state of the economy and the non-availablity of financial resources for Plan purposes kept down the size of development outlay during this period.

The Fourth Plan (1969-74) aimed at accelerating the tempo of development and reducing fluctuations in agricultural production as well as a the impact of uncertainties of foreign aid. It sought to raise the standard of living through programmes designed to promote equality andsocial justice. The Plan laid particular emphasis on improving condition of less privileged and weaker sections especially through provision of employment and education. Efforts were also directed towards reduction of concentration and wider diffusion of wealth, income and economic power.

The Plan aimed at inincreasing net domestic production at 1968-69 factor cost from Rs. 29,071 crore in 1969-70 to Rs. 38,306 crore in 1973-74. In terms of 1960-61 prices, this implied an increase from Rs. 17,351 crore in 1968-69 to Rs. 22,862 crore in 1973-74. Average annual compound rate of growth envisaged was 5.7 per cent.

The Fifth Plan (1974-79) was formulated against the backdrop of severe inflationary pressures. Major objectives of the Plan were to achieve self-reliance and adopt measures for raising consumption standards of people living below the poverty line. This Plan also gave high priority to bring inflation under control and to achieve stability in the economic situation. It targeted an annual growth rate of 5.5 per cent in national income. Four Annual Plans pertaining to the Fifth Plan period were completed. It was subsequently decided to end the

Fifth Plan with the close of Annual Plan 1978-79 and initiate work for a new Plan for next five years with new priorities and programmes.

The Sixth Plan (1980-85) was conceptualised keeping in view achievements and shortcomings of the past three decades of planning. Removal of poverty was foremost objective of the Plan even though it was recognised that task of this magnitude could not be accomplished in a short period of five years. The strategy adopted for the Plan consisted essentially in moving simultaneously towards strengthening infrastructure for both agriculture and industry so as to create conditions for an accelerated growth in investments, output and exports and provide through special programmes designed for the purpose, increased opportunities for employment especially in rural areas and unorganised sector and as well meeting minimum basic needs of people. Stress was laid on dealing with inter-related problems through a system approach rather than in separate cmpartments, greater management efficiency and intensive monitoring in all sectors and active involvement of people in formulating specific schemes of development at local level and securing their speedy and effective implementation.

Sixth Plan's actual expenditure stood at Rs. 1,09,291.7 crore (current prices) as against the envisaged total public sector outlay of Rs. 97,500 crore (1970-80 prices) accounting for a 12 per cent increase in nominal terms. Average annual growth rate for the Plan was 5.2 per cent, targeted growth rate for this period.

The Seventh Plan (1985-90) emphasised on Policies and programmes, the aim of which had been rapid growth in foodgrains production production, employment opportunities and productivity within the framework of basic tenets of planning, namely, growth, modernisation, self-relience and social justice. Due to overall fovourable weather conditions, implementation of various thrust programmes and with concerted efforts of the government and the farmers, foodgrains production during the Seventh Plan grew by 3.23 per cent as compared to along term growth rate of 2.68 per cent during 1967-68 to 1988-89 and a growth rate of 2.255 per cent in eighties. To reduce unemployment and, consequently, the incidence of poverty, special programmes like Jawahar Rozgar Yojana were initiated in addition to the already existing programmes. Due recognition was also accorded to the role small scale and food-processing industries can play in this regard. Various policy instruments were used to improve the productivity and the international competitiveness of the Indian economy. Instead of creating new facilities, the thrust was on improvement of existing facilities, and fuller capacity utilisation.

The total expenditure during the entire Seventh Plan stood at Rs. 2,18,729.62 crore (current price) as against the envisaged total public sector outlay of Rs. 1,80,000 crore, resulting in a 21.52 per cent increase in nominal terms. During this Plan period, Gross Domestic product (GDP) grew at an average rate of 5.6 per cent per year exceeding the targeted growth rate by 0.6 per cent

The Eight Five Year Plan (1990-95) could not take off due to the fast changing political situation at the Centre. The new government which assumed power at the Centre by June 1991 decided that the Eighth Five Year Plan would commence on 1 April 1992 and that 1990-91 and 1991-92 should be treated as separate Annual Plans. Formulated within the framework of the earlier Approach to the Eighth Five Year Plan (1990-95), the basic thrust of these Annual Plans were on maximisation of employment and social transformation.

The Plan proposes a growth rate of 5.6 per cent per

annum on an average during the Plan period. The level of national investment is proposed at Rs. 7,98,000 crore and the public sector outlay of Rs. 4,34,100 crore. Consistent with the expected resource position, the size of the plans of the states and union territories is projected at Rs. 1,86,235 crore and of the Central Plan at Rs. 2,47,865 crore.

The Annual Plan 1992-93 envisaged a total public sector outlay of Rs. 80,771.96 crore, actual expenditure came down to Rs. 72,853 crore which is lower by one per cent than the Budget Estimates for the Plan. The actual size of the Plans for states and union territories was lower by nearly 10 per cent i.e. from Rs. 32,364.88 crore (BE) to Rs. 29,159 crore. The main reasons for the shortfall in State Plans were deterioration in the balance from current revenues, erosion in the contribution of state electricity boards and in some cases of state road transport corporations, negative opening balances,mounting non-plan expenditure, shortfalls in the collection of small savings, etc.

The envisaged total public sector outlay of Rs. 1,00,120.16 crore for the Annual Plan 1993-94 on revision came down to Rs. 92,623.64 crore which is lower by 7.48 per cent that the budget estimates for the Plan. In the Central Sector, the approved outlay was Rs. 61,453.53 crore. The total outlay of the plans for states and union territories on revision was lower by 13.84 per cent i.e. from Rs. 36,184 crore in the budget estimates to Rs. 31,175.11 crore in revised estimates. The main reasons for the shortfall in states plans were deteriorating in the balance from current revenues, erosion in the contribution of state electricity boards and in some cases of state road transport corporations, negative opening balances, mounting non-plan expenditure, shortfall in the collection of small savings, etc.

The Annual Plan 1994-95 provides for a public sector outlay of Rs. 1,12,197 crore at current prices. At 1991-92 prices it would be about 20 per cent of the envisaged Eighth Plan public sector outlay. The state plans outlay is Rs. 39,992 crore at current prices, which works out to 35.64 per cent of public sector outlay and 17.17 per cent of the Eighth Plan provision for the states at 1991-92 prices. In the first three years, assuming that the actual outlays will be the same as the revised estimates of 1993-94 and the budget estimates of 1994-95 will be reallised, the public sector outlays in the Central Plan and the State Plans will work out to 59 per cent and 44 per cent of the respective Eighth Plan provisions, at constant prices.

The role of planning, therefore, continued to be highly relevant. The nature of instruments available to implement the Plan, however, has undergone a significant change in the wake of liberalization and economic reforms. Fixing specific targets for various sectors and deciding who should produce what, when and how is no more the responsibility of the Plnning Commission. Market signals will decide these. To ensure that market signals are consistent with the society's requirements, however, will continue to be a planning function. The planning process will have to focus on planning for policy so that the signals that are sent out to the economic system induce the various economiic agents to behave in a manner which is consistent with the national objectives.

Recognizing the federal character of our system and to encourage meaningful fiscal federalism involving the Centre, the States and local bodies, the planning process has to develop a common policy stance which would be adopted both by the Centre and the States. The role of planning in the coming years would, therefore, involve a considerable degree of policy co-ordination between the

Centre and the States, among the States and between the States and the Sub-state level tiers of government.

The role of the government, in general, has to shift from being the provider to the facilitator for people's participation in the development process by creating right types of institutional infrastructure and environment conducive to broad based economic development of people's initiatives cannot be achieved without the active support and involvement of the political system at all levels. In the IX Plan, the Panchayati Raj bodies in rural areas and municipalities in urban areas will be directly involved in the development process. People's involvement via their elected representatives is expected representatives is expected to be realized through genuine democratic decentralization.

The approach to the IX Plan recognezes the need to restore the fiscal health of the government at all levels. The fiscal deficit, especially the revenue component of the deficit, will remain a central concern of macro-economic management. Every effort will have to be made to contain the non-plan, non-development revenue expenditure will be minimized. The borrowings of the government will be regulated so as to maximize the productive potential of the economy.

Subsidies, both direct and indirect, constitute a heabvy burden on the public exchequer. Most of them are untargeted or open-ended. While the costs of indirec6subsidies are hard to measure. Fixation of administered prices of goods and services produced in the public sector on extra-economic considerations is an important element of non-transparent subsidies. Such subsidies are openended and often accrue to those who are not envisaged to benefit from them. Further, th;ey lead to misallocation of resources in l;the economy resulting from wrong price signals apart from placing heavy burden on the exchequer.The Ninth Plan is expected to move away from untargeted hidden subsidies to a system of transparent subsidies directed towards specific target groups in a selective manner.

Adequate quantity, quality and reliability of infrastructure are essential preconditions not only for economic growth and development but also to make the country internationally conpetitive and attractive for investment. The investment needs in this sector are of magnitudes that are beyond the resources available to the government. There is an imperative need, therefore, to motivate the private sector to participate in the development proces, if the infrastructure gap has to be bridged. The public sector which has carried the burden of infrastructure development so far will also benefit by the competition and partnership with the private sector. Successful development of this crucial sector will require bold policy initiatives, framing of schemes and seting up of an institutional environment which would provide a level playing field to all competitors whilst simultaneously safeguarding the rights of consumers.

The overview of the approach to the Ninth Five Year Plan outlined in the preceding paragraphs clearly indicates that it Plan'. The true test, of course, is in the implimentation. The deprived sections of our society certainly deserve a better deal than what they have got so far. Let us hope that their time has come.

Coming to specifics of the Ninth Plan, it may be noticed that as compared to the earlier approach plan documents which used to give prominence to growth of aggregate GDP, the Ninth Plan gives prominence to growth of agriculture. This is based on the logic that it is agricultural prosperity which brings down povety and generates more employment and, therefore, higher rate of growth of GDP should be achieved through achieving higher rate of growth of agricultural output. In the earliear plans, industrial development was given prominence and the public sector usually occupied commanding heights. But during th Ninth Plan, it is agriculture which is going to occupy commanding heights and the public sector outlay constitutes only about 35 per cent of the total estimated plan investment of Rs. 8,75,000 crore. So this is a shift of emphasis in terms of priority from public sector industrial development to agricultural development which is mostly in the private sector. This was necessary because the public sector investment in agriculture had stagnated in the name of providing inputs subsidies like fertilizers subsidy. Correspondingly, public sector investment in agriculture infrastructure like irrigation had come down. This was rectified even during 1996-97 by allocating Rs. 900 crore for accelarated irrigation development. But that amount was diverted from other sectors and the overall public sector investment in agriculture remained around 12.8 per cent. Therefore, the Ninth Five Year Plan has decided to increase budgetary support and public sector investment in irrigation, rural roads, rural markets and a host of other infrastructures. What is more, while the overall growth of GDP envisaged during the Ninth Plan is seven per cent, which was made mandatory by the Common Minimum Programme, the rate of growth of agriculture envisaged during the Ninth Plan is as high as 4.5 per cent. This can be achieved only by promoting commercial agriculture through modernization and bringing in vast amount of private invesment. This pattern of development is envisaged for agriculture during the Ninth Five Year Plan.

Industrial development will continue to receive priority as it received during the Eighth Five Year Plan but there will not be much public sector investment in new industrial units. Most of whatever investment that will be undertaken will go for providing industrial infrastructure for small-scale industries paricularly in food processing activities. Recently, the Government of India enhanced the investment limit of small-scale industries to Rs. 3 crore. This will help technological upgradation of small-scale industries. Foreign direct investment is assumed to play a very prominent role in the development of industry. In this context, several measures have been taken. all of them are aimed at mobilizing private investment for industrial development.

Other than agriculture, the second most important priority of the Ninth Plan is infrastructure development like power generation, ports, railways, national highways, etc. Most of these except railways are left to the private sector. But wherever necessary, such as in the case of power generation and distribution and development of railways, public sector investment will continue. But the magnitude of the problelm is so much that these infrastructure facilities cannot be provided without massive investment from the private sector both domestic and foreign.

Finally, the Ninth Plan recongnizes the failure of the past efforts to provide basic minimum services to the rural areas. Accordingly, this task was taken up during 1996-97 itself. It is going to be a prominent programme during the Ninth Plan. it is hoped that by the end of the Ninth Plan, the people in rural areas will have access to basic minimum services like safe drinking water, roads, primary health and primary education.

The Planning Commission has also decided to pay more attention to protection of biodiversity in Himalayan region and cleaning the rivers polluted by industrial and urban effluents. Besides, the State governments are asked to formulate appropriate development strategies and programmes to reduce intra-State economic disparities.

No doubt, creation of employment opportunities, reduction of poverty, empowerment of women and other weaker sections of the society, fostering environmentally sustained development and promoting self-reliance are all continued in the Ninth Plan. but most of these programmes are ongoing which are carried forward from the previous plans. Relative emphasis may differ. But the top priority is given to agriculture, infrastructure and basic minimum needs during the Ninth Plan. They are the priorities of the Ninth Plan and they are intended to make the country a reasonably decent plane to live in.

A reappraisal of the country's Science and Technology (S&T) policy is called for in the wake of economic liberalization and the emerging globalization research and development (R&D) The basic object of the reappraisal would be to provide better assistance to the country's industrial growth and exports, industrial growth and exports, besides enhancing the quality of life of the people.

Several eminent scientists and technocrats have highlighted the inadequacies of the current approach to S & T. The government's S & T policy has been termed "short sighted" at the recent 84th session of the Indian Science Congress. In the words of a well-known scientist, if the government went on "underplaying S & T at it has been doing since the economic reforms started", there would be hardly any science left in this country in another 5-10 years.

Though S & T is to be given high priority in the Ninth Plan, it should address several fundamental problems hindering its effective application. A brief overview of the main issues that need to be addressed would reveal several soft options but few hard choices for the planners.

The country' R&D expenditure declined from a little

over one per cent to 0.86 per cent of the gross national product (GNP) during 1990-95 and the trend has not been reversed. Though this is relatively high among developing countries, it is very small compared with 2.5 per cent of GNP spent by developed countries in general. India's R&D expenditure is around $ 1 billion. The United States spends 200 times more than India on R&D, while Japan and South Korea allot 140 times more. Though we have the third largest manpower with some science and technology qualification, we do not have any advantage in terms of specialized skills and training.

No doubt the Plan allocation for S&T has considerably increased from Rs. 15 crore in the I Plan to Rs. 9,180 crore in the VIII Plan. However, a major share has gone to Defence, Space and Atomic Energy. For example, the 1995-96 budget estimates of the Departments of Atomic Energy and Space were Rs. 1,001 crore and Rs. 911 crore, respectively.

More than money, young people today shy away from science. In 1950-51, there were 1,27,000 students enrolled in the science stream and in 1993, we have 10 million of them. But, the percentage of students opting for science at the undergraduate level was 32 in 1950-51, which declined to 19 in 1993. Again, the top 32 per cent opted for science in 1950, but today only the middle and the lower 19 go for it. Management, accountancy and financial disciplines attract more. Computer software is the lone exception in terms of popularity but the numbers for employment will soon become limited, especially at the specialization level. Over the past one decade., the number of students enrolling for degrees in science has stagnated at the same level.

Indian S&T is at a crossroads. Globalization and the need for self-reliance, apparently contradictory in terms of their objectives, call for a realistic mix of policies. The myth of import of technology has been blasted loud and clear by unequivocal and frank warning by no less a person than Dr. A.P.J. Abdul Kalam and a few other scientists. Dr. Kalam pointed out that there is no such thing as a free lunch in the import of technology. It we are not careful, we would often end up with less relevant, obsolete, eco—unfriendly technologies from developed countries, except in a few cases. We should accept the reluctance of developed countries to transfer technology in frontier areas and take up the challenge of developing our own technology in critical fields.

Unfortunately, liberalization has misled some people into believing that self-reliance has no relevance! Nothing could be more harmful to the interests of the country. In fact, at one time, the Confederation of the Indian Industry suggested the elimination of all restrictions on technology imports and foreign collaboration. While the removal cannot be 100 per cent, considerable liberalization has indeed taken place. Since the new Industrial Policy (1991), automatic approvals by the Reserve Bank for technology imports are allowed in cases pertaining to specific industries, where the total lump sum payment does not exceed Rs. 1 crore and the royalties on domestic sales and exports do not exceed five per cent and eight per cent, respectively. In 1994, for instance, 340 out of 915 cases got automatic approval. Hidden behind the plea for a 100 per cent automatic approval is a reluctance on the part of the industry to undertake any R&D so long as foreign products and processes are available and can be sold at high profit. In other words, this is described as "black box" approach, where one deals with technology as if it is a black box meant for trade only! It is an easy option but it cannot be adopted in the long-term interests of the country.

The truth is globalization is not a one-way street. Where there is expertise and resources, it becomes a two-way street, as for example, in India. Today, a wave of collaborative R&D is sweeping the world. Networking with premier R&D organizations around the world is becoming profitable. The evolution of a worldwide information network has made real time-management of production and marketing possible anywhere in the world. Leading companies from the US are coming to India since the country offers research facilities at low cost, a good science base, a fair legal framework and freedom and flexibility of operations. There is new breed of entrepreneurs in India who value quality and prompt delivery. With adequate intellectual property safeguards, more and more R&D firms are tying up with Indian counterparts, known for their world class research. For example, the National Chemical Laboratory(NCL),Pune, has licensed some of its patents to a Us firm. The Indian Institute of Chemical Technology, Hyderabad, has collaboration with DuPunt in agrochemical research. NCL is offering its services to China.

The Council of Scientific and Industrial Research (CSIR) has responded to this trend effectively. CSIR will soon have a "virtual" laboratory to monitor the data on what is being perfected or experimented in its laboratories. CSIR is no longer dependent entirely on government funds. It is supposed to earn up to 50 per cent of its experditure through commercial use of its products and processes. CSIR's external cash flow is expected to reach Rs. 145 crore during 1995-96. There is a suggestion from the private sector that the CSIR laboratories be converted into corporations and made the to compete in the market and sell their products and processes. However, many of the laboratories do not have effective competitors in the private sector.

About 75 per cent of the R&D expenditure is ment by the government on laboratories under its control. Only 25 per cent is met by the industry. However, the R&D

expenditure by companies accounts for less than 0.1 per cent of their turnover. But the industry is slowly realizing the value of collaboration with research instiutions. For instance, three Indian Pharmaceutical companies have recently signed long-term agreements with government research laboratories for R&D in new drugs.

Industry is accused of not interacting closely with universities. It is a pity that the interaction between government laboratories and academic institutions has remained minimal. The Mashelkar Cpmmittee (1993) had made several specific recommendations for providing incentives to researchers and for exposing them to the international scientific community.

The Ninth Plan approach paper has indicated that emphasis would be made on networking between the research institutions/nationl laboratories both for development and marketing of technology. In order to achieve these objectives, the existing S&T infrastructure will be modernised through major investment by industry. Efforts would alsobe made to dispense with hierarchical bureucracy in the R&D institutions adequate delegation of powers, according to the approach paper.

Some initiatives from academic institutions are noteworthy. The Indian Institute of Science, Bangalore, is setting up special research cells for dealing with wpecific industrial problems in areas such as telecommunication, food processing, software engineering and drug design. The IIT, Chennai has set up a Center for Industrial Consultancy and Sponsored Research.

One test of technological excellence is the number of patents sealed in critical areas. A survey (1994) of the National Council for Applied Econmic Research of scientists working in Central government laboratories showec that the average number of patents applid for a scientist wa 0.13 and the patents obtained was 0.09. In terms of technology, the perceived gaps between the status quo and the state-of-the-art technology is 15-20 years in the paper industry, 10-15 years in cement, 10 years in polymers and 5-10 years in the paint industry. In specific cases, the gap would have since narrowed but the figures indicate the long road ahead in catching up with the state-of-the-art technology.

Several initiatives have been taken to address the problem of enhancing the level of technology. The Technology Development Fund (TDF), created in 1994-95 to be financed from the five per cent cess on imported technologies through collaboration is expected to procure around Rs. 100 crore for the Department of Science and Technology. The TDF is expected to promote indigenous technology, especially in the small-scale sector. A Technology Development Board has been set up to assist in the use of the TDF.

The approach paper says that besides continuing the initiatives taken during 1996-97, a Corpus Fund for financing research projects in frontier areas of scinece by distinguished scientists of any age, will be created. Efforts would also be made during the Ninth Plan to generate maximum resources for R&D from the production and service sectors.

Another initiative is the setting up of mission mode projects such as the one on fly-ash disposal and utilization. Yet another idea being tried is the location of clusters of industries (e.g. leather and jute) and supporting them with better facilities such as housing and health care.

However, the scheme offering tax deduction for sponsored research has not taken off in a big way. Only a few industries have responded to the broadcasting of 125 per cent weighted tax deduction for sponsored research in a national laboratory. This shows that the industry cannot be motivated by limited tax cuts alone. Market-driven demand seems to be a better incentive.

The challenges

As said, formidable challenges lay before the Ninth Plan. In the first instance, it may be interpreted as the challenge of a seven per cent rate of GDP growth, which would be a break with the historical rate of growth of Indian planning of some 3.5 per cent to 6 per cent, depending on the moods of rain gods and the gods have been exceptionally kind to us consecutively for the last eight years, and let us hope and pray that they would be in the Ninth Plan also. It may seem an amazing assertion to say that the seven per cent growth rate is the least of the challenges of the Plan. Without exaggeration and bravado 8-10 per cent rate of growth is within the reach of the economy. What is seven per cent after all for a plan of nearly Rs. 1 m crore investment to which the plan investment should be rounded off. If a seven per cent rate of growth is not within the grasp of the economy, then what is all this liberalization, globalization, opening of the economy, etc. for? With improved management and evaluation and monitoring, an eight per cent rate of growth would be within easy reach.

That is, by all reckoning the seven per cent rate of growth appears to be a pessimistic rate of growth which in all likelihood would end up in an eight per cent rate of growth. That is the experience of the VIII Plan and there is no reason to believe that it won't repeat itself in the Ninth Plan with the economic fundamentals of inflation, forex, FDI, etc. more in place. Like the export pessimism of the yester-years, the economy appears to be afflicted with growth pessimism bordering on defeatism and self-deprecation. This is evident in the panic reaction of the national industrial houses against MNCs and their threat of take-over. It is sorrowful if the Indian industry had not yet come of age. When would it? Never?

The whole planning debate is being expended on the rate of growth, the rate of saving (26.2%), the rate of investment (29.6%), ICOR (4.2%) and so, in a great exercise of not seeing the wood for the trees. There can be no doubt concerning the attainability and validity of these figures, which are the minor points of the plan. The economy in these respects appears to suffer from underestimates. The savings potential and rate of the Indian economy should not be underestimated, so also the size of the economy. There is a labyrinthine part of the economy which is quite formidable. There is no proper planning, strategy and foresight to utilized the economy's potential. In addition, there is an estimated 20 m Indian community abroad who still have their roots in the country. Their savings are estimated anywhere between $ 100 billion to $ 300 billion.

Triggering off rural economic revolution: The real challenges of the Ninth Plan are in the areas of rural development. The real planning and economic action must be planned in that vast rural sector. The strength as well as weakness of the economy is in the rural sector. Agriculture needs not just a 4.5 per cent rate of growth, which is most likely to be unattainable. There is no second Green Revolution in sight, even after nearly three decades of the first one. Economic revolution of the country, yet to take place, has to come about from the countryside or rural areas. One looks forward hopefully to an Indian economic miracle like the Japanese ad the South Korean ones. When is it likely to be? Not even after nearly 50 years of planning and planned economic development? Where are the millions of jobs to be created except in rural areas for quite some time? If urbanization of the 80s of less than five per cent is any indication, a lot of economic action ought to take place in the countryside from HRD to social economic infrastructure to environmental planning.

We have had enough of Malthusianism. It, without enough of rural development, is aggravating land wars. Only increased agricultural productivity, still a long way behind the world standards by about 60 per cent even in the 'developed' agricultural State, could considerably bring down the agrarian tensions. In other words, the Indian economic revolutions to be set from the countryside and it would be an indigenous revolution with all economic reforms and foreign capital participation confined to industry, services and urban areas. It must be the task of the Ninth Plan to trigger off the rural economic revolution and bring forth a second Green Revolution countrywide.

The economy, first, is suffering from improper house keeping and management on account of which it is caught in thick cobwebs. The first task of the Plan would be to clear the economy of these cobwebs, which are of social and economic overheads, infrastructural and improper and uneconomical plan and economy management.

The economy on the eve of the 21st century and the Ninth Plan is in need of stock-taking, spring cleaning, proper housekeeping and management, having grown without proper management and housekeeping over the last so many years. This is the first task and challenge of the Ninth Plan. Later on, it has challenges of proper housekeeping and management resources development.

Formidable tasks and challenges lay at the doorsteps of the Ninth Plan. The great task of rural development, fighting poverty employment generation, food security, HRD, population control, etc. The said thankless and profitless jobs would be the responsibility and challenges of the Plan, so also public enterprises profitability and viability.

Not that one is making too much of the Ninth Plan and trying to entrust with formidable tasks and challenges. They are very much there.

The approach paper of the Ninth Plan was approved by the National Development Council (NDC) on 16 January. In conformity with the objectives specified in the Common Minimum Programme (CMP), the Ninth Plan aims at increasing the annual growth rate to seven per cent of GDP during the plan period. To achieve such a high rate of growth, the approach paper suggests to increase the savings rate to the extent of 26.2 per cent and investment rate to the extent of 28.6 per cent while putting a ceiling on the current account deficit at 2.4 per cent of GDP. While a high ıate of economic growth is desirable for increasing the overall size of the economy, it is doubtful whether we can be able to achieve the target envisaged in the Plan.

There seems to be a number of constraints which may hinder the process of increased capital formation. First, we may not increase domestic savings to the extent of 26.2 per cent. Public sector savings in the VIII Plan were only 1.6 per cent. To increase this rate to the extent of 2.8 per cent seems hardly feasible. there has been no improvement in the operational efficiency of public sector enterprises during the last five or six years. and the government sctor may have to increase its expenditure on the basis of the recommendations of the fifth Pay Commission and on account of subsidies which may continue for a long time, because of political uncertainty. It is estimated that open subsidies absorb nearly 20 per cent of the tax revenues of the government, both the Centre and the States taken together. Besides, there are a number of hidden subsidies whose magnitude and quantum are probably much moe than open subsidies. According to some estimates, 16 per cent of GDP goes into subsidies both explicit and implicit. No attempt is made to reduce these subsidies. On the other hand, competitive politics and populism (as we see in Punjab and Andhra Pradesh) may dreve many state governments towards bankruptcy. A target of seven per cent annual growth requires hard decisions. But there is little political will to take such decisions.

There is no guarantee that the government can increase tax revenue to meet such additional expenditure. The Deputy Chairman of the Planning Commission feels that public savings can increase through improvement in the taxes net of subsidies. He believes that tax compliance can be improved and the tax GDP ratio increased. He says, as against 85 per cent of the population in Denmark and Sweden which pay income tax, in India only 0.8 per cent pays income tax. He therefore, proposes to tax the visible expenditure of the creamy layer and include more people in the tax net. He also hopes to rope in some of the black money through apropriate schemes. But the uncertainty that has been created with the Minimum Alternative Tax (MAT) and the reverses that have taken place in the case of Presumptive Tax do not give encouraging results.

The private corporate sector and the household sector and the household sector may not also increase their savings due to inflation which may increase to the extent of nine to 10 per cent. The government will have to increase th administered prices of petroleum products since the oil pooln deficit is expected to increase to Rs. 18,000 crore by the end of March 1996. If the administered prices of petroleum products are not inreased, the current account deficit may be much more than 2.4 per cent of GDP which may increase fiscal deficit to a large extent. To improve the household savings, the Deputy Chairman has plans to introduce a set of incentives for small savers. But experience, however, shows that more incentives for small savers do not bring about a higher savings rate; on the other hand, they may only channilize more savings rate; on the other hand, they may only channelize more savings into financial assets, leaving the totality unchanged.

Secondly, the accelerated rate of growth of seven per cent per annum is again based upon 4.5 per cent growth in agriculture and 9.3 per cent in industry. In spite of favourable monsoons for a period of consecutive se ven to eight years, the rate of growth of agriculture in the VII Plan was 3.35 per cent and may be 3.5 per cent in the VIII Plan. There is no guarantee that monsoon would be as favourable in the coming years. If the fiscal deficit increases in the plan period, the government may not have adequate resources to increase investment in agriculture. And the poor infrastructure may retard the growth of industries.

It admitted by the planners that sustained growth of the economy depends on adequate availability of basic infrastructural facilities, such as power, transport and communications and irrigation of adequate quality. The VIII Plan has fallen significantly short not only of the targets, but also of the VII Plan in these areas, as indecated in primarily due to the slower pace of investment than had been contemplated.

Fiscal deficit: It has been mentioned in the approach paper that efforts at containing the fiscal deficit of the government have fallen diproportionately on public investment, particularly in those sectors which are more dependent on budgetary support. The share of capitall expenditure in the total expenditure of the government has declined sharply from around 30 per cent at the beginning of the VIII plan to 24 per cent The IX plan may also face the same difficulty. Further, it is noticed that public investment as a whole is targeted to be no more than 33 per cent of the total investment against the 36.5 per cent realized during the VIII Plan (The VIII Plan targeft was 43 per cent). This is justified on the ground of reducing the fiscal deficit to the extent of four per cent of GDP. But the state of the economy as it prevails now does not proviede any optimism either in regard to growth or reduced rate of fiscal deficit.

Another area which again seems doubtful is lower incremental capital-output ratio [(ICOR) 4.08% as against 4.24% during the VIII plan]. If investment from external sources comes to 2.4 per cent as envisaged in the approach paper in the shape of Foreign Direct Investmint, they are bound to be capital-intensive projects. But the approach paper indicates three areas which may reduce ICOR. One area is to encourage small-scale labour-intensive industrial development with short gestation periods. According to statistics, 40 per cent of total manufacturing is labour-intensive. If this balance can be maintained, it is possible to realize lower ICOR, particularly with shorter gestation periods.

Further, it is assumed that reforms will phase out obsolete technologies and usher in higher material and energy efficiency. Thirdly, improvement in the efficiency and productivity of the five infrastructural sectors, viz irrigation, mining, power, railways, and communications. No definite proposal has been given to implement these assumptions. In many cases, the actual implementation of some of these proposals is in the hands of State governments, most of whom openly divert their plan funds for non-plan expenditure. All this implies that the rate of growth envisaged in the approach paper leaves too many loose ends which may frustrate the hopes and aspirations of the planners.